CONFESSIONS OF AN INFALLIBLE MAN

THE SECRET MEMOIR OF POPE LEO X

Translated from Latin by

Stanley Wallerstein

©2010

All rights reserved.

© Copyright 2010 Stanley Wallerstein

ISBN 978-0-557-28394-1

Publisher: Lulu.com

Lulu Publishing ID: 8227138

O Lord, help me to be pure, but not yet.

St. Augustine

TABLE OF CONTENTS

Prologue	7
The Medici	13
The Pazzi Conspiracy	29
Savonarola	45
The Borgia	63
Pope Julius II	101
Pope Leo X	137
Hanno	149
Journal	165
Translator's Afterward	241
Select Bibliography	248
Partial Genealogical Tables:	
Medici	251
Borgia	252
della Rovere	253
Sforza	254
Este	255
Map of Italy (1494)	257

PROLOGUE

It is not easy to be the son of a great man. My father, Lorenzo, "The Magnificent", de Medici, had expectations of me. From the moment of my birth, he charted the course of my life. He decreed for me a vocation in the Church and spent vast sums to purchase my benefices. My father once remarked: "I have three sons – one good, one wise and one foolish." I was the wise son (or so Lorenzo believed). I have devoted my entire life to fulfilling my father's expectations.

Lorenzo has been dead for over twenty years and he is universally hailed as a great man, even in Florence where the fickle citizenry twice drove our family into exile. I believe that, five hundred years from now, men will still celebrate his contributions to learning, art, architecture and politics. But how will history judge me? A sodomite, a pagan, a glutton, a spendthrift, an underhanded intriguer – I have heard all of these slanders said of me.

But is it not true that my father, through his inattention to the family business and his excessive liberality, squandered the Medici fortune and set the stage for our family to be driven from Florence; our palaces and possessions confiscated and looted? And have I not restored our family to its former honor, wealth and power?

You may find it strange that I feel the urge to argue my case. After all, I am Pope Leo X, the Vicar of Christ, the Bishop of Rome, the Successor of the Apostles, the Patriarch of the West, the Primate of Italy, the Vice-Regent of the Prince of Peace, the Ambassador of Heaven. No man on earth occupies a loftier position.

However, in truth, who can speak ten intelligent words about the nine Leos who preceded me? For that matter, who remembers the great majority of the 215 prior occupants of the Seat of St. Peter? Even here in the Vatican, possessor of the greatest library in the world, the lives of most popes are but dust.

I do not belittle my office. The Roman Church is the oldest, richest and most powerful institution in the history of the world. Protecting it from the forces of Satan and nurturing its expansion for the glory of God and the salvation of mankind is a humbling responsibility.

It is also an insecure, even dangerous, office. Many of my predecessors have been murdered, mutilated or driven from Rome by angry mobs. My namesake, Leo III, had his eyes and tongue gouged out by the nephews of his predecessor, Pope Adrian I. Leo was forced to seek protection from Charlemagne, King of the Franks, who demanded and received the titles King of the Romans and Holy Roman Emperor in return. My namesake, Leo V, was murdered by his successor, Pope Sergius III.

Sergius was quite mad. While occupying the supreme dignity, he exhumed the decade-old corpse of Pope Formosus from the crypt at St.

Peter's and cut three fingers from the hand, as well as the late Pope's head, and tossed them into the Tiber. Miraculously, the head was recovered in a fisherman's net and returned to the crypt.

What makes this story truly remarkable is that Pope Formosus had been exhumed once before. In 897 AD, Pope Stephen VII disinterred his predecessor, dressed the corpse in pontifical robes, sat it on the throne and excommunicated it for heresy. After removing the papal vestments and cutting off two fingers, Stephen flung Formosus' body into the Tiber. Formosus' supporters fished him from the river and, after Stephen was strangled to death later that year, returned his body to St. Peter's, where Sergius repeated the desecration years later.

I digress. I confess that I am not a disciplined man. My mind often strays and wanders down alleys. In setting down this narrative, I shall do my best to remain focused on the subject at hand (but I make no promise to succeed).

Is it the sin of pride that motivates me to pick up my quill? I cannot deny the possibility and do not claim to be faultless. But in truth I write because I live in exciting times. Among my acquaintances are men whose memories will no doubt outlast my own – Raphael, Michelangelo, Leonardo and Botticelli in the fine arts; Poliziano, Ficino, Mirandola and Bembo in philosophy and the literary arts. But without the generous patronage and patient nurturing of the Medici, these stars would not shine so brightly.

In politics, I have intrigued with and against, allied with and waged war upon the Sforza of Milan, the Estes of Ferrara, the Montefeltro of Urbino, the Orsini and Colonna of Rome, the diabolical Borgias and the kings and emperors of France, Spain, Naples and the Holy Roman Empire. As Christ's representative on earth, I have battled witches, heretics and Mohammedans.

I sometimes ponder why, after a millennium of darkness, the glory of ancient Rome has now revisited Italy. Our modern basilicas, palaces, statuary, art, music, theater and philosophy now rival or surpass the best work of the ancient Greeks and Romans. Some suggest it is the ever presence of sudden death that spurs us on to great accomplishments. Certainly death lurks everywhere in our age. Plague, malarial fever, small pox, cholera and consumption strike down both the high and low born at will. Great pox, that new disease called the French boils by the Italians, the Naples' disease by the French and the priests' disease by nearly everyone,° works it evil slowly but horribly. Add to that famine, flood, fire, war, accident and murder (not to mention the incompetent physician) and death is our consent companion. With my stomach

---

° Translator's note: Syphilis.

complaint and suppurating anal fistula, I have lain at death's door more often than I would choose.

But I say this is nonsense. Death is as much part of God's order as life and our ancestors were no more immune from an abrupt departure than us. It cannot adequately explain the rebirth of learning, art and culture which flowers in Italy. While one can never rule out divine will, I postulate a more prosaic explanation – money.

Italy is today awash in florins and ducats. Advances in transportation, navigation and manufacture have stimulated a volume of trade unknown since the Roman Empire and Italy is the fulcrum of Europe.   Italian dyes, textiles, silks, brocades, leather, glass and ceramics are sought throughout the world. Italian olives, hams and wines grace the table of every monarch, nobleman and merchant in the barbaric north. The merchant fleets of Venice, Genoa and Pisa supply all of Europe with slaves, spices, gems and exotic goods from the Orient. Italian bankers finance it all and the gold florin is the international coin of exchange. At the center of this web of commerce sit the Medici.

Of course, one cannot overlook the Church's contribution to Italian prosperity. From every far-flung parish and diocese throughout the world, Peter's Pence flow in rivulets, joined by the remittances from the lands, vineyards and monasteries of the Dominicans, Franciscans, Augustinians and other Holy Orders, which flow into rivers mingled with the tribute of monarchs and the proceeds from the sale of indulgences and benefices and the confiscated property of heretics forfeit to the Holy Office of the Inquisition and the taxes imposed upon the Papal States, until a great floodtide of gold cascades upon Rome. And who has the heavy responsibility to dispose of this fortune in a manner that brings honor upon our Lord, His Church and its servants? Me – Giovanni de Medici. Certainly, no one can accuse me of shirking my duty.

It is an interesting tale that I have to tell. I am not a literary man – I have no genius with words. I shall endeavor to present my story without excessive flourish and with as much objectivity as any man can muster in writing about his own life. Because this is a private document (at least for the balance of my life) I shall dispense with the customary papal "we" in referring to myself. If I put words in quotations, it will represent my best recollection or understanding of what was said, but I cannot vouchsafe that the words are absolutely precise.

I shall commence this narrative with a brief history of my family, followed by my childhood, my adventures as cardinal and my papacy. I shall abbreviate discussions of religious dogma and political intrigue as such subjects are both convoluted and of little lasting interest. It is my fervent hope that, after my death, some of the harshest slanders about the Medici will be dispelled by this history.

I shall take prudent precautions to protect the secrecy of this memoir, which I know will offend many within the Curia. Only one man knows of its existence, my cousin Giulio, the Cardinal Medici, who is my most loyal friend and the man I trust above all others on this earth.

THE MEDICI

The origin of the Medici family is shrouded by the mists of time. My family believes that we descended from Averardo, a bold knight in the army of Charlemagne, who slew an evil giant who had been terrorizing the peasants of the Mugello, that verdant valley of the Sieve River nestled between the peaks of the Apennines to the north of Florence. In the savage battle, Averardo's shield was dented in several places by furious blows from the giant's mace. Charlemagne himself decreed that the great deed be memorialized by a coat of arms upon which the dents are represented by raised red balls ("palle" in vernacular Italian) upon a shield of gold; the insignia of the Medici for many generations.

Less imaginative historians suggest that we are descended from a family of apothecaries (hence our name) who left the Mugello for Florence around the year 1200 and that the balls on our shield actually represent medicinal pills. Still others suggest the balls represent coins, the traditional symbol of the pawnbroker.

While the Medici's origin may never be known (not that it truly matters), that of Florence can be stated with absolute certainty. In 59 B.C., Julius Caesar decreed that a trading settlement be established on the banks of the Arno River, just below the ancient Etruscan hilltop town of Fiesole. For a millennium, Florence remained a backwater of first the Roman and then the Holy Roman Empires, but by 1200 AD it had become a major manufacturing and trading center.

Around this time, the first of my ancestors migrated from the Mugello. In 1296, Ardingo de Medici was elected Gonfaloniere° of Florence, followed by his brother Guccio in 1299 and Averardo de Medici in 1314.

In 1348, the most significant event in Florence's history occurred. That summer, the Black Death swept through the city, inflicting unprecedented suffering and death. Approximately 80,000 souls (almost two-thirds of the inhabitants) perished that year. Entire families, convents and monasteries were wiped out. The Medici and other rich fled to their country estates, but the poor had no place to go. Farmers refused to deliver food to the city for fear of contracting the disease and many otherwise healthy residents died of hunger. To this day, Florence has not regained its population of 1348.

The Great Plague did more than devastate the population. It cleaved the souls of the survivors and their descendants into two disparate halves. One half is best represented by Boccaccio's *Decameron*. Life is hard, fate is random and death lurks everywhere. Therefore, enjoy life to the fullest and live every day as if it were your last. No city on earth celebrates like Florence. Scores of religious and secular holidays, festivals and receptions for distinguished visitors (many underwritten by

---

° Translator's note: Mayor.

my family) mark the calendar, each an occasion for revelry and feasting, pageants, processions and tournaments, music, songs and merry-making. On these days, the houses and shops are festooned with tapestries and gold and silk cloths, the women parade in exquisite gowns, bedecked with pearls and jewels and the men play practical jokes, sing ribald songs and drink fine Tuscan wine until they drop.

However, competing for the Florentine soul is the stern admonishment of the Church, as forcefully represented by the Franciscan friar, Bernardino of Siena. He thundered in Lenten sermons that pestilence and plague were visited upon this modern Sodom by a wrathful God as punishment for Florence's multitude of sins. While he railed against "gambling, blasphemy of God and the saints, gluttony, frequenting of taverns and other places of ill repute, lying, mistrust, deception and theft," he addressed his most vitriolic denunciations against the Florentines' practice of sodomy.

Like in ancient Athens, sodomy is an integral part of Florentine social life and culture. It is not considered unnatural or evil by most people. Girls are kept under close supervision by their watchful parents, to be preserved intact for an advantageous marriage. Men do not generally marry until their early thirties and a substantial number of men never marry at all, lacking the money or connections to contract a suitable match. So, with prostitutes being both expensive and subject to foul diseases, most adolescents and young men satisfy their natural urges with their peers.

The practice of sodomy permeates every level of Florentine society and makes Florence famous throughout Europe. Indeed, the German word for sodomite is "florenzer." According to municipal records, two out of three male Florentines under the age of forty have been denounced by the Officers of the Night.

Mothers dress their boys enticingly in short, brightly colored doublets and stockings with convenient buttoned flaps in the front and back. Fathers encourage their young sons to seek relationships with older men with money and political influence. An attractive young boy can put food on the family's table.

Upon marriage or after forty, few men continue their relations with boys. Some, like Donatello, Botticelli and Leonardo (all denounced to the Office of the Night) and, truth be told, me, were exclusive sodomites, but most Florentines (like my father and brother Giuliano) were catholic in their passions and would bed a boy, a slave girl°, the wife of a friend or their own wife with equal pleasure.

The Church was, and continues to be, unequivocal in its condemnation of sodomy as a grave and mortal sin, but, of course, priests are among its most prolific practitioners. There is an amusing letter from 1470 preserved in the Medici library at San Marco monastery from the Officers of the Night to the Archbishop of Florence:

> Most reverend and just father . . . our magistracy is entrusted with safeguarding the convents and also with obviating, as much as possible, the horrible vice of sodomy. Wishing to fulfill a part of our duty, we have arrested several young boys who have been sodomized not only by laymen, but also by numerous priests. This was made known to the representative of your most reverend lord, yet nothing has been done about it. For this reason we are most scandalized.

Nothing has ever been done about it.

No man better illustrates the conflict in the Florentine soul than Michelangelo. The artist, born the same year as me, was apprenticed by my father when he was thirteen and lived with me, as a brother, in the Medici palace. There, Michelangelo and I were tutored by Angelo Poliziano and Marsilio Ficino, leaders of Lorenzo's Platonic Academy, who introduced us to both Greek philosophy and Greek love.

While I always have found it pleasurable, Michelangelo, like my mother Clarice, took seriously the teachings of the Church and was thus miserable during his entire life. Uninterested in women (he once wrote in a poem: "when I look down upon each of your breasts they look like two watermelons in a bag") and restrained by guilt from satisfying his natural inclination, he could exorcise his passion only through his art.

In 1508, Pope Julius II (whose lust for young boys was insatiable) commissioned Michelangelo to fresco the ceiling of the chapel constructed by his late uncle, Pope Sixtus IV. Sixtus himself was a sodomite, most notably with his "nephew", Pietro Riario (whom he elevated to cardinal and whom some believe to be the natural issue of an unnatural liaison between Sixtus and his sister). It is ironic but fitting that Michelangelo's ceiling of the Sistine Chapel, the most venerated painting in all of Christendom, is also the most passionate tribute in all of art to the transcendent beauty of the naked male body.

° Translator's note: Florence authorized slavery in 1336 after an outbreak of plague led to a shortage of Italian servants. Most slaves were imported from Greece, Turkey and the Caucasus.

Enough! This is not a treatise on sodomy, although it weighs heavy upon my soul that I must, as pontiff, condemn that which I practice and enjoy. I have digressed yet again. At this rate, my papacy will have ended before the story of my life begins.

The metamorphosis of the Medici from a provincial Florentine merchant house to an international banking colossus was the work of my great-great-grandfather and namesake, Giovanni di Bicci de Medici. Born in 1360, he was apprenticed to his cousin Vieri di Cambio de Medici, director of the small Rome branch of the Medici bank. Giovanni was a quiet, humble and industrious businessman who cultivated an image of being a friend of the workingman while amassing a giant fortune. He avoided ostentatious displays, preferring to work behind the scenes. He proffered to his son, Cosimo, the advice that became the touchstone for our family over four subsequent generations:

> Never hold an opinion contrary to the will of the people, even if this same people should prefer something that is perfectly useless. Do not speak with the air of giving counsel, but prefer rather to discuss matters gently and benevolently. Be as inconspicuous as possible.

But while Giovanni may have been quiet and unassuming, it was a risky financial gamble that catapulted the Medici bank to international domination. He financed the ecclesiastical career of Baldassare Cossa.

Cossa was born on the Italian island of Procida where, in his youth, he was a seafaring pirate, preying on merchant ships in the Gulf of Naples. While he had the requisite skills for a successful life of crime, he was also extremely intelligent and ambitious and recognized that the life expectancy of a pirate was short and the work demanding. So, like many other young men of great ambition, he decided to make a career in the Church, where the potential for riches dwarfed the most optimistic dreams of the captain of a corsair.

Baldassare enrolled in the canon law program at the University of Bologna, where he continued his predatory ways, assaulting, robbing and extorting his fellow students.°

In time, Cossa's talents drew the attention of Pope Boniface IX, a fellow Neapolitan, who offered him a job as private chamberlain in Rome. There, Cossa handled the Pope's sales of benefices, indulgences and dispensations. True to his nature, Cossa embezzled some of the papal funds which passed through his hands and Giovanni, the young

---

° Translator's note: In defense, the students formed a secret society, *Kappa Sigma*, the first university fraternity in Europe.

17

apprentice at the Medici bank's Rome branch, handled the illicit proceeds "under the table" taking the customary ten percent commission. When, in 1402, Boniface offered Cossa a cardinal's hat, it was Giovanni who funded the 10,000 ducat purchase price.

In that year, Gian Galeazzo Visconti, the Duke of Milan, declared war on Florence and Bologna and succeeded in capturing Bologna (which had been sold to the Church by the Visconti in 1360 for some quick cash). Boniface named his new cardinal the papal legate to Bologna with instructions to retake the city by force. Given command of the papal army, the former pirate proved a most able ground commander and drove the Visconti out. Cossa then took up residency in Bologna as its virtual dictator, murdering his rivals, extorting its merchants and raping at least 200 of its women (most of them nuns). But his relationship with Giovanni remained strong.

In 1409, Cossa, with Giovanni's backing, organized his boldest undertaking. He invited friendly cardinals and bishops to a new Church Council at Pisa. He intended that the Council would bring an end to the Great Schism by deposing the recently elected Pope Gregory, together with the Avignon Pope, Benedict XII.

As he had hoped, the Council declared the two sitting Popes heretics and named Cossa's nominee, his good friend Cardinal Filargi of Milan, as the one true Pope (Alexander V) of a united Christendom. Unfortunately, neither Gregory nor Benedict abdicated and each Pope immediately excommunicated the other two. Christendom now had three pontiffs, each claiming the backing of the Holy Spirit and the obedience of the world's Catholics. The King of France supported Benedict, the King of Naples supported Gregory and the Emperor supported Alexander.

Having failed at Pisa, Cossa now embarked on a course of action more consistent with his character. He raised an army (with Medici florins) and marched south to Rome, where he captured the Vatican on behalf of Alexander, driving deposed Pope Gregory into exile. Shortly thereafter, Alexander died (some libelously suggest that Cossa poisoned him). Seven days later, Cossa was crowned Pope John XXIII.

Giovanni's bold gamble had paid off. Cossa immediately named the Medici bank as the Depository of the Papal Chamber, which meant that all worldwide papal income, debt collections and expenditures passed through Medici hands. We were now God's Banker and unimaginable profits flowed to the family.

In 1429, Giovanni died of the Medici family curse, gout, and was succeeded by my great-grandfather Cosimo. While Giovanni catapulted the Medici to primacy in wealth, it was Cosimo who established the family's primacy in politics. And to properly tell the tale of Cosimo, I must now intentionally digress and provide a brief explanation of fifteenth century Italian politics (I flatter myself that this narrative may eventually be read by men of other times and nations).

Beginning in the south, in 1260 Naples was sold by Pope Clement IV (together with Sicily and the rest of southern Italy) to the French lord, Charles of Anjou, for an annual tribute of 800 ounces of gold. However, in 1442, King Alfonso of Aragon conquered Naples with a Spanish army and, since that time, French and Spanish nobility have fought countless battles for control of Naples and the south (bringing, in addition to the French boils, great misery to all the people of Italy). The Pope, its titular sovereign, has shifted his allegiance as often as the military and political situation required.

To Naples' north, Rome nominally belonged to the Pope, but in reality it was a centuries old killing ground. Ancient Roman tribes, the Orsini, Colonna and Frangipani, fought each other and the Popes for control of the city and its surrounding towns in the Compagna.

In the Papal States of central Italy, the Pope was once again the titular sovereign, but the important towns were ruled (and misruled) by petty tyrants who declared their obedience to the Pope (and paid token tribute as papal vassals)but acted independent of papal authority in all material respects.

The situation was similar in the Lombardy Plain, except that the titular sovereign was the Holy Roman Emperor. However, the region was dominated by the Visconti (and later the Sforza), the Dukes of Milan, in the west and the Republic of Venice in the east. Venice, a republic in name only, was ruthlessly ruled by the Council of Ten, whose political enemies were quickly and efficiently strangled, beheaded, drawn and quartered, drowned in the lagoon or buried upside down in the Piazza San Marco, depending upon the severity of the indiscretion or the whims of the Council.

Finally, Tuscany was dominated by the Republic of Florence, although Florence was never able to conquer its historic enemies, Siena to the south and Lucca to the north. Florence's day to day operations were overseen by the nine Priori of the Signoria and the Gonfaloniere, whose names were selected by lot and who served only two month terms, living together in the Palazzo della Signoria. But, in truth, it was the rich merchants and bankers who really ran the city.

The only constant in Italian politics was war. There was virtually no time when any Italian city was not at war with at least one other rival. How did Italy flourish despite nearly continuous warfare?The answer is that we Italians elevated warfare to an art form, as unique as Italian gastronomy or painting.

Unlike the feudal lords of the barbaric north, who maintained standing professional armies which ravaged the lands through which they passed like locusts through a field, Italians contracted war to bands of roving mercenaries commanded by condottieri. The condottieri were businessmen, first and foremost, had no allegiance other than to gold and took care not to waste their most valuable assets – their fighting men. So, Italian warfare was an intricate ballet of maneuver and siege, carefully choreographed by opposing captains (often related to one another) to minimize wasteful bloodshed and maximize the opportunity for plunder. Prisoners who could be ransomed for profit were far preferable than dead opponents who had no value. Entire wars could be prosecuted without either army coming in sight of the other. And, by common practice, all warfare was suspended as winter approached so as not to subject the participants to undue hardship (with new contracts to be negotiated the following spring).

Wars were resolved in an equally artful manner. When one condottiere gained the upper hand, the losing city might negotiate a peace treaty; or contract marriage between the families of the rulers; or bribe the condottiere to abandon his campaign or even switch sides and attack his former employer. Often, other cities would intervene, bidden or unbidden, to maintain the pre-existing status quo.

It was therefore rare for a town to be brutally sacked in an Italian war and rape and pillage were principally (but not always) inflicted upon the lower classes. The rulers of Italian cities usually had far more to fear from their closest relatives. Indeed, the Medici was one of the few noble families where parricide and fratricide were not part of the family history. Unfortunately for Italy, this civilized form of warfare became obsolete in 1494 when Ludovico Sforza, in a moment of madness, invited Charles VIII to invade Italy with his army of 50,000 bloodthirsty and diseased Frenchmen.

With this brief lesson in Italian history concluded, I return to the story of my great-grandfather. Cosimo was born in 1389 and, as the eldest son, was destined to inherit the family business.

After making a tour of the Medici branch banks in northern Europe, Cosimo returned briefly to Florence. Giovanni then dispatched him to Rome where he served as the manager of the Rome branch for three years.

When Giovanni's health deteriorated, Cosimo was brought back to Florence. At this time, Florence was controlled politically by the Albizzi, an old merchant family whose wealth had been eclipsed by the Medici. While Giovanni avoided politics like the plague, Cosimo believed that control of Florence's government was essential to the continued prosperity of the Medici. So, a collision between the Albizzi and the Medici was inevitable.

For several years, an uneasy stalemate prevailed between Cosimo and Rinaldo Albizzi, the young head of the family. Rinaldo and his supporters controlled the Signoria, but Medici money, lavished on the Florentines through the underwriting of festivals, public works and many acts of charity, enamored the Medici to the lower classes. Cosimo's embrace of humanism also made him a favorite (and major benefactor) of Florence's cultural elite.

In 1431, Rinaldo struck directly at the Medici's purse by sponsoring a decree that permitted Jews to engage in money lending in Florence, a profession heretofore forbidden to them. Cosimo retaliated by orchestrating sodomy indictments against Rinaldo's political supporters.

Cosimo tried personal diplomacy to heal the rift with Rinaldo. His words:

> Now it seems to me only just and honest that I should prefer the good name and honor of my house to you: that I should work for my own interest rather than for yours. So you and I will act like two big dogs that, when they meet, smell one another and then, because they both have teeth, go their ways. Wherefore now you can attend to your affairs and I to mine.

This tactful approach bore no fruit. In August, 1433, Rinaldo stacked the Priori with allies and, with the government firmly in his pocket, launched what he expected to be a fatal blow against his enemy.

Cosimo, who was summering at his villa at Cafaggiolo, received a summons demanding his attendance at a meeting of the Signoria. He returned to Florence and went to the council chamber, but the Captain of the Guard, instead of granting him entry, escorted him to the Alberghettino, the tiny prison cell near the top of the bell-tower.

With Cosimo locked up, Rinaldo convened a parliament° and his armed supporters prevented all Medici adherents from entering the Piazza della Signoria. The parliament obediently nominated a balia° which then indicted Cosimo for treason. Rinaldo demanded the death penalty and seizure of all Medici property which, given his control of the balia, seemed a near certainty.

But Rinaldo underestimated his opponent (as many men have underestimated me). With a modest bribe to his jailer, Cosimo was able to turn his cramped cell into the command center of a coordinated

---

° Translator's note: A meeting of all citizens during which the government could be recalled or the constitution changed.

° Translator's note: A committee charged with carrying out the policies adopted by the parliament.

campaign to influence the outcome. Coded messages, as well as sumptuous meals, went back and forth between the Medici palace and the Alberghettino. The Gonfaloniere was turned with a 1,000 florin bribe and other leading members of the balia were subverted as well.

Venice and Ferrara, deeply indebted to the Medici bank, dispatched ambassadors to Florence to demand Cosimo's release, as did the bank's most esteemed customer, Pope Eugenius IV. Cosimo's brother, Lorenzo, raised an army at Cafaggiolo and the condottiere, Nicolo da Tolentino, was engaged to move his mercenaries from Pisa to the outskirts of Florence.

The pressure proved too much for the balia. Instead of executing Cosimo and confiscating his property, the balia merely exiled him to Padua, where he was welcomed with the pomp usually reserved for royalty. Rinaldo, glumly acknowledging his tactical errors, noted: "One should either not lift a finger against the mighty or, if one does, one must do it thoroughly."

Cosimo, in turn, made no errors in extracting his revenge. Using his international connections, Cosimo engineered a boycott of credit for Florence, so that its government could not borrow "so much as a pistachio nut." The squeeze on credit soon extended down to the merchants and the city's economy began to crumble.

When Florence's entire 9,000 man army was routed and taken prisoner by Milanese mercenaries at the battle of Imola on August 28, 1434 (consistent with the art of Italian warfare, only four Florentines died and thirty wounded on the field of battle), Florence turned against the Albizzi. A Signoria favorable to my family's interests was selected, the banishment was revoked and Cosimo was invited back.

Cosimo started home that very day, accompanied by an honor guard of 300 Venetian soldiers. All along the route, men gathered to cheer him and the citizens of Florence welcomed Cosimo back like a conquering hero.

Wasting no time, Cosimo exiled the Albizzi family and their principal supporters. Florence now belonged to the Medici and would remain so for another sixty years. As his friend, Pope Pius II, said of Cosimo:

> Political questions are settled at his house. The man he chooses holds office. He it is who decides peace and war and controls the laws. He is King in everything but name.

In 1447, Cosimo made a decision as bold and consequential as Giovanni's sponsorship of Baldassare Cossa – he decided to underwrite Francesco Sforza's campaign to rule Milan. Let me provide some necessary background.

The Visconti family had ruled Milan for 170 years. The last Visconti, Filippo Maria, was a grotesquely fat man with a penchant for rolling about naked in his garden during hot summer days. He was so ugly that he refused to have his portrait painted. He was so suspicious that he had his first wife executed as a possible adulteress and so superstitious that he had his second wife locked away when a dog howled on their wedding night. But despite these quirks, Filippo was an astute politician and tactician who greatly expanded Milan's power and influence in Lombardy.

Filippo's chief instrument was the great condottiere, Francesco Sforza. Sforza was the illegitimate son of an illiterate peasant who had been kidnapped as a child by a gang of brigands. Giacomo Sforza rose to take command of the gang and converted it into a mercenary band, taking assignments from Naples and the Pope. Upon his father's death, Francesco succeeded him and greatly expanded the band into one of the largest, most disciplined and effective private armies in Italy. Francesco, unlike most of his contemporaries, was not only competent, but honest and he took contracts from virtually all of the cities in Italy. Since Milan was the richest city in Italy (if not the world), he developed a special relationship with its Duke, Filippo Maria.

Sforza was both intelligent and ambitious and desired dynastic lands to pass down to his heirs. He set his sights on Bianca, Filippo's natural daughter and only issue. Filippo distained marrying Bianca to the bastard son of an illiterate peasant and she had no shortage of noble suitors. However, Francesco remained persistent and, as the years passed, became increasingly aggressive in his arguments.

Filippo, being a perceptive man, ultimately concluded that having Italy's most formidable condottiere as a son-in-law was better than having him as an enemy; so he finally consented to the match, which was consummated in 1441.

In 1447, Filippo died and Milan was viewed by all as a fruit ripe for picking. The Emperor asserted his ancient claim against the city (the Visconti Dukes were nominally his vassals). King Alfonso of Naples lay claim as the legatee under Filippo's will. The Duke of Orleans made a claim through his late mother, Valentina Visconti, the natural daughter of the first Duke of Milan. Venice asserted a claim as the dominant power in Lombardy. And, of course, Sforza claimed Milan as Bianca's husband.

The Milanese themselves had other ideas and declared an independent republic, but none of the disputants took this as a serious obstacle. Sforza had the requisite military skills to press his claim, but lacked the vast sums of money required to successfully vanquish his formidable adversaries. And as the illegitimate son of an outlaw brigand, he lacked the breeding thought necessary to rule Italy's premier city. Only one man in Italy could provide what Sforza needed – Cosimo de Medici.

Of course, Florence and Milan had been enemies for decades and Sforza had personally led his army against Florence on numerous occasions. But that stopped neither Francesco nor Cosimo from doing mutually advantageous business. From Cosimo's perspective, allowing Venice to dominate Milan would forever upset the delicate balance of power in Italy. Venice's oligarchs were already too powerful and threatened the Medici's mercantile empire. So Cosimo opened his purse (and that of Florence) to Francesco and used his innumerable connections with Europe's leaders to check the Venetian advance against Milan.

The military and political jockeying went on for three years, but Sforza triumphantly entered Milan in 1450 and declared himself the Duke of Milan, bringing an end to the short-lived republic. Once again, a bold Medici gamble had paid off and the ruler of Italy's richest city was deeply beholden to the head of Italy's richest family.

Venice, of course, was livid at having been out-maneuvered by Cosimo and Sforza and thirsted for revenge. It signed an alliance with Naples to jointly invade both Milan and Florence and both cities expelled all Florentine bankers and merchants. Venice then prevailed upon the Emperor and the Eastern Emperor to expel the Florentines from Germany and Greece. Cosimo countered by signing a mutual defense treaty with France and negotiated trading concessions with Venice's greatest enemy – the Mohammedan Turks.

In 1453, a Neapolitan army commanded by Alfonso's bastard son, Ferrante, marched north towards Tuscany, while a French Army commanded by Rene of Anjou (who considered Naples still to be Angevin property) marched south. It appeared that all of Italy was about to ignite into war.

But then an unexpected and calamitous event occurred that made the petty territorial disputes of Italy suddenly trivial – the Turks captured Constantinople, the city of Constantine and birthplace of Eastern Christianity. The Byzantine Empire had fallen to the Mohammedans. All of Christendom was now at risk and nowhere was the risk graver than in Italy, whose eastern coastline was exposed to the Turkish fleet.

The Pope convened an emergency meeting at Lodi to end the intramural bickering and unite all of Italy in a holy crusade to retake Constantinople. The Venetians, now confronted with a direct threat to their very existence, were eager to abandon the war they had fomented. In the Treaty of Lodi, signed in 1454, all of the principal cities of Italy entered into a non-aggression pact and formed a Most Holy League with the Pope. Sforza was now universally recognized as the legitimate ruler of Milan and Ferrante's army was recalled to Naples.

After the treaty of Lodi, Italy experienced a rare period of extended peace, which was fortunate since Cosimo had become increasingly disabled by gout. He refocused his remaining energy on expanding the Medici's commercial empire (in 1466 he obtained an exclusive concession from the Pope to exploit Italy's only alum mine[°]) and acts of beneficence. He was especially active in his architectural commissions. Cosimo once presciently remarked: "I know the humors of my city; before fifty years have passed we shall be expelled, but my buildings shall remain."

According to Cosimo's books of account, he spent 663,755 florins on buildings, charities and taxes. I modestly note that I spent a greater sum in just the first year of my pontificate.

Cosimo died on August 1, 1464 and was interred in the vault of San Lorenzo, the Medici's church. The Signoria, which had expelled Cosimo from Florence in 1433, now confirmed upon him the posthumous title "Pater Patriae."[°]

The story of my grandfather Piero is short, as he was afflicted by severe gout from an early age (his nickname was "il Gottoso") and headed the family for only five years before he succumbed. Because of his disability, Piero did not serve a long apprenticeship in the bank like Cosimo. Actually, Cosimo was grooming his second son, Giovanni, to succeed him, but Giovanni, to everyone's surprise, died of apoplexy before his invalid older brother.

Despite the pain that plagued him throughout his life, Piero had an amiable disposition and King Louis XI of France, where Piero had served as ambassador, enjoyed his company (and Medici loans) so much that he issued a diploma authorizing the Medici to incorporate three of the lilies of the royal house of Valois into our coat of arms.

After Cosimo's death, Piero quietly but forcefully attended to the needs of the Medici bank and other mercantile concerns. Under his stewardship, the family's wealth grew even greater, surpassing that of both his father and grandfather.

But, as historically has been the case, our enemies, tempted by Piero's bodily weakness, underestimated the strength of the family's leader and attempted, once again, to destroy the Medici by treasonous intrigue.

A cabal of second-rate merchants, led by Lucca Pitti (whose monstrously ostentatious palace has destroyed a beautiful hillside in

---

[°] Translator's note: Alum was a mineral salt, essential to tanning, dyes and glass-making.

[°] Translator's note: "Father of his Country."

Oltrarno) schemed to foment an armed rebellion and execute Piero and his sons.

The conspirators secretly approached Venice (still smoldering from Cosimo's thwarting of its ambitions against Milan) and Ferrara for military assistance. Shortly after old Francesco Sforza died on March 8, 1464, Duke Borso d'Este of Ferrara signed onto the plot (the successor Duke of Milan, twenty year old Galeazzo Maria Sforza, was known for his cruelty and lechery, but not his military skills).

When Piero took ill that August and retired to his villa at Careggi, the conspiracy was launched. Este's army marched west from Ferrara through Bologna towards Florence and armed assassins set out for Careggi. But Cosimo's old friend, Giovanni Bentivoglio, the tyrant of Bologna, sent a swift messenger with word of the approaching danger.

Piero did not hesitate. He ordered his servants to place him on a litter and carry him back to Florence, taking back roads to avoid the hired thugs. Surrounded by armed Medici supporters, Piero made a dramatic entrance into the Signoria, where he called Florence to arms to resist the foreign army that was approaching its border.

This bold move crushed the conspiracy. Lucca Pitti, fearing for his life (and fortune) hurried to the Medici palace to beg forgiveness and pledge his undying loyalty. Like his father, Piero demanded a parliament and 3,000 Medici soldiers guarded the entrances to the Piazza della Signoria to assure its outcome. The conspirators (with the exception of the repentant Pitti) were banished from Florence and their property seized (in any other city, they would have been executed). The rebellion was over.

I now come to the challenge of setting down my father's story. As much as I desire to aggrandize the history of my family, I must be honest in this account. While it is indisputable that Lorenzo de Medici had many great qualities, I shall not sweep his defects under the carpet.

Lorenzo was born on New Year's Day, 1449. He was exceedingly intelligent and the first Medici to receive an entirely humanistic education. His interests were broad. He loved philosophy and literature, poetry (he was an accomplished poet), art and architecture, music (he was an exceptional lute player), farming and hunting, sports, practical jokes, tournaments, pageants and love-making of every type. Lorenzo was a true man of the Renaissance. Unfortunately, my father's varied interests failed to extend to banking and commerce, which was to have disastrous consequences for our fortune.

Piero, his health quickly deteriorating, decided to contract an early marriage for nineteen year old Lorenzo. Shunning Florentine society (from which all prior Medici brides had been selected), he set his sights on one of the most ancient, noble and powerful families in all of Italy –

the Orsini of Rome. In many respects, this potential match mirrored Cosimo's backing of Francesco Sforza. The Orsini were a military powerhouse, having been in a near constant state of war against their fellow Roman barons as well as various popes for several hundred years. Medici gold could underwrite numerous future battles and Orsini arms could protect the far-flung Medici interests.

Piero settled on sixteen year old Clarice Orsini, daughter of Jacopo Orsini and niece of Cardinal Latino. After negotiation of a 6,000 florin dowry, Lorenzo and Clarice were married by proxy, with Filippo de Medici, Archbishop of Pisa, representing the groom.

To assuage the Florentines, who were not pleased that Piero had ignored their many eligible daughters, Piero sponsored a splendid tournament at a cost exceeding 10,000 florins. Clarice made her own entry into Florence four months later, which of course called for another round of celebrations. For three days, the Medici feasted the citizens of Florence, who consumed two and a half tons of sweetmeats and 300 barrels of wine.

Piero died shortly after the marriage and a delegation of Florence's leading citizens arrived at our palace to express their condolences and request Lorenzo, then just twenty-one, to take on his father's and grandfather's role as the de facto ruler of the city. My father graciously accepted this unofficial coronation.

For several years, my father gave the Florentines what they most desired – an almost continuous succession of pageants, tournaments, festivals, spectacles, revels and processions. Lorenzo sponsored carnivals, dances, horse races, circuses, mock battles and football games. He financed these distractions with profits from the Medici bank, but was oblivious to the fact that, in the absence of vigilant oversight, the branch managers were beginning to make unsound loans and investments.

Lorenzo's first political misstep occurred in the Tuscan town of Volterra in 1472. The magistrates of Volterra, a dependency of Florence, had awarded a lucrative mining concession to a consortium of Florentine and Volterran businessmen. The local citizens, believing that bribery accounted for the generosity of the concession, elected new magistrates who voided the contract and seized the mine. Naturally, Florence could not condone such treatment of its businessmen, so Lorenzo dispatched the condottiere, Federico da Montefeltro, Duke of Urbino, to restore the mine to its rightful owners. Montefeltro besieged the town, which quickly capitulated, promising return of the mine in exchange for withdrawal of his mercenary army. However, the Duke's men, asserting their customary privileges, entered the town, raped some women, murdered some men and looted and burned a few businesses.

None of this would have been noteworthy had not my father, upon receiving news of the second-rate sack, personally rushed to Volterra, apologized for the destruction and distributed money to the victims. This display of weakness was duly noted by the enemies of the Medici throughout Italy.

On December 10, 1475, my pregnant mother, Clarice, awoke from a vivid and frightening dream. She dreamed she was lying on the floor of the Duomo, writhing in pain as she gave birth. What emerged from her loins was a lion, immense in size but docile in nature. The next day, I entered this world.

THE PAZZI CONSPIRACY

The earliest direct memories I have of my life are the events of Sunday, April 26, 1478, when I was just two and a half years old. It was a sunny spring day and our palace was strewn with fresh flowers and bustled as the servants prepared a magnificent feast for an important visitor. My older brother Piero and I were dressed in matching scarlet doublets with white silk stockings and black leather shoes with silver buckles (I confess my memories of fashion and food are far more vivid than my recollections of canon law).

I recall my father leaving for Mass with our young guest, who looked wonderful in his scarlet robes and tasseled hat. Later, my Uncle Giuliano, who was nursing an injured leg, limped off to church in the company of two strangers. I was in the courtyard of our palace, stealing marzipan from a table laden with sweets, when I heard an awful commotion in the street. Suddenly, armed men streamed into the courtyard. One of them, whom I recognized as one of my father's bodyguards, grabbed me in his arms and rushed me inside, my nurse screeching at the top of her lungs as she followed behind.

My brother and I, along with our nurse, were locked in our bedchamber and I heard men stationed outside our door. I heard the palace filling with shouting men and wailing women. From our window, I saw the Via Larga filled with bands of armed men and soldiers on horseback. I smelled smoke. I cried from fear and my nurse did nothing to comfort me.

Sometime later, our door opened and my father and mother entered. My father's face was ashen white and a bloody bandage was wrapped around his neck and his brocaded waistcoat was stained with blood. Tears ran down my mother's cheeks. Lorenzo hugged Piero and me and told us not to be afraid. Then he left us, leaving our mother behind.

The next morning, my mother and brother and sisters and I left Florence in our coach, accompanied by more than 100 armed soldiers. As we passed through the Piazza della Signoria, I saw dead men hanging by their necks from the upper windows. Some were naked. One was dressed in vestments. We traveled to Pistoia, where we stayed with our friends, the Panciaticci family. It would be more than a year before we were permitted to return home to Florence.

This is what I can remember myself. Later, of course, I learned the details of what is now universally called the Pazzi conspiracy. To put it in proper context, I must go back in time to 1471, when Francesco della Rovere was elected as Pope Sixtus IV, succeeding my father's friend, Paul II. Della Rovere was a Franciscan from Savona with a large family who elevated six of his "nephews" (of whom several were his natural issue) to the purple shortly after attaining the supreme dignity. This, of course, was a time-honored tradition, although Sixtus somewhat overdid it.

In 1473, Sixtus successfully negotiated with Duke Galeazzo Maria Sforza of Milan to marry Galeazzo's bastard daughter, Caterina, to his nephew, Girolamo Riario. The contract required Sixtus to purchase the town of Imola from Sforza for 40,000 ducats and present it to the young couple as a wedding gift. Sixtus naturally went to God's Banker for a loan to complete the purchase.

Now, as I have repeatedly written, the foundation of the Medici fortune was its appointment as Depository of the Papal Chamber. All of my ancestors since Giovanni di Bicci had made excellent relations with the pontiff the keystone of their business policy. My father did not.

Imola, while inconsequential in size and revenue, was strategically located on the main road between Rimini and Bologna and was highly desired by Florence, which was engaged in parallel negotiations with Sforza. So Lorenzo, putting Florence's interest above that of the Medici, refused Sixtus' request for a loan. In one inexcusable blunder, sixty years of mutually beneficial relations between my family and the Vatican was destroyed. From that moment on, the path of the Medici fortune descended from its zenith to its nadir.

Lorenzo's refusal was not only stupid, but ineffectual. Sixtus immediately went to the Rome branch of the Pazzi bank, which was happy to provide the loan. The Pazzi were one of Florence's oldest families, tracing their lineage all the way back to Pazzo de Pazzi, supposedly the first knight to breach the walls of Jerusalem during the First Crusade. However, the Pazzi bank was a mere shadow of the Medici bank. That changed in an instant when Sixtus terminated the Medici contract and rewarded the Pazzi bank by naming it the new papal depository.°

It was a measure of Lorenzo's hubris that, instead of begging the pontiff's forgiveness, he escalated the rivalry. In 1474, Lorenzo supported Nicolo Vitelli, a condottiere who had occupied the fortified town of Citta di Castello in defiance of Sixtus, who rightfully claimed the town as part of the Papal States. When the Pope sent an army to re-take the town, Lorenzo reinforced Vitelli with 6,000 hired mercenaries, but to no avail. Vitelli was routed and forced to retreat to Florence where, to Sixtus' disgust, he was welcomed as a hero.

The relationship between Sixtus and Lorenzo went from bad to worse when the Pope named a Pazzi relation, Francesco Salviati, as the new Archbishop of Pisa upon the death of Filippo de Medici. Traditionally, popes had sought the concurrence of Florence prior to naming bishops within cities in Tuscany under Florentine control. The Signoria, under

---

° Translator's note: Sixtus later awarded the Pazzi the Medici's enormously profitable alum concessions.

Lorenzo's prompting, declared Salviati persona non grata and subject to arrest if he ventured into the province.

My father made another grave miscalculation in 1475 when he attempted to replace the existing alliance between Florence, Milan and Naples with a new alliance between Florence, Milan and Venice. This not only infuriated the Pope, but angered King Ferrante of Naples who was not even consulted. Sixtus responded to my father's machinations against him with a thinly veiled threat: "We may have to use our irons, so as to help Lorenzo see that he is a citizen and we are the Pope, because thus has it pleased God."

Sixtus struck back spiritually at Lorenzo and threatened Florence with interdict and excommunication if the ban on Salviati was not lifted. In October, 1475, the Priori submitted to the Pope and accepted Salviati as the new Archbishop of Pisa.

The following year Duke Galeazzo of Milan was assassinated, leaving his seven year old son as heir. The boy's mother and four ambitious uncles became locked in a struggle for control of the regency, diverting Milan's attention and arms from the simmering dispute between Lorenzo and Sixtus.

Sensing Lorenzo's weakness, and hating him with an unholy passion, Archbishop Salviati hatched a plot to assassinate Lorenzo and Giuliano. He enlisted two co-conspirators, the Pope's nephew, Girolamo Riario, now Count of Imola, and Francesco de Pazzi, manager of the Rome branch of the Pazzi bank. Each had an interest in seeing the Medici destroyed.

The three conspirators journeyed to Florence to enlist the support of Jacopo de Pazzi, head of the family. Jacopo was a compulsive gambler but these odds were too long for him and he turned them down. Francesco next approached the condottiere Gian Battista da Montesecco, whom he wanted to handle the actual bloodshed. Montesecco, who was on the payroll of the Curia, told Pazzi that the Pope's blessing would be required before he would undertake such a dangerous mission. Girolamo arranged a meeting with his uncle.

> "But this matter, Holy Father, may turn out ill without the death of Lorenzo and Giuliano, and perhaps of others," Montesecco informed Sixtus.°

° Translator's note: Montesecco wrote a detailed confession after his capture and torture.

"I do not wish the death of anyone on any account since it does not accord with our office to consent to such a thing. Though Lorenzo is a villain, and behaves ill towards us, yet we do not on any account desire his death, but only a change in the government."

"All that we can do shall be done to see that Lorenzo does not die," Girolamo said. "But should he die, will your Holiness pardon him who did it?"

"You are an oaf. I tell you I do not want anyone killed, just a change in the government. And I repeat to you, Gian Battista, that I strongly desire this change and that Lorenzo, who is a villain and a despicable rascal, does not esteem us. Once he is out of Florence, we could do whatever we like with the Republic and that would be very pleasing to us. Go and do as you wish."

One can imagine the gruff old Pope smiling wryly as he stated, for the record, that he could not condone the murder of a Christian. In any event, the conspirators left the audience convinced that the required blessing had been extended.

From there, the plot moved quickly. Montesecco recruited soldiers from the Pope's strongholds of Tolentino, Imola and Citta di Castello. He then traveled to Florence to inform Jacopo de Pazzi of Sixtus' endorsement of the venture. The duplicitous condottiere even visited my father at Cafaggiolo to give assurances of Count Riario's continued friendship and good will.

How to smuggle dozens of armed men into Florence presented a problem. This was solved when Riario arranged for his nephew, Raffaele Riario, a seventeen year old student at the University of Pisa, to be invited to Florence for a visit. The young collegian had just been named the Cardinal of San Giorgio by his great-uncle Sixtus and it was customary that a prince of the Church traveled with an armed retinue.

Originally, the assassination of Lorenzo and Giuliano was planned to take place at a luncheon at the thinly defended Medici villa at Fiesole. Mercenaries would then storm the Signoria and kill the Gonfaloniere and Priori. However, Giuliano, with his injured leg, was unwilling to make the long trip up the hill and the luncheon was moved to the Medici palace on Via Larga. Since the heavily fortified palace was impossible to infiltrate, Salviati decided the Medici would be murdered at the Duomo during High Mass.

Montesecco was a professional killer, but more pious than the Archbishop. He refused to commit sacrilege on consecrated ground. So his place was eagerly taken by two young priests, Antonio Maffei and Stefano da Bagnone, who both bore grudges against my family.

On the morning of April 26, Cardinal Riario arrived at our palace, changed into his vestments (the beautiful scarlet ones I saw) and walked with Lorenzo to the Duomo. Giuliano remained in his bedchamber. Seeing that the Medici brothers had separated, Francesco de Pazzi and one of his employees, Bernardo Baroncelli, hurried to the palace to coax Giuliano into attending the service. My uncle relented and limped to the Cathedral. Pazzi threw his arms around him, surreptitiously checking for body armor or weapons.

The signal for the assassination was the ringing of the sacristy bell upon the raising of the Host. At that most sacred of moments, Father Antonio drew his dagger and braced his other hand on Lorenzo's shoulder. Feeling the hand, my father quickly turned and the dagger's point grazed his neck instead of severing the artery. Lorenzo jumped back, drew his own sword and went on the attack, driving the two cowardly priests away. Surrounded by loyal friends, Lorenzo leaped over the alter rail and rushed into the new sacristy, bolting the door behind him.

Giuliano did not have Lorenzo's luck. Upon the ringing of the bell, Baroncelli's dagger pierced my uncle's skull. Francesco de Pazzi, in a paroxysm of rage, stabbed Giuliano's corpse time and time again with great ferocity. One of his nineteen blows missed and plunged into his own thigh. As Pazzi limped out through the panicked congregation, Baroncelli ran after Lorenzo, but was intercepted by two of my father's friends, Francesco Nori, whom Baroncelli killed with a single blow, and Lorenzo Calvalcanti, who was wounded in the arm. Thanks to these brave men, Lorenzo successfully escaped.

The second half of the conspiracy simultaneously played out at the Signoria. Archbishop Salviati, with a gang of Perugian mercenaries in tow, requested an immediate audience with the Gonfaloniere, Cesare Petrucci, to convey an urgent message from the Pope. Petrucci, who was in the middle of Sunday dinner, had the Archbishop shown to his waiting room, while the Perugians were directed to the Chancery chamber.

When Petrucci arrived for the meeting, Salviati cried out for the attack to begin, but, unbeknownst to him, the Chancery chamber had a self-locking door and the Perugians were trapped inside. Petrucci grabbed an iron spit from the fireplace and beat the Archbishop to the ground. He then called for the Signoria's guards and gave orders for the Vacca, the Signoria's alarm bell, to be rung to bring out Florence's citizens.

In the streets, Jacopo de Pazzi attempted to take the Piazza della Signoria with a band of mercenaries, but men loyal to my family drove them away. About fifty Medici soldiers entered the Signoria and when they exited a short time later they carried the severed heads of the Perugians on their lances.

Retribution commenced almost immediately. The wounded Francesco de Pazzi was taken from the Pazzi palace and dragged naked to the Signoria, where he was hung from the high window of the Council chamber. His body was soon joined by Archbishop Salviati (hung in his full regalia) and several other Pazzi. The two priests who unsuccessfully tried to murder my father were castrated and hung. Jacopo de Pazzi, the family's patriarch, fled Florence, but was captured by peasants and returned, where he was stripped naked, tortured and hung next to the Archbishop. Later, his body was exhumed from its grave at Santa Croce and returned to the Pazzi palace, where the decomposing head was used as a door knocker. The body was then thrown into the Arno, fished out by children who re-hung the decomposing corpse from a willow tree and finally flung back into the river. All together, almost 100 conspirators and Pazzi relations were executed after the failed plot.

The young cardinal, Raffaele Riario, was just an innocent dupe, but was held by the Priori as a bargaining chip with the Pope, who was furious at both the failure of the conspiracy and the unsanctioned hanging of the Archbishop and priests. Sixtus' revenge was swift. The Florentine Ambassador was arrested, but this breach of diplomatic immunity provoked such heated protests from Milan and Venice that he was soon released. Sixtus then had all Florentine merchants and bankers in Rome arrested and their properties seized, but released them in exchange for Cardinal Riario's safe return to Rome.

The Pope then issued a lengthy Bull of Excommunication. He thundered:

> That son of iniquity and foster-child of perdition, Lorenzo de Medici, and those other citizens of Florence, his accomplices and abettors, are pronounced culpable, sacrilegious, excommunicate, anathematized, infamous, unworthy of trust and incapable of making a will. All of their property is to revert to the Church; their houses are to be leveled to the ground, their habitations made desolate so that none may dwell therein. Let everlasting ruin witness their everlasting disgraced.

Not content with just theological weapons, Sixtus next declared war on Florence and quickly convinced King Ferrante of Naples (who bore a grudge against Lorenzo for his attempt to create a northern alliance with Milan and Venice) to join him in a joint military campaign of conquest. Ferrante dispatched his son Alfonso, Duke of Calabria, with a large army which quickly captured the southern Tuscan town of Montepulciano. Sixtus engaged the Duke of Urbino, Federico da Montefeltro, to command the papal army.

On the Florentine side, Milan, Bologna and the Orsini sent small contingents of mercenaries and the King of France weighed in with moral support. Florence engaged the Duke of Ferrara, who happened to be the Duke of Calabria's brother-in-law, to command its forces. The two relatives maneuvered carefully during the fall of 1478, being sure to maintain at least two days' march between the opposing armies. In November, the two Dukes declared a winter truce and returned to their sister wives.

Florence did not fare so well in 1479. Ludovico Sforza, intelligent, cultured, but a back-stabber of the first order, connived with Count Girolamo Riario, the instigator of the Pazzi conspiracy, to have Milan switch sides and join Naples in an attack on Florence. On the war front, Alfonso managed to capture the key Florentine strongholds of Poggio Imperiale in September and Colle Val d'Elsa in November. Foreign troops were decimating Tuscany's farmland and the cost of bread was soaring in Florence, provoking riots. On top of it all, plague once again broke out in the city.

The situation was desperate and desperate measures were required. In early December, my father dramatically addressed a meeting at the Signoria. He told his stunned fellow citizens that he would personally travel to Naples and offer himself to King Ferrante. If he lost his life, it was a small price to pay to save his beloved Florence from ruin.

Lorenzo, while brave, was also no fool. For months before, he had been conducting secret diplomacy with Ferrante and Alfonso, from whom he received assurances of safe passage and a favorable reception. Two Neapolitan galleys picked up my father and his entourage at Pisa's port and delivered them to Naples. Upon arrival, he began distributing the 60,000 florins he brought with him (raised by mortgaging all the Medici lands in the Mugello since our bank was on the brink of insolvency) to aid in his diplomatic negotiations. Gifts were lavished upon the King, his children, Ippolita Sforza, Alfonso's highly political wife (and sister of Ludovico Sforza) and the King's principal political advisors.

But my father engaged in more than crass bribery. Over the course of three months of difficult negotiating (made palatable by lavish banquets, pageants, falconry and hunts), Lorenzo made compelling arguments as to why Naples should desert the Pope and call off the war against Florence. Ferrante ultimately recognized that a resurgent Vatican, led by a nepotistic Pope with dozens of relations clamoring for personal fiefdoms, posed a real threat to neighboring Naples. In addition, the French King, Louis XI (my late uncle Giuliano's good friend), was reasserting the old Angevin claim to Naples and Sicily. So a treaty of friendship between Naples and Florence was drafted and presented to the outmaneuvered pontiff.

Lorenzo was welcomed back to Florence as a conquering hero. All of the city's notables and foreign ambassadors met him outside the gates and escorted him to our palace. Of course, when the fine print of the treaty became known, triumph turned to dismay. Florence was required to pay a huge indemnity to the Duke of Calabria; King Ferrante retained sole authority to decide when to return the captured Tuscan fortresses and the papal interdict remained in place.

But good fortune shone upon Lorenzo (as it had on Cosimo twenty-six years before). In August, 1480, the Turks crossed the Adriatic Sea and captured the Neapolitan town of Otranto, massacring 12,000 inhabitants and taking another 10,000 off as slaves. The dreaded Mohammedans now had a foothold in Italy and Sixtus could not afford the diversion of a continued feud with Lorenzo and Florence. On December 3, a delegation of twelve leading citizens of Florence (my father not among them), bowed before the Pope and begged forgiveness. Striking each of them lightly with his staff, the Holy Father magnanimously absolved Florence and the Medici of their sins.

I can write much more about the Pazzi conspiracy, but this is my story, not my father's, so I shall return to April, 1478 when Lorenzo sent the family to Pistoia. There, I gained a new brother, for Lorenzo adopted Giulio, the infant son of my murdered uncle Giuliano and his mistress, Fioretta Gorini. My cousin has remained by my side to this very day and is my most trusted friend and advisor.

I have no memory of the spring and summer at Pistoia, but I shall never forget the cold, rainy, miserable winter we spent at Cafaggiolo, the fortified villa high in the Mugello to which Lorenzo sent us for safekeeping. Because of the horrible weather, we could rarely play outside, so Poliziano, the Platonic Academy member whom my father ordered to serve as our tutor, devised indoor games to keep us amused. He decreed that the losers of the games must forfeit courses at dinners, which led to many tears (even as a toddler, my passion for food was intense). Poliziano was quick to comfort me with hugs, kisses and gentle caresses, which may account for my later predilection.

By the age of four, I was already reading. This provoked a major dispute between Poliziano and my mother. Clarice, descended from the ancient Orsini, was medieval in all respects and superstitiously religious. She despised Poliziano's teaching of Greek philosophy (and, of course, Greek love, to which he was openly disposed, occasionally with Lorenzo) and she insisted that I should learn Latin exclusively from the Psalter, not Cicero and Virgil. Indeed, she demanded that my tutor be banished from Cafaggiolo entirely, to which Lorenzo reluctantly conceded and ordered Poliziano to our villa at Fiesole.

As I stated at the beginning of this memoir, my father decreed for me a vocation in the Church. Before I turned seven, my head was shaved into a tonsure and I received holy orders. From that day on, I was addressed by all as "Messire Giovanni." My family's friend, King Louis XI, granted my first benefice, naming me abbot of Fonte Dolce on May 19, 1483 (the timing was fortunate because Louis died just three months later). He also named me the Archbishop of Aix, but had to retract the grant a few days later when he learned that the old Archbishop was still alive. Lorenzo called in his favors and additional benefices flowed upon me, twenty-seven in all. Even our nemesis, Sixtus IV, presented me with the lucrative abbey of Passignano. These benefices provided me with an independent income for life, which was fortunate since my father's neglect, incompetence and feud with the Pope had nearly destroyed our bank.

In August, 1484, Sixtus died of apoplexy. The two principal contenders for his replacement were the deceased Pope's nephew, Cardinal Giuliano della Rovere, and Cardinal Rodrigo Borgia of Spain. Neither could summon the requisite support in the conclave and so Giovanni Battista Cibo was blessed by the Holy Spirit as a compromise candidate and assumed the name Innocent VIII.

My father was a friend of Innocent (as he was with everyone of note in Europe) and immediately commenced a campaign to buy me a cardinal's hat (even though I was not yet nine years old). My fourteen year old brother Piero was dispatched to Rome to congratulate the new pontiff on his election and to request for me "any promotion which you may think proper to bestow." Cardinals Borgia and Ascanio Sforza (the brother of Ludovico Sforza) were retained to intervene on my behalf. Lorenzo regularly wrote long flattering letters to Innocent, accompanied by gifts of fine Tuscan food, wine and cloth.

But it was my sixteen year old sister Maddalena who made the ultimate sacrifice for my career. Forty year old Franceschetto Cibo was slow-witted, rotund and addicted to drink and gambling, but he was Innocent's acknowledged son. And so Lorenzo negotiated a marriage contract with the Pope. In May, 1487, the two were betrothed. My father was barely able to scrape together a 4,000 ducat dowry, but sweetened the pot by presenting the newlyweds with the confiscated Pazzi palace in Florence and Pazzi estates in Montughi and Spedaletto.

The match was mutually beneficial. Innocent, the son of a former Roman Senator, was a friend of the Colonna and therefore, by default, an enemy of the Orsini (a dangerous thing to be in Rome). Lorenzo, married into the clan, was able to check the Orsini's enmity. Innocent also had no experience in international diplomacy, while Lorenzo was "the needle of the Italian compass" with privileged entry into every capital in Europe. For the Medici, the match restored us to the status of God's Banker and the political back-door to the Vatican.

My mother died of consumption the following year. This may seem a rather abbreviated and callous way of relating the death of the woman who gave me life, but in truth we were never particularly close during the twelve years we shared this earthly realm. Clarice Orsini de Medici was a Roman baroness in exile, haughty, detached, distaining of Florentines and ignorant of art, literature and politics. Only the Church and her daughters interested her. I was relegated to the care of nursemaids.

Her Orsini blood flowed into my brother Piero, but not to me. Even as a child, Piero was arrogant, impatient and impolite; with a fiery temperament, but an empty head. He was handsome, well-built and extremely strong, a superb athlete, skilled in the martial arts and he bullied me incessantly.

I was the opposite of my older brother in virtually every respect. I was tall, but predisposed to corpulence. My complexion was pasty, my body soft and my eyesight gravely deficient. From an early age, I required the assistance of a glass to see objects more than a few feet from my eyes. As a result, my coordination, sporting and martial abilities were virtually non-existent, which naturally led to Piero's cruel amusements at my expense.

However, my mind was as agile as my body was stolid. I read at an early age and absorbed information like a sponge. I delighted in aesthetics. I loved poetry and literature, art and especially music. Food and fashion were passions. I was fascinated by the political and philosophical discussions in which Lorenzo and the Platonic Academy regularly engaged.

The natural inclinations of my personality were encouraged and sharpened by my father and tutors. As I was being groomed for a life of high clerical dignity, I was trained to respond to all provocations with equanimity; to be genial, but reserved; humorous, but serious; accommodating, but ambiguous; spontaneous, but studied; agreeable, but non-committal. I learned to be a friend to all, but a confident to none (except, of course, my cousin Giulio). Clarice played little role in all of this. Her interest in the Church was religious, Lorenzo's was political and I found the gods of antiquity far more appealing than the wrathful God of the Hebrews.

But there was one manly pursuit that obsessed me – the hunt. After that terrible winter at Cafaggiolo, spring bloomed in the Mugello, the air smelled fragrant with the scent of pine and wildflowers and game animals abounded in the forest. Lorenzo and a large hunting party rode off, resplendent in their fine hunting costumes, and returned in the late afternoon, their boots and britches soiled, smelling of sweat, moist earth and blood. Later that evening, there was a feast of the slaughtered game and the men drank and sang and bragged of their exploits until after midnight when they departed, one by one, each with a young servant of his selection.

I was smitten. I begged my father to accompany him on the next hunt. On my fifth birthday, Lorenzo gave me a pony and by eight I was an accomplished horseman. My defect in vision was of no consequence on a well-trained horse. He was my eyes as we galloped through field and forest. Of course, I couldn't actually see the game. But servants would snare or net a hare, stag or boar, which allowed me to dismount and dispatch the animal with a lance or sword. Words cannot adequately describe the exquisite thrill I felt at such moments.

I have digressed yet again. Lorenzo received word from Rome, early in 1489, that Innocent was soon to name five new cardinals and that I was likely to be one. My father quickly arranged for major orders to be confirmed upon me, as well as a doctorate in canon law (although I had never attended any university). The newly invigorated Medici bank transferred 95,000 florins to the Apostolic Chamber (perhaps a record price for the purchase of a red hat).

On March 8, 1489, Innocent formally nominated me the Cardinal Deacon of Santa Maria in Domenica. However, he attached conditions to the nomination. Because, at thirteen, I was by far the youngest man ever elevated to the purple, Innocent decreed that I could not wear the vestments or exercise the privileges of my rank for three years; that my nomination be kept secret (although, strangely, people celebrated on the streets of Florence the very day Lorenzo received the letter of nomination); and that I study canon law at the University of Pisa during my probation period.

I left for Pisa with Giulio (who was enrolled in the Knights of Jerusalem, where he remained until he discovered he had no military aptitude) and Bernardo Dovizi (nicknamed "Bibbiena" after the town of his birth). Bibbiena, although only five years my senior, was one of my father's private secretaries and Lorenzo ordered him to supervise my education and, especially, my finances (even then, I could not hold a florin in my purse).

Bibbiena was brilliant. His urbanity and wit sparkled like a diamond, and like a diamond, he was many-faceted on the surface and incomparably hard throughout. The soul of a predator lurked within the dazzling exterior. In intellectual debate, he was not content to merely express his opinions; he needed to devour his opposition. In matters financial, he was sharp as a Jew. Lorenzo recognized these traits (and their lack in me) and delegated to him the role of my manager. Bibbiena recognized that an intimate attachment to a prince of the Church was the ticket to a life of power, luxury and riches, and so he accepted the assignment without protest.

Above all, Bibbiena was a predator in matters carnal. He was profligate and ruthless in his pursuit of women (particularly those of beauty, wealth or influence) and boys. I do not believe he ever once had a solicitous feeling towards his partner. For Bibbiena, conquest and subjugation were the principal objectives of the game (unlike gentle Poliziano, for whom intimacy was but a physical manifestation of love). At all times, Bibbiena was dominant and I submissive in our positions (a preference on my part that has remained constant throughout my life, at great injury to my private orifice).

At Pisa (whose faculty was endowed by the Medici), I studied civil and canon law with Filippo Decio and Bartolommeo Sozzini. I confess I enrolled in few courses of theology, because within the Curia lawyers, not theologians were the principal interpreters of God's words. However, I did study with the two great Camaldolese theologians, Pietro Delfino and Paolo Justiniano, with whom I developed intimate bonds.

Shortly before my mother died, Lorenzo purchased for her a beautiful walled garden with a casino and loggia down the Via Larga from our palace towards the Piazza San Marco. It was a quiet place of refuge to which she could escape from the bustle of the palace. After Clarice's death, Lorenzo converted the property into a school for young sculptors in the hope that the great traditions of ancient Greece and Rome could be revived. He hired Bertoldo di Giovanni, a student of Donatello and Italy's greatest living sculptor, to run the school.

Lorenzo ordered Florence's master artists to nominate their most promising apprentices for retraining as sculptors. Domenico Ghirlandaio recommended a boy my own age, Michelangelo Buonarroti, the son of a distant relation of the noble Ridolfi family, into which my young sister Contessina would shortly be betrothed.

My father observed Michelangelo chiseling a remarkably exact copy of a bust of an antique faun and became enamored with the boy. Lorenzo invited him to live with us in the palace and to take his meals with the family (although I was studying at Pisa, I returned often to Florence). He also insisted that Michelangelo attend the Platonic Academy where he could improve his mind and broaden his understanding of the ancients. Lorenzo was so smitten that he actually paid Michelangelo a monthly stipend, which was unheard of.

So, I gained another de facto brother (Giulio being the first). I welcomed the addition because Piero was an arrogant bully and Giuliano (born in 1479) was a good-natured dreamer without ambition. Michelangelo was unique. I have never met a man so singularly obsessed with his talent. From the moment I met him as a fourteen year old boy to this day, I have never once observed him properly washed, shaved or dressed. He lived and slept in one set of clothes, covered with marble flakes and grime, and he usually smelled rank. He was totally indifferent to food and would ignore meals for days at a time. From dawn until dark, he chiseled and polished his precious statues and then would sketch by candle light until he dropped off to sleep. He was quite intelligent and did well at our sessions with the Academy (where he became an instant favorite), but every conversation invariably turned to art (which has also been a lifelong preoccupation of mine, but properly balanced with other interests).

I suppose great genius is a curse as well as a blessing. Michelangelo is one of the least happy men I have known. His work drives him incessantly, but he seems to derive no pleasure from the beautiful works he creates. When I was sixteen, Lorenzo, whose health was rapidly deteriorating, delegated the organization of the hunt to me (my own obsession). Several hundred of Florence's most illustrious men were invited to attend. I extended the honor of an invitation to Michelangelo and he refused it. He said he could not bear to be parted from his work for even a day. This not only insulted me, but the entire Medici family, to whom he owed everything. I was furious.

My sister Contessina intervened and Michelangelo glumly attended the hunt, unarmed except for a sketchpad onto which he penciled cartoons of the hunters and game. I believe Contessina had fond feelings towards him, which could have had scandalous implications if Michelangelo had a reciprocal interest (Lorenzo had already contracted her to Piero Ridolfi). But, as I have previously written, Michelangelo's natural inclination was to men and this too had been subsumed into his art.

As Lorenzo's gout and many other ailments worsened, Pope Innocent's own health declined in lockstep. This caused my father (and me) grave anxiety as my confirmation as cardinal had yet to be finalized. By February, 1492, Lorenzo could no longer walk or even hold a pen, but he dictated letter after letter to Innocent beseeching him to complete my elevation.

Lorenzo's nagging bore fruit (and just in time since Innocent died that August) when word arrived from Rome that the required Brief had been signed. My investiture ceremony was held on Sunday, March 9, 1492, at the Badia Fiesolana monastery at Fiesole (underwritten by the Medici). Because Lorenzo was too ill to make the trip up the hill (and Piero too busy with other pressing matters), I was accompanied only by Giulio, Bibbiena, Pico della Mirandola (of the Platonic Academy), my brother-in-law, Jacopo Salviati, and a notary. After taking the sacrament from Canon Bosso at Mass, the papal Brief was read and I was invested with the insignia of my high office – the pallium, biretum, galerus and sapphire ring. The monks then chanted *Veni Creator Spiritus*.

I immediately exercised the prerogative of my exalted rank by granting an indulgence to all who had attended the ceremony and all who, in the future, would visit the monastery on the anniversary of my elevation. I then mounted my humble mule and rode back down the hill towards Florence. As I approached the city gate, Piero galloped up, exquisitely dressed and mounted on a horse of extraordinary size and spirit, caparisoned with gold. He was surrounded by a large group of his friends and did everything in his power to divert the attention of the cheering citizens of Florence from myself to him (to little avail). On the way to our palace, I stopped at the church of the Annunciata and the Duomo to grace each pulpit with my presence and give my benediction. When I reached the palace, I mounted the roof and blessed the cheering throng. After a sumptuous feast (at which the Priori presented me with a gift of silver plate, worth at least 25,000 florins), the night sky was illuminated with a brilliant display of fireworks and the entire population of Florence rejoiced.

I departed for Rome three days later. On the eve of my departure, I blessed my dying father and received in return his famous letter to me (I say famous because it seemed everyone in Florence was quoting from it within hours of its delivery to me, although I showed it to no one). The letter rambled on for pages, but I shall excerpt some of his more memorable words of instruction:

> It would be indeed highly disgraceful, and as contrary to your duty as to my hopes, if at a time when others display a greater share of reason and adopt a better mode of life, you should forget the precepts of your youth, and forsake the path in which you have hitherto trodden. Endeavor therefore to alleviate the burden of your early dignity by the regularity of your life and by your perseverance in those studies which are suitable to your profession.
>
> I know well that as you are now to reside in Rome, that sink of all iniquity, the difficulty of conducting yourself by these admonitions will be increased.
>
> Guard against all ostentation either in your conduct or your discourse. Affect not austerity, nor even appear too serious.
>
> You are now devoted to God and the Church, on which account you ought to aim at being a good ecclesiastic, and to show that you prefer the honor and state of the Church and of the Apostolic See to every other consideration. Nor, while you keep this in view, will it be difficult for you to favor your family and your native place.
>
> On public occasion let your equipage and dress be rather below than above mediocrity. A handsome house and a well-ordered household will be preferable to a great retinue and a splendid palace. Endeavor to live with regularity, and gradually to bring your expenses within those bounds which in a new establishment cannot perhaps be expected. Silks and jewels are not suitable for persons in your station.
>
> Invite others to your house oftener than you yourself receive invitations. Let your own food be plain, and take sufficient exercise, for those who wear your habit are soon liable, without great caution, to contract infirmities.
>
> There is one rule which I would recommend to your attention in preference to all others: *Rise early in the morning*.
>
> With respect to your speaking in the consistory, it will be most becoming for you at present to refer the matters in debate to the judgment of His Holiness, alleging as a reason your own youth and inexperience.

Etc., etc.

When I left for Rome, I was a sixteen year old boy, eager to fulfill to the letter all of my father's admonitions. Looking back over the past twenty-five years, I confess that I missed the mark on virtually all of them (particularly early rising). Nonetheless, I have not done badly.

SAVONAROLA

I contend that zealots, particularly those of the religious persuasion, have caused more misery than all of the duplicitous, ruthless and ambitious condottieri, politicians and lawyers combined. I understand this is a bold statement, since some would suggest that the Apostles and saints themselves were zealots.

Yet there is sometimes a fine line between angel and devil and we in this earthly realm are often unable to accurately distinguish between them. Certainly, no man has done more harm to my family than that Devil's Instrument, Girolamo Savonarola.

Savonarola was born in Ferrara in 1452 into a common, but respectable, family. His childhood was unremarkable. As a young man, Savonarola developed an infatuation for Laodamia Strozzi, the natural daughter of Roberto Strozzi (whose ancestor had been exiled from Florence by Cosimo de Medici). Ignoring custom, Girolamo proposed marriage directly to the shocked young lady, who haughtily rejected the impertinent offer. Although she was a bastard, the thought of a Strozzi stooping to align with a Savonarola was laughable.

This cruel rejection apparently unhinged Savonarola's mind (beginning with Eve, the root of much evil can be traced back to casual remarks by women). He soon developed an unhealthy antipathy for all things worldly or pleasant. In 1475 (the year of my birth), he journeyed to the monastery of St. Dominic in Bologna, announced his intention to take vows and requested to be assigned the meanest and humblest services as penance for his imagined sins.

Girolamo's fevered mind was able to indulge in gratuitous self-abuse (disguised as sanctimonious piety) at the monastery. He fasted, even on days not appointed for abstinence, to the point that his body appeared more like a specter than a living man. He slept on a grating with a sack of straw for a mattress and one ratty blanket. He dressed in the coarsest of clothes and favored hair shirts. His superiors were frequently obligated to curb his zeal.

By 1481, the Dominicans in Bologna had enough of this strange bird and ordered him to fly back to Ferrara. There, he proved less than a sensation. The best said of him was the old proverb from Luke: "Nemo propheta in patria sua." In less than a year he was sent packing to Florence, where he took up residence at the monastery of San Marco.

° Translator's note: "No man is a prophet in his home country."

I must now say a word about San Marco. It originally belonged to the Order of St. Sylvester, but the monks allowed the building to fall into ruin and their scandalous behavior precipitated numerous complaints to the Curia. In 1437, Cosimo de Medici obtained papal permission to evict the monks and turn the monastery over to the Dominicans of the Lombard Congregation. He then assigned his architect, Michelozzo Michelozzi, to oversee its renovation and personally lavished 36,000 florins to cover the cost. Cosimo hired Fra Angelico to adorn its walls with frescoes of great piety and he purchased and entrusted to the Dominicans Niccolo Niccoli's vast collection of ancient manuscripts (San Marco becoming the first public library in Italy). So, for all intents and purposes, Savonarola owed his magnificent new home to the generosity of the Medici.

Savonarola made no more favorable an impression in Florence than he had in Ferrara. He was invited to give the Lenten sermon at San Lorenzo. By the end of his turgid oration, the overflow congregation had dwindled to less than two dozen women and children.

His frustrated superiors then sent him first to the Tuscan backwater of San Gimignano and next to Brescia in Lombardy. Savonarola found his calling in Brescia. With the apocalyptic *Book of Revelations* as his loadstone, Girolamo would starve and flagellate himself into catatonic trances and then emerge professing "visions" of horrible consequences for the "evils" of his congregants. Brescia, he thundered in a Lenten sermon:

> would fall a prey to raging foes; they would see rivers of blood in the streets; wives would be torn from their husbands, virgins ravished, children murdered before their mothers' eyes; all would be fire, and bloodshed unless the people repented for their sins, inasmuch as the Lord would have mercy on the just.

These "prophecies" of course made a sensational impression on the simple minds of the Brescians. The monk who could not hold a congregation in Ferrara or Florence was now playing to packed churches. Unfortunately, one of men who became enthralled with Savonarola's predictions of doom was Giovanni Pico della Mirandola.

Pico was a rich young nobleman of prodigious, but shallow, learning who attached himself to my father and the Platonic Academy. He was a great sycophant who once declared that Lorenzo's poems were superior to those of Dante and Petrarch. He was also enamored with his own opinion of himself. In 1486, Pico published 900 theses which he pompously asserted elucidated the whole of science, philosophy and religion. He sent letters to the world's leading scholars challenging them to come to Rome and debate him on his propositions (and offering to pay their expenses).

Unfortunately (for Pico), Pope Innocent was less than impressed with his erudition. The pontiff declared the 900 theses:

in part heretical, in part the flower of heresy; several are scandalous and offensive to pious ears; most do nothing but reproduce the errors of pagan philosophers; others are capable of inflaming the impertinence of the Jews; a number of them, finally, under the pretext of "natural philosophy," favor arts that are enemies to the Catholic faith and to the human race.

That ended Pico's dream of a grand debating tournament. Not being a man of great courage, Pico issued a lengthy written apology, but the Pope was not appeased. Pico fled Italy, but was arrested and imprisoned in France at the urging of the papal nuncio. My father, loyal to a fault, interceded with Innocent who allowed Pico to return to Florence, where Lorenzo installed him at our villa in Fiesole.

It was there that Pico brought the monk's visions to my father's attention and entreated him to bring Savonarola back to Florence. Lorenzo declared: "with good will and good ink I am always ready to serve you" and dispatched the request under his seal to the Lombard Dominicans (which request, of course, was forthwith granted).

Savonarola returned to Florence in 1489, shortly after I left for Pisa in obedience to Innocent's injunction that I study canon law. On August 1, Savonarola delivered a sermon at San Marco to a large throng of curious Florentines. The monk whose last address emptied the pews at San Lorenzo now captivated his audience with his assertions of a corrupt clergy and predictions of the looming Apocalypse.

By 1491 (the Apocalypse inconveniently having failed to appear on cue), Florence became evenly divided between the monk's true believers and those who regarded him as an ignorant fanatic and fraud who made an effect rather by dint of loud words and fantastic imagery. And so Savonarola decided to up the ante.

Savonarola spread word that an extraordinary Lenten sermon was forthcoming and so many Florentines (myself and father included) demanded admission that the venue was moved from San Marco to the Duomo. He started his address with his usual rant about sin and corruption. But then the friar preached the following:

> Fathers make sacrifice to this false idol, urging their sons to enter the ecclesiastical life, in order to obtain benefices; and thus you hear it said: Blessed the house that owns a fat curate. But I say unto you: A time will come when rather it will be said: Woe to that house; and you will feel the edge of the sword upon you. Do as I bid you; rather let your sons follow the way of all others, than undertake the religious life for gain. In these days there is no grace, no gift of the Holy Spirit that may not be bought and sold.

> On the other hand, the poor are oppressed by grievous burdens, and when they are called to pay sums beyond their means, the rich cry unto them, Give me the rest. When widows come weeping, they are bidden to go to sleep. When the poor complain, they are told to pay and pay again. Bethink you well, oh you rich, for affliction shall smite you. This city shall no more be called Florence, but a den of thieves, of turpitude and bloodshed. Then shall you all be poverty-stricken, all wretched, and your name shall be changed into a terror.

I am certain you can imagine my consternation as all eyes in the Duomo cast furtive glances in the direction of the Medici pew and my humiliation when I was referred to as a "fat curate." Savonarola had declared holy war on the Medici, the family that housed him in its monastery and arranged for his recall to Florence. He was seeking to turn the poor of Florence against the one noble family that had always been their champion; and all for his personal aggrandizement.

Had I been the head of the family, the devil would have hung before sunset from the same window as the late Archbishop of Pisa. But Lorenzo was weak, always preferring to be loved than feared. As his mind deteriorated with his body, I think Lorenzo half-believed the ravings of the lunatic.

In any event, the enemies of the Medici (of which there were many among Florence's lesser noble families) became emboldened by Lorenzo's appeasement. Savonarola was invited to address the Signoria in April, 1491 and he repeated his venomous attack on Lorenzo:

> I must tell you, then, that all the evil and all the good of the city depend from its head, and therefore great is his responsibility even for small sins, since, if he followed the right path, the whole city would be sanctified. Tyrants are incorrigible because they are proud, because they love flattery, and because they will not restore ill-gotten gains.

Still, my father did nothing and, in July, Savonarola was elected the Prior of San Marco. Since Cosimo's time, it was a tradition that each newly-elected Prior would visit the head of the Medici and pay respects and homage. Not Savonarola. Refusing the exhortations of his fellow friars to make the visit, he declared: "I consider that my election is owed to God alone, and to Him alone will I vow obedience."

What did Lorenzo do? He went to San Marco, attended Mass and then wandered in the garden, limping from his gout, awaiting Savonarola, who contemptuously refused to acknowledge his existence. Lorenzo then sent rich gifts and alms to the monastery, which only fed Savonarola's contempt and the new Prior delivered the gifts and alms to the brothers of San Martino for distribution to the poor.

My father's partisans became alarmed by Lorenzo's blatant display of weakness and a delegation of five leading supporters went to Savonarola and warned him to cease his attacks on pain of exile. Girolamo was not cowed:

> I know you have not come of your own will, but at that of Lorenzo. Bid him to do penance for his sins, for the Lord is no respecter of persons, and spares not the princes of the earth. I fear not sentences of banishment. I will stay while he will depart.

He then predicted that Lorenzo, Pope Innocent and King Ferrante of Naples would all soon die. Given that each man was in seriously poor health, this did not, in my estimation, elevate Savonarola to the rank of prophet. But it did unnerve Lorenzo.

After my investiture and departure for Rome, Lorenzo ordered that he be carried on a litter to his beloved villa at Careggi, where he desired to spend his remaining days. On April 5, 1492, two of Florence's lions, mascots of the Republic, were killed in a fight in their cage. That night, a bolt of lightening struck the lantern atop the Duomo, a piece of which fell from the cathedral in the direction of the Medici palace. Upon receiving word of these portents, my superstitious father announced that they presaged his imminent demise.

Lorenzo's doctor, Piero Leoni, did not concur with this diagnosis and suggested that bed rest, warmth and avoidance of pears and grape pips would lead to a full recovery. Unfortunately, Ludovico Sforza dispatched his own Milanese physician, Lazaro di Pavia, to attend to Lorenzo and he prescribed bleeding, accompanied by a potion of pulverized pearls and precious stones. Within a day after ingesting this concoction, Lorenzo fell into a coma. He was given the last sacraments by a local priest and died in the company of my brother Piero, Pico della Mirandola, Poliziano and a Camaldolensian friar. Piero Leoni, heartbroken at his failure to cure my father, threw himself down a well to his death.

I now must correct an insidious rumor that began to circulate within days of Lorenzo's passing. According to this gossip, Lorenzo, after receiving the sacraments from a local priest, requested Savonarola be summoned to his bedside to bless him. This monk, who had refused to acknowledge my father at San Marco, supposedly rushed to his bedside. Savonarola allegedly demanded, as the price of absolution (which my father had already received), that Lorenzo relinquish his fortune and restore liberty to Florence. When my father turned his face away and remained silent, the Prior of San Marco then cursed Lorenzo to eternal damnation, upon which my father died.

This story is a fabrication. Piero, Pico and Poliziano have each individually assured me that Savonarola never appeared at Careggi and that Lorenzo died in their collective presence, at peace and absolved of sin, his eyes fixed upon a silver crucifix as the Camaldolensian friar read to him the story of Christ's Passion.

Pope Innocent died that July, adding further renown to Savonarola's reputation for prophecy (King Ferrante lasted until January, 1494). Innocent was succeeded by Rodrigo Borgia, who took the name Alexander VI.

Now I am in a quandary. Borgia and his infamous issue clearly merit a chapter of their own, but Savonarola's tale is not yet fully told. It may confuse and distract if I commingle their stories. So, I will continue with the Devil's Instrument, giving passing mention to broader events and then shall circle back to this point and give a detailed recitation of my early years as cardinal under the reign of Alexander.

Upon Lorenzo's death, Piero became master of the House of Medici. He immediately prevailed upon the superiors of the Lombard Congregation in Milan to have Savonarola transferred out of Florence for a second time. The monk was ordered to Bologna, where he was closely watched and muzzled by our friend, Giovanni Bentivoglio, the tyrant of Bologna.

While Savonarola was a fraudulent prophet, he was a masterful politician, as attuned to the nuances of Italian rivalries as my late father. He traveled twice to Venice, where he convinced Giovacchino Turriano, the Vicar-General of the Dominicans, to support independence for San Marco (which was not difficult, the Venetian being no lover of the Milanese). He also solicited support from Cardinal Caraffa of Naples, the Protector of the Dominican Order (who was also no friend of Milan). He even convinced my idiot brother that it was insulting that a Tuscan monastery should be under the thumb of Lombardy. Piero attempted to enlist my support for Savonarola's independence campaign, which I rejected in no uncertain terms. But he refused to listen. His Orsini blood would not continence accepting advice from his younger brother.

In Rome, Pope Alexander was not favorably disposed to sign the brief granting independence to San Marco (which had been drafted by Savonarola and brought to Rome by his chief sycophant, Fra Domenico). Borgia owed his throne to the switched vote (purchased for five donkey-loads of silver) of Cardinal Ascanio Sforza of Milan and was also not enamored by Savonarola's constant harping upon corruption in the Church.

Nevertheless, one night after a particularly difficult consistory, Alexander and Caraffa were relaxing in the Pope's private chamber and Caraffa took the opportunity to present the brief. After Alexander refused it, Caraffa gently removed the seal-ring from Borgia's finger and sealed the brief himself. The pontiff merely smiled at this audacious and sacrilegious act. Moments later, a delegation of Milanese arrived to press their case. Alexander waived them off, stating: "Had you come sooner your request would have been granted, but now what is done is done." Savonarola had triumphed.

Events then moved swiftly. Vicar-General Turriano immediately ordered Savonarola transferred back to San Marco and even extended his authority by naming him Provincial of Tuscany. The Lombard Congregation was ordered to discontinue its efforts to annul the unlawfully sealed brief.

Savonarola returned to Florence for a second time in May, 1493, again with the active assistance of the Medici. At least my father had no forewarning of the danger he posed to our family. Piero's support was inexcusable.

Once back, Savonarola wasted no time imprinting San Marco with his own brand of zealotry. He ordered the beautiful paintings, statues and tapestries which the Medici had donated over the years to be sold and the money distributed to the poor. The friars were forced to exchange their beautiful flowing robes for coarse woolen frocks with pinched hoods. The fine food for which the monastery was famous vanished, replaced by gruel. The friars were now required to work and to surrender all personal possessions. Illuminated manuscripts and gold and silver crucifixes were banned.

Many of the older monks grumbled and quite a few became ill from the abrupt change of diet. But this militant asceticism sparked the imaginations of impressionable youths, who flocked to join the Order. Needless to say, the lower classes of Florence were favorably disposed to the changes and Savonarola's temporal powerbase grew along with the spiritual.

Back in the pulpit, Savonarola began where he had left off in 1492. Throughout late 1493 and 1494, he relentlessly attacked Florence's rulers in general and Piero in particular. He excoriated the people of Florence for their evil (in his mind) ways. In a sermon at the Duomo, he thundered from *Genesis 6:17*: "Behold, I bring the waters of a great flood upon the earth!" and told the frightened congregation of an impending scourge.

Once again, Savonarola was able to capitalize upon his intimate knowledge of politics in order to issue a prophesy assured to be fulfilled. For at the very time he was making these predictions, a massive French army was crossing the Alps on its way to conquer Naples.

I will address the roots and consequences of this calamity in great detail in the following chapter. For now, suffice it to say that a 50,000 man army, commanded by the young French King, Charles VIII, entered

Italy in August, 1494 and reached Florence in November. With the army camped outside Florence's gates, a general revolt, orchestrated by Savonarola, took place and the Medici were driven from Florence and our properties and assets confiscated.

As soon as we were gone, Savonarola moved to fill the void. In a sermon at the Duomo, he declared:

> The Lord has driven my ship into the open sea. The wind drives me forward. The Lord forbids my return. I spoke last night with the Lord and said, 'Pity me, O Lord. Lead me back to my haven.' 'It is impossible,' said the Lord. 'See you not that the wind is contrary?' 'I will preach, if so I must, but why need I meddle with the government of Florence?' 'If you would make Florence a holy city, you must establish her on firm foundations and give her a government which favors virtue.'

Awed by God's personal endorsement, Florence's citizens acclaimed Savonarola as their de facto dictator and the Devil's Instrument quickly applied the same strictures to the Republic as he had to San Marco. He abolished the parliament; a puppet Signoria did his bidding. He enforced with fanatical zeal the old sumptuary laws, forcing Florentines to abandon their elegant dress, jewels, art, books and cuisine. He demanded death for all remaining supporters of the Medici. He outlawed "the pestiferous affliction and cankerous worm of usury." He recruited an army of delinquent boys, cut their hair short, dressed them in white uniforms and sent them out in gangs, carrying red crosses, to strong-arm any citizens who resisted his new moral order.

And then he exceeded his reach. Not being a native, Savonarola could not appreciate the Florentines' attachment to sodomy. In December, 1494, he promulgated a new sodomy statute. The old law, instituted during Cosimo's rule, prescribed fines for occasional offences. Savonarola's law required standing in the pillory and loss of civic privileges for the first offence, branding for the second and burning at the stake for the third.

This was too ruthless for even those Florentines who did not practice sodomy. Denunciations dropped off markedly and opponents loosely coalesced into an organization known as the Arrabbiati. Savonarola railed from the pulpit: "If you do not want to kill them, at least drive them out of your territory." When that did not happen, Savonarola demanded that his lackeys in the Signoria prescribe burning for the first offence: "Make a pretty fire, or two or three, there in the square, of these sodomites. Don't punish with money or secretly, but make a fire that can be smelled in all of Italy."

Soon, word reached the ear of Alexander (I may have played my own small part) of Savonarola's purported conversations with God, his false prophesies and his suggestion to King Charles that he depose the Pope on his journey south to Naples. The Holy Father was not amused. Being Christ's exclusive representative on earth, he took a dim view of stigmatics, hysterics, heretics, false prophets and others who claimed direct communications with the Lord.

Alexander dispatched a papal brief to Savonarola:

> Beloved son, greetings and Apostolic benedictions! We hear that among all who labor in the vineyards of the Lord, you toil with most zeal: for which we rejoice and give thanks to Almighty God. We hear likewise that you claim that your predictions of the future come not from you but from God; we desire, therefore, as it is our Pastoral duty, to converse with you, that being better informed through you of the will of God, we may fulfill it. We charge you, therefore, by virtue of holy obedience, to come to us with all speed, and we shall welcome you with love and charity.

Prudent men, upon receiving a friendly summons from Borgia, checked to make sure their personal affairs were in order and their testaments up to date. Savonarola was no fool; nor did he rely upon his confidant, the Lord, to protect him from Alexander. Instead, he pleaded illness and took to his bed.

Six weeks passed and God had not yet seen fit to cure his prophet's mysterious malady. But Alexander had run out of patience. He dispatched a second brief to Florence, returning San Marco to the supervision of the Lombard Congregation and ordering Savonarola and his three chief lackeys, Fras Domenico, Silvestro and Tommaso, to quit San Marco and repair forthwith to Bologna. But the impudent monk rejected the Holy Father's order. He wrote back:

> Our reunion with the Lombard friars at this moment would only deepen the rancor already, unhappily, existing between the two congregations, and give rise to fresh dispute and fresh scandal. And, inasmuch as your Holiness declares that you desire this union so as to prevent others from lapsing into my errors, and inasmuch as it is now most plain that I have not lapsed into error, the cause being non-existent, neither should its effect remain. Having therefore proved the falsity of all the charges brought against me, I pray your Holiness to vouchsafe a reply to my defense, and to grant me absolution.

This Dominican combined the craftiness of a Jew with the virtuosity with words of a most skillful lawyer. But Satan imbues his instruments with powers beyond those possessed by the mere mortal.

Alexander, attempting to meet the monk halfway, sent a third brief ordering Savonarola to cease from all public preaching until such time as he had recovered his health sufficiently to journey to Rome and explain himself.

In disregard of the pontiff's new order, and to divert attention from this disobedience and rile the people, Savonarola launched another series of vituperative sermons against my family. In October, 1495, he declared that Piero must be killed on sight ("Cut off his head, were he even the chief and head front of thy house; cut off his head!"). His lackeys in the Signoria immediately responded by authorizing a 4,000 florin reward for anyone murdering Piero and a 2,000 florin reward for murdering Giuliano. I was spared this insult only by virtue of my high office.

If there is one lesson to be learned from this story, it is that madmen, when appeased, only grow bolder. As will be explained in the next chapter, Alexander was beset by many difficulties at this time, and so was not as vigilant as he should have been to this demonic threat to the very foundation of the Church. Perhaps, he hoped that the people of Florence would simply tire of their false and sanctimonious prophet.

Even though Alexander countenanced his disobedience, Savonarola, furthering Satan's designs, directly attacked the papacy. In a sermon in early 1496 explaining his refusal to obey the Alexander's order not to preach, he declared:

> The Pope may not give me any command opposed to charity, or contrary to the Gospel. We are not compelled to obey all commands. When given in consequence of lying report they are invalid; when in evident contradiction with the law of charity, laid down by the Gospel, it is our duty to resist them.

In other words, he, not the Holy Father, was the ultimate interpreter of Scripture; he, not the Pope, was the ultimate authority in the Church; he, not the Vicar of Christ, was God's representative on earth.

And yet Alexander continued to temporize. But God did not and brought down his wrath upon Savonarola's "reformed" Florence. In the spring of 1496, a famine of epic proportion afflicted Tuscany, as did an epidemic of the French boils (courtesy of the departed French army). In the field, the Pisan army crushed the Florentine army and its popular commander, Piero Capponi, was killed. Under the strain of famine, pestilence and war, Florence's economy collapsed and its population became destitute. Florence's municipal bonds traded at only ten percent of their face value.

How did Savonarola explain these calamitous events, which occurred after more than two years of his dictatorial rule? Of course, he blamed the Florentines:

> Do you see now that, unless you change your life, you will suffer? O Florence, vice still flourishes; men game and blaspheme, and thus you bring down this scourge upon you.

But the Florentines were not buying it and the Arrabbiati were gaining strength in the Grand Council, the popular body that Savonarola had created to replace the parliament. Like any good dictator, Savonarola proposed restricting membership to all but his disciples:

> Ungrateful people! God has given you this Grand Council, and you are seeking to ruin it by admitting enemies of the country. I did not mean that the wicked should be included, as they are now.

So Savonarola ordered his boy gangs into the streets to enforce his authority. An army of 5,000 uniformed young thugs blocked the streets and went door to door, terrorizing the occupants, confiscating all "vanities" (fancy clothes, jewelry, wigs, rouge pots, perfumes, fans, bracelets, secular books, musical instruments, chess boards, playing cards and anything else that struck the boys' fancies) and extorting alms. The boys made a huge pile of the vanities in the Piazza della Signoria and on Palm Sunday a great bonfire was made of the vanities. Lorenzo di Credi, Fra Bartolommeo and even Botticelli threw their own precious paintings into the flames.

In Rome, Alexander, desiring to muzzle the monk without creating a spectacle, quietly sent word that a cardinal's hat was available for Savonarola should he quit Florence and journey to Rome as had been ordered two years before. The Pope should have known better. Upon receiving the offer, Savonarola took to the pulpit:

> Come here, wretched Church; I gave you, saith the Lord, fair vestments, and you have made idols of them. You have given my vessels to vainglory and my sacraments to simony; in your lechery you are a shameless whore; you are worse than a beast, you are an abominable monster. Once you blushed for your sins, but not now. The priests used to call their sons nephews; now they are not nephews, but sons, sons plain and simple! You have made a public place of the Church, you have built brothels everywhere. And so, O Whore of a Church, you have shown your foulness to the whole world, and your stench rises to Heaven.

Savonarola had sealed his fate. One did not directly attack Borgia and survive. Cardinal Caraffa could no longer protect his protégé and a long-overdue Bull of Excommunication was sealed by Alexander on May 12, 1497.

The monk, having vanquished the Medici, now issued a declaration of war against the Church:

> This excommunication is invalid both in the sight of God and man, inasmuch as it is based on the false reasons and accusations devised by our enemies. Nor does the Christian commit sin in accepting the aid of the secular power, in order to escape from unjust excommunication; for unjust sentences of this description are mere violence, and the law of nature prescribes that we should repulse force by force.

With the protection of his lackeys in the Signoria, this excommunicated friar continued to celebrate Mass at San Marco and even gave Christmas communion at the Duomo.

I attended the consistory in February, 1498, when Alexander called in the Ambassador to account for Florence's continued protection of Savonarola. I have rarely seen Alexander so riled. He raged against Florence and threatened to have all Florentine merchants in Rome arrested and their property confiscated (just as Sixtus had threatened during his war with Lorenzo). The message Alexander dispatched to the Signoria left nothing to doubt:

> Your conduct has profoundly incensed us. You have not only encouraged the disobedience of this Friar; but by preventing all others from preaching, you have made him almost your oracle of Apollo. And we shall never relent, until reparation has been made to the dignity and honor of the Holy See, which this worm has been able, with your aid, to insult. Weigh your decision maturely; for only as you show yourselves ready to obey will we concede your requests for the material welfare of your Republic. In any event, reply with no more letters but with acts; for we are firmly resolved to tolerate your disobedience no longer; and we will place the interdict on your city, to last as long as you continue to favor this monstrous idol of yours.

It was no coincidence that, shortly after the Pope's outburst, armed thugs attempted to force their way into the Ambassador's residence and murder him.

Savonarola also left nothing to doubt. He dispatched letters to the rulers of Europe, demanding a General Council and proclaiming:

> I testify, in the name of God, that this Alexander is no Pope, nor can he be considered such, since, leaving aside his most execrable sin of simony, by which he bought the Papal throne and daily sells ecclesiastical benefices to the highest bidder and his other manifest vices, I affirm that he is no Christian and does not believe in God, which passes the limit of every infidelity.

Back in Florence, the people were in a quandary and the government was paralyzed with indecision. Excommunication was a serious matter to the faithful and Savonarola's venomous attacks on the papacy unnerved even his strongest supporters. Savonarola's prophesies had not come true, daily life was miserable and the economy in tatters. The tide had finally begun to turn.

The Devil's Instrument then played what he thought to be his trump card. In March, 1498, holding the Blessed Sacrament in his hands, Savonarola addressed the congregation at the Duomo:

> I entreat each one of you to earnestly pray to God that if my doctrine does not come from Him, he shall send down a fire upon me, which shall consume my soul in Hell.

Perhaps the monk should have been more circumspect in his entreaty, because God was apparently listening that morning and, in His inimitable and mysterious manner, set in motion a chain of events which ended with the prayed for fire.

There existed from the earliest days an antipathy between the followers of St. Dominic and those of St. Francis. While the Dominicans of San Marco rallied around their Prior, the Franciscans of Santa Croce were among his most vociferous critics. Thus, it was a Franciscan, Fra Francesco of Apulia, in a sermon at Santa Croce, who issued a challenge to an ordeal by fire:

> I fully believe that I shall be burnt, but I am ready to sacrifice myself to free the people from this delusion. If Savonarola is not burnt with me then you may believe him to be a prophet.

Consistent with his cowardly nature, Savonarola evaded the challenge, writing: "As for myself, I reserve myself for a greater task, in behalf of which I shall always be ready to lay down my life." His belief in God was clearly just metaphorical. But his lackey, Fra Domenico, was a rabid true believer and accepted the challenge as Savonarola's proxy. Florentines of all persuasions, always eager for a bloody spectacle, clamored for the Signoria to sanction the contest, which it did with some reluctance.

The Ordeal by Fire was set for Saturday, April 7, 1498 and the participants were ordered to arrive at 8:00 AM, with the actual Ordeal scheduled for noon. The Signoria erected a great platform in the Piazza della Signoria to provide an unrestricted view of the Ordeal for the nobles and leading citizens of Florence and prepared two piles of wood, forty yards long and saturated with oil and pitch. Armed guards were posted at all entrances to the Piazza and spectators were searched for weapons before entry was allowed. Women and children were turned away.

At eight in the morning, Fra Francesco timely arrived, accompanied by a small band of his brothers. He was directed to the section of the Loggia reserved for the Franciscans, where he took a seat and quietly contemplated his fate. And then the proceeding took on the elements of farce.

It was a hot and humid day and the crowd grew restive as the hours passed and there was no sign of the Dominicans. Then, shortly before noon, a procession of 200 chanting Dominicans entered the Piazza, led by Fra Domenico, decked out in a cap of fiery red velvet and carrying a giant crucifix, and Savonarola carrying the Host. Behind them, hundreds of supporters paraded carrying lighted torches.

The crowd eagerly cried out for the faggots to be lit and the Ordeal commenced. But Piero degli Alberti, who had been deputized to preside over the Ordeal by the Priori, grew concerned that Fra Domenico was concealing a magic potion or charm under his cap to protect him from the fire. He ordered Domenico to remove the cap, but the Dominican refused. The parties then retired to the Palazzo to resolve the issue. They argued for hours, until Fra Francesco interceded and stated that he had no objection to Domenico wearing his cap.

Meanwhile, a riot had broken out in the Piazza between supporters of Savonarola and the Arrabbiati. The armed troops of the Signoria had to intervene and drive apart the warring factions. No sooner had order been restored than a thunderstorm rained down on the Piazza, soaking the faggots. The Priori tried to cancel the Ordeal, but the crowd would not have it. They had come to smell burning flesh and would not be deterred by a little rain.

Once the controversy over the cap had been resolved, the disputants returned to the Piazza. But then another issue arose. Domenico insisted on being allowed to carry the crucifix with him into the fire, to which Francesco objected. The parties retired yet again to the Palazzo. After additional hours of debate, Francesco conceded and they returned again to the Piazza.

The fires were about to be lit when Domenico now insisted on carrying the Host, as well as the crucifix, into the fire. He claimed that Fra Silvestro had had a vision in which an angel demanded that he carry the Host into the flames. This was, of course, an abomination. The body of the Lord was never intended to be used for such a tawdry purpose. It became clear to the Priori that Domenico had no intention of entering the flames and would come up with excuse after excuse to avoid his fate. It was also now evening and growing dark. So the Priori declared the Franciscan the winner by default and canceled the Ordeal.

Well, the huge crowd had come for blood and would not be denied. Even Savonarola's supporters were outraged by the Dominican's refusal to submit to the Ordeal. The next morning, Palm Sunday, a riot broke out at the Duomo. The mob then converged upon San Marco, carrying torches to submit Savonarola and Domenico to an impromptu ordeal. The Dominican friars had secreted a large cache of weapons at the monastery and now dressed themselves in mail and armed themselves with halberts and swords. But the mob was not to be denied and stormed San Marco. Savonarola's brother (braver than the monk) was killed in the attack, together with eight friars. When troops from the Signoria arrived, Savonarola, Domenico and Silvestro were taken prisoner and marched to the Palazzo as crowds jeered Satan's disciples. San Marco itself was sacked and burned.

With Savonarola safely locked in a cell, the Priori opened negotiations with Alexander. They requested that the interdict upon Florence be lifted and that the mob that had murdered eight priests and sacked a consecrated monastery be granted absolution. The Pope agreed. They requested a decision on a long-standing petition to impose a ten percent tithe on the property of the clergy in the city. The Pope consented. Alexander requested a secular trial forthwith for the imprisoned friars, under the supervision of papal envoys. The Priori agreed and the deal was sealed.

On April 9, 1498, Savonarola's trial commenced, as was customary, with torture to elicit a confession. No sooner had the monk caught sight of the rack than he began to babble his confession (the torturer declared that he had never known anyone to break so quickly). He confessed that he had never had divine revelations; that he had violated the confidentiality of the confessional; that he had not been confessed for any mortal sin since he was twenty, although he had committed many sins of the flesh; and that he had given communion to many with unconsecrated Host.

Fra Domenico was made of sterner stuff. For two weeks, he was subjected to every cruel device in the torturer's arsenal, but to no avail. The simple-minded dog remained true to his master. However, Fra Silvestro quickly turned on Savonarola and begged for forgiveness (as did the rest of the friars of San Marco, who apologized to Alexander noting: "Not merely ourselves, but likewise men of far greater talent, were deceived by Fra Girolamo's cunning").

While Savonarola was quickly convicted by the secular court on the basis of his own confession, he could not be punished without the sanction of the Church. Alexander dispatched three papal commissioners to Florence and they arrived on May 19. This necessitated a new round of torture to confirm the prior confession, which the cowardly monk readily ratified.

Savonarola and his two lackeys were executed on May 22. A large scaffold and stake was erected in the Piazza, upon which a gibbet with six chains was fixed. The prisoners were led to the base of the gibbet, where the Bishop of Vasona had them striped of their robes and separated from the Church Militant. They were then granted absolution for their sins and turned over to the secular authorities for punishment.

The Committee of Eight unanimously sentenced them to death for their atrocious crimes and decreed that: "each of the three be hung from the gibbet, and then burnt, so that their souls are entirely parted from their bodies."

Silvestro was hung first, then Domenico and finally Savonarola. The executioner reached for a torch to light the pyre, but was beaten to the task by a man from the crowd, a sodomite who proclaimed as he lit the fire: "at last I can burn the Friar who would have liked to burn me!"

As the bodies burned before the vast crowd in the Piazza, young boys danced around the pyre and threw rocks at the disintegrating corpses. The Committee of Eight ordered that the bodies be burned until all parts were completely consumed, so as to prevent any scavenging for false relics. The ashes were then loaded into a cart and dumped into the Arno.

The Devil's Instrument had returned to his master.

THE BORGIA

I had just departed Florence after my investiture when I digressed in this memoir to correct the misinformation which circulates to this day regarding the life and death of Savonarola. Now I shall return to the proper chronology.

Bibbiena and Giulio accompanied me on my journey to Rome, as did a large contingent of servants and guards and a train of wagons loaded with my possessions and gifts for the Holy Father and my new colleagues. All of the notables of Florence paid their respects by accompanying us for the first two miles of the trip. I stayed at my abbey at Passignano on the first night.

From there, we traveled to Siena, Florence's traditional rival in Tuscany. However, I was welcomed most graciously and entertained and feted for several days by its rulers and leading merchants. I next stopped at Viterbo, where I was hosted by the Pope's son (and my brother-in-law), Franceschetto Cibo, who accompanied me for the rest of my journey to Rome.

After several nights visiting Orsini relations, I arrived in Rome on March 22, 1492, in a pouring rain. Notwithstanding the inclement weather, many of Rome's notables turned out to greet me and escort me to the monastery of Santa Maria di Popolo, where I spent my first night. The next morning, my fellow cardinals paid their respects and then escorted me to the Vatican, where Innocent received me in full consistory and gave me the holy kiss. Giulio and Bibbiena were granted the honor of kissing the Pope's feet. For the rest of the day, I attended to Rodrigo Borgia, the Vice Chancellor and Ascanio Sforza, who had both been instrumental in securing my red hat.

Rome was just awakening from its thousand year sleep. Its antiquities had fallen into ruin; the Forum was a cattle market and the Palatine Hill a trash heap. Pestilential slums rose upon the mud flats and marshes of the Tiber. The only industry in the city was the Church and Rome's 40,000 inhabitants (of whom 7,000 were registered prostitutes) preyed upon the 50,000 pilgrims who visited the holy sites each year.

But new palaces were rising among the squalor, built with marble and stone scavenged from the ancient temples. The wealthiest cardinals, Giuliano and Domenico della Rovere, Raffaele Riario, Ascanio Sforza and Stefano Nardini vied with each other to build the grandest abode, but none rivaled the opulence of the Borgia palace, which I visited directly after attending to the Pope.

The main entrance hall was probably twice the size of that in our palace in Florence and was splendidly decorated with heavy tapestries. From there, I was escorted through a drawing room, where Borgia's vast collection of gold and silver plate was displayed, and then an anteroom, heavy with fine satin and Persian carpets and finally, to Borgia's private study, where he sat upon a couch covered in cloth of spun gold.

Borgia was as imposing as his palace. He was a large man, both in height and girth. He had a broad face with a fleshy nose and his head rested upon a powerful neck. His lips were sensual, his eyes bright and his demeanor genial. It was no wonder that women found the cardinal irresistible (and he returned the favor).

The difficulty in writing about the Borgia is that every heinous crime (violent, financial or carnal) in Italy over the past forty years has been attributed to one or more of the Borgia. Owing to the extraordinary character of the family, each attribution is at least plausible. I shall endeavor, in writing about them, to separate established fact from unsubstantiated rumor.

Borgia was christened Rodrigo Lenzuoli, a minor family in Valencia, Spain, but when his maternal uncle, Alfonzo Borgia, assumed the Seat of St. Peter as Calixtus III, Rodrigo changes his name to Borgia and was soon rewarded with the bishopric of Valencia. When Rodrigo was twenty-five, his uncle elevated him to the purple and in 1457 named him Vice Chancellor of the Roman Church, ranking only behind the pontiff in the Church hierarchy. Needless to say, over his thirty-five years in that powerful position, Rodrigo had accumulated a great fortune.

Cardinal Borgia was an able administrator and a skillful negotiator and the Vatican flourished under his stewardship. But he was perhaps best known for his carnal affairs. As a young cardinal, Rodrigo had entertained concurrent relations with a Roman woman and her two beautiful teenaged daughters. He fell deeply in love with one of the daughters, Vanozza Cataneis (the wife of an accommodating Curia functionary, Giorgio San Croce), who bore him four children, Cesare, Juan, Lucrezia and Jofre (more on them later), whom Rodrigo acknowledged as his own.

While Rodrigo's love for Vanozza is beyond dispute, it is also certain that he was liberal in spreading his seed widely. In the most scandalous provable incident, Borgia and Cardinal d'Estouteville presided at a baptism in Siena and, at the celebration after the ceremony, evicted all men from the party and had their way with the young mother and her female friends for six hours. When word of this atrocity reached Pope Pius, he issued a most scathing private letter of reproach to the Vice Chancellor.

Rodrigo also consorted with beautiful Giulia Farnese, the wife of Orsino Orsini (thus a relation of mine through the wives of my father and brother Piero). Later, she was referred to as "the Bride of Christ" and "the Pope's Whore" (but only outside of Borgia's hearing, of course).

Returning to my first meeting with Borgia, Rodrigo complemented me on the decorum I exhibited at my first consistory with the Pope and on the generosity of my father. I, in turn, expressed gratitude for the assistance Borgia had provided in obtaining my recent promotion. Borgia did not directly request my support in the upcoming conclave (Innocent's health was fast deteriorating) and I did not directly offer it. At the conclusion of the audience, we were both pleased and exchanged vows of close affection. I had done well for a sixteen year old boy.

Later that day, I attended a similar meeting with Ascanio Sforza, another leading contender for Innocent's chair, and achieved a similar result. Even the della Rovere cardinals sought me out and assured me of their love (just as Montesecco had assured Lorenzo years before). Applying my lessons well, I was polite and accommodating to all, but ambiguous in my commitments.

I purchased a modest palace near the Pantheon which had been recommended to me by the manager of the Rome branch of the Medici bank. Due to the deterioration of the bank under Lorenzo's management, I needed to pawn some of my new plate to secure the balance of the purchase price.

In early April, I received the sad but not unexpected news that my father had died. I immediately dispatched a letter to Piero, pledging him my complete support. In the letter, I tactfully suggested that he exhibit some discretion in his relations with others:

> I implore you, Piero mine, for my sake to contrive to show yourself generous, courteous, friendly and open towards all, but especially towards our own followers, for by such qualities there is nothing one cannot achieve or keep.

Not surprisingly, Piero did not grace my epistle with the courtesy of a reply. Rather, word reached me in Rome of Piero's street brawling and nocturnal amours. He also opened a feud with our cousins, Lorenzo and Giovanni Pierfrancesco de Medici, who were both influential in Florence and richer than us (my father had appropriated their trust funds before his death and Piero refused to acknowledge the debt). His governance was limited to sponsoring sporting and martial tournaments, in which he victoriously participated.

In May, I approached Pope Innocent and sought his leave to journey to Florence to repair Medici affairs. The Holy Father not only granted my request, but appointed me the papal legate to Tuscany, which gave me direct control over all Church interests in the province.

I was greeted by cheering throngs in Florence like a conquering hero returning from the campaign, which gratified me deeply. Piero's welcome was less exuberant, but civil and correct. To avoid unnecessary friction, I took my own palace in Sant Antonio near the Faenza Gate, leaving Piero to occupy the family seat on Via Larga unencumbered.

My first task was to attend to the Platonic Academy. Piero was deeply suspicious of men of intellect and had cut off their allowances immediately after Lorenzo's death. He could not appreciate the degree to which these eminent scholars and philosophers influenced the political climate in Florence. I had Marsilio Ficino appointed a canon of Florence and provided pensions and commissions to Demetrius Chalcondyles and other nearly impecunious members (Pico della Mirandola could take care of himself).

I was turning my attention to the woeful state of the Medici bank when word reached me from Rome that Innocent was about to expire. Forthwith, I assembled my train and retraced my recent steps. The Signoria designated Paolo Orsini to accompany me with a large contingent of soldiers, because Rome was even more violent and dangerous than normal during a papal interregnum (a modest 220 Romans were murdered by the mobs during this conclave).

On July 24, Innocent slipped into a coma. His doctor, a Jew, tried a new remedy. Three boys were brought to the papal bedchamber and drained of their youthful blood, which was exchanged with Innocent's tired blood. Needless to say, the three youths expired. Unfortunately, so did Innocent on the following day. I arrived just in time to escort Innocent's body to St. Peter's.

As always, the conclave was an intensely political affair, with the Holy Spirit remaining aloof until the bartering was concluded. King Charles VIII of France had pretensions against Naples (the old Angevin claim) and thus supported the Milanese, Ascanio Sforza (even though Sforza's sister was married to King Ferrante's son Alfonso). Ferrante supported Giuliano della Rovere (even though Giuliano was the papal legate to France and was highly esteemed there) and deposited 200,000 ducats in della Rovere's bank account (Genoa added 100,000 ducats). Borgia represented the independent block and withdrew so much coin from the Spannocchi bank that it nearly failed.

I was caught in the middle. I owed debts for my elevation to both Borgia and Sforza and my family's strong ties to France suggested joining the Sforza contingent. However, Piero, for reasons which were inexplicable to me, was publicly supporting Naples and della Rovere. So, I tried to maintain neutrality, aligning myself with Cardinals Piccolomini and Caraffa, two of the most pious and respected members of the College.

After three scrutinies, it was clear that no faction could garner the required two-thirds majority, so intense horse-trading commenced. This is where Borgia excelled. In addition to the aforementioned mule-loads of silver, Rodrigo deeded to Ascanio his magnificent palace (along with the town of Nepi) and promised to appoint Sforza to the Vice Chancellor post that he was shortly to vacate. Ascanio, for his part, deeded his now superfluous palace to Raffaele Riario, della Rovere's cousin, and Borgia promised him the position of Cardinal Chamberlain. Borgia then distributed his own benefices, including the abbey of Subiaco, the castles of Soriano and Civita Castellana, the bishoprics of Cartagena, Majorca and Porto and about twenty cities and towns among the Cardinals Orsini, Colonna and Savelli. By the end of the conclave, only Cardinals Piccolomini, Caraffa, Costa and I had not received gifts from Rodrigo. Even Giuliano della Rovere accepted the fortress of Ronciglione and the legation at Avignon in order to make Borgia's elevation unanimous. I had politely declined Rodrigo's offers; I did not want to be any more indebted to Borgia than I already was.

Upon examination of the last scrutiny, just before dawn on August 11, 1492, Rodrigo exclaimed joyfully like a child with a new toy: "We are Pope, Pontiff and Vicar of Christ." He immediately assumed the name Alexander VI (fitting for a man who intended to conquer the world). As we rose to make obeisance to the Holy Father, I turned to Cardinal Cibo and whispered to him: "We are in the jaws of a rapacious wolf. If we neglect to flee, he will devour us!"

Alexander's coronation took place two weeks later and was the most spectacular pageant since ancient Rome (until mine surpassed it). Thirteen squadrons of cavalry led the procession from St. Peter's to the Church of the Lateran, followed by Borgia's household and the diplomatic corps. I and the rest of the cardinals followed on richly caparisoned horses, each accompanied by twelve attendants. The Captain-General of the Church rode behind us bearing his drawn sword. The Pope himself rode under a canopy to shield him from the burning sun, but he nonetheless fainted twice during the ceremonies. Alexander was followed by the Papal Guard and the senior members of the Curia. I can attest it was a most exhausting day.

The Florentine delegation was the first to arrive bearing homage to Alexander. Piero, magnificently attired, led the embassy accompanied by Poliziano, Pico and Puccio Pucci (the Bride of Christ's brother-in-law) among others. I naturally offered Piero hospitality at my palace, but he accepted Alexander's invitation to lodge at the Vatican. We barely spoke during his stay in Rome.

Alexander's first consistory was held on August 31, 1492, during which he confirmed the grants of the benefices which had secured his election. He also named his son Cesare the Archbishop of Valencia. The seed Alexander planted this day would one day blossom into an evil flower for Rodrigo, his family and all of Italy.

To understand why, I must delve into the Borgia family history. Before immigrating to Italy to serve his uncle, Rodrigo had fathered a boy and two girls (mothers unknown) in Spain. The boy, Pedro Luis, served in the army of King Ferdinand of Aragon and, after distinguishing himself at the siege of Ronda, was given the title Duke of Gandia and the estates that went with it.

As previously written, Rodrigo fathered four children in Italy with Vanozza Cataneis. Cesare was born first, just a few months before me in 1475. Like me, he received his first benefices in 1483 and was later dispatched to Pisa to study canon law. His brother Juan (like mine Giuliano) was born a year later, followed by Lucrezia and Jofre. Cesare, like my brother Piero, was handsome, athletic, extraordinarily strong, skilled in martial arts and lustful towards women. Unlike Piero, he was also highly intelligent and cunning in his dealings with people. Like a true Borgia, Cesare was totally amoral, lacking in empathy and prone to extreme violence (Rodrigo is rumored to have committed his first murder at age twelve).

From Rodrigo's perspective, Cesare was his second son and thus was destined for a clerical career. However, from Cesare's perspective, he was the first son born of his father and Vanozza and was due a secular career. Thus, when Alexander named Cesare Archbishop of Valencia, he confirmed his son to a vocation which Cesare detested (and for which he clearly was not suited), exciting jealously and hatred towards his younger brother. It also galled Cesare that it was Juan who had inherited the title and estates of the Duke of Gandia when Pedro Luis died in 1488.

On September 13, 1492, Piero did the only commendable service in his short and undistinguished life – he fathered a son (Lorenzo) with his wife, Alfonsina Orsini (a relative of our mother), thus assuring a legitimate male heir to the House of Medici. Unfortunately, in that same month the idiot made political blunders that destroyed the tenuous relationship I was forging with Alexander and brought ruin to our family and Italy itself.

Italian politics is like a spider's intricate web; if you pluck a single strand, the entire web will vibrate. In the fall of 1492, Piero yanked on so many strands that the web nearly collapsed. Franceschetto Cibo (our brother-in-law) had been given by his father, Pope Innocent, the papal castles of Anguillara, Clodia and Cerveteri, all of which dominated strategic roads approaching Rome. Franceschetto was a compulsive gambler and, when Innocent died, he quickly became in dire need of immediate cash. Borgia's nemesis, Giuliano della Rovere (who, heeding my advice to Cardinal Cibo, had fled Rome for the safety of his fortress at Ostia), brokered a sale of the castles to Virginio Orsini for 40,000 ducats.

Orsini was already the most powerful baron in Rome (he had nearly exterminated the Colonna during the reign of Sixtus) and his purchase of the castles would greatly upset the delicate balance of power between the Orsini, Colonna and Pope (it being no secret that Alexander intended to change the balance in his favor as quickly as possible).

Making the situation worse, Virginio was currently serving as the commander of the Neapolitan army and King Ferrante had lent him half of the purchase price. And even worse, the sale was consummated without proper notice to Alexander, whose consent was required since the castles were papal fiefs.

There was no need for the Medici to involve ourselves in this affair and I begged Piero to steer clear of it. I had learned well the lesson of our father's blunder regarding papal real estate, which had led to war between Sixtus and Florence and the loss of our banking and alum concessions. But Piero's meddlesome wife joined with our sister Maddalena (Cibo's wife) and urged Piero to publicly endorse the sale, which he foolishly did.

Alexander's reaction to the completed sale was totally predictable and I found it prudent to immediately depart Rome for the relative safety of Florence. The Pope dispatched briefs to all the rulers of Italy and Europe denouncing Orsini, Ferrante and the Medici and requesting armed assistance to recover the purloined castles.

Borgia was not the only ruler infuriated by Piero's very public tilt in favor of Neapolitan interests. As you may recall, when Duke Galeazzo Maria Sforza was assassinated, his heir, Gian Galeazzo, was only seven years old. The young Duke's mother and uncles fought over his regency and Ludovico Sforza ultimately prevailed. In 1490, the Duke came of age, but Ludovico refused to cede power to the rightful heir. The Duke, being feeble minded and interested only in horses and dogs, did not particularly care that his uncle continued to rule Milan, but his ambitious wife (and first cousin), Isabella of Aragon, was another matter. She chafed at the short leash and inadequate allowance that Ludovico keep her husband on and complained bitterly to her grandfather, King Ferrante, her father, Alfonso, Duke of Calabria and her mother (Ludovico's sister). Ferrante and Alfonso, surrendering to the female chatter, began pressuring Ludovico to relinquish power.

Now, Cosimo de Medici had put the Sforza on the throne of Milan and Lorenzo had backed Ludovico in the intramural disputes over the regency. Consequently, Florence and Milan had been close allies for sixty years. Thus, it completely unnerved Ludovico (a pathologically suspicious, insecure and cowardly man) that Piero was tilting Florence away from Milan and towards a now-threatening Naples.

So, the two aggrieved parties, Borgia and Sforza, signed a new treaty in April 1493, the League of St. Mark, to which Venice (Florence's political and mercantile foe) happily joined. Florence and the Medici were now squeezed between two powerful states to the north and east and the Pope to the south. This being Italy, the political connection was supplemented by a marital one. In June, Rodrigo's thirteen year old daughter, Lucrezia, was married at the Vatican to Ludovico's bastard cousin, Giovanni Sforza, the Count of Pesaro. The fact that Lucrezia had already been contracted to a Spanish nobleman, Don Gaspare d'Aversa, was of little consequence; nobody lightly crossed the Borgia and a 3,000 ducat severance payment soothed the insult. While I (being self-exiled in Florence) did not attend the wedding, I am reliably informed it was a most ostentatious affair. Alexander, knowing no shame, had the Pope's Whore, Giulia, walk beside the bride to the papal throne and co-host the celebration. Rodrigo himself witnessed the deflowering of his young daughter later that evening.

As in any good chess game, Ludovico's move prompted a counter-gambit by Ferrante. He complained bitterly to his cousin, King Ferdinand of Aragon and Castile, that Borgia was betraying Spain by his tilt towards Milan. At this time, Ferdinand had his own need for Borgia's good will. Christopher Columbus had just discovered new lands lying to the west of the Azores and Canary Islands. Portugal claimed the new lands belonged to it under the authority of earlier papal Bulls. The Pope, as Vicar of Christ, had sovereignty over all uncharted areas of God's earth and their heathen inhabitants.

The three Spaniards worked out a mutually beneficial arrangement. Alexander issued the Bull *Inter Caetera*, granting sovereignty to Spain over most of the New World. Ferdinand gave his cousin, Maria Enriquez to Rodrigo's son Juan Borgia, the Duke of Gandia. Ferrante gave his granddaughter Sancia (the bastard daughter of Alfonso) to Jofre Borgia and bestowed upon him the title Prince of Squillace (a town south of Naples). Ferrante also forced Virginio Orsini to pay a 35,000 ducat indemnity to Borgia for purchasing Cibo's castles without papal consent. Alexander, in turn, renounced his just completed pact with Sforza.

Needless to say, Ludovico felt betrayed (indeed, he was, but that was nothing new in Italian politics). His supremely ambitious wife, Beatrice d'Este, was beside herself. Beatrice, the daughter of Duke Ercole d'Este of Ferrara (and granddaughter of King Ferrante), had married Ludovico in a double marriage ceremony in 1491 orchestrated and decorated by Leonardo da Vinci (Beatrice's brother Alfonso simultaneously married Anna Sforza, the sister of Duke Gian Galeazzo). Beatrice, who engaged in a life-long status contest with her older sister Isabella, the Marchesa of Mantua, was jealous of her cousin, Isabella of Aragon, the wife of the rightful Duke of Milan. To Beatrice, the Pope's betrayal foreshadowed that Ludovico's despotic rule of Milan would shortly come to an end, thereby depriving her of the richest court in Italy. So, she convinced Ludovico (who did not need much convincing) to invite King Charles VIII of France to invade Naples and overthrow the Aragon regime (notwithstanding her own Aragonese blood). Ludovico backed his invitation with a 100,000 ducat contribution towards the cost of the war (borrowed from a Genoese bank at fourteen percent interest).

However, Charles had his own tangled affairs to unwind before he could launch an invasion of Italy (which France's aristocracy and military opposed as wasteful and diversionary). He had inherited the crown of France in 1483 upon the death of the Spider King, Louis XI (the Medici's good friend). Charles was only twelve at the time and Louis had decreed before he died that his daughter, Anne, being "the least insane woman in France", serve as regent until Charles came of age in 1491.

In 1493, two pressing disputes with Europe's most powerful monarchs needed to be resolved before Charles could safely depart for his Italian adventure. Under the 1482 Peace of Arras, Maximilian, the Holy Roman Emperor, had pledged his daughter Margaret to Charles (with the provinces of Artois and Franche-Comté as dowry) and sent the infant girl to Paris to be properly educated for her future role as Queen of France. But Charles was infatuated with fourteen year old Duchess Anne of Brittany, a far more comely young lady than Margaret. Unfortunately for Charles, Anne had been married by proxy to Maximilian (but had never met the man to consummate the marriage).

In 1491, Charles invaded Brittany (a rich prize in itself) and took Duchess Anne hostage, forcing her to renounce her marriage to Maximilian and agree to marry him. She was not pleased by the prospect of a connubial connection with the dwarfish, misshapen (his feet were so large in comparison with his bent limbs that it was rumored he had six toes on each foot), pallid, twitchy, nearly illiterate monarch; indeed, she brought two beds with her to the palace. But Charles was in Brittany with a powerful army and Maximilian was sitting impotently in Germany, so the poor girl really had no options.

Charles not only had the audacity to steal the Emperor's betrothed, but he also refused to return Margaret and the two provinces given as the dowry. He wanted to auction his ex-fiancée to the highest bidder. Obviously, Maximilian was not pleased.

The Emperor was not the only monarch offended by the high-handed tactics of the youthful king. Ferdinand of Spain had borrowed 100,000 ducats from Louis XI and had given the provinces of Perpignan and Roussillon as security. When Ferdinand tried to repay the loan, he was rebuffed by Charles, who preferred keeping the provinces. Unless amity was restored between Charles and the two elder monarchs, an invasion of Italy was out of the question.

So Ludovico brokered another grand deal. In the Treaty of Senlis, Charles agreed to return the two dowry provinces to the Emperor, along with officially recognizing the Emperor's claim to Flanders. Ludovico gave his niece Bianca Maria to Maximilian as replacement for the purloined Anne. Margaret was given to Ferdinand's son John, Prince of Castile. Charles returned Perpignan and Roussillon to Ferdinand and waived repayment of the loan. Ferdinand and Maximilian, in return, pledged not to interfere with Charles' invasion of Naples.

I imagine you are quite confused by the complexity of the maneuvering that took place during 1493. I confess I found it difficult myself to keep track of all of the shifting alliances and matrimonies. Suffice it to say that Ludovico had trumped Ferrante and nothing now stood in the way of 50,000 savage Frenchmen marching south.

When Ferrante learned of Ferdinand's perfidy, he descended into a deep melancholy (not even his collection of embalmed enemies, posed like statues in a museum chamber off his bedroom, gave him solace). He died in January of that fateful year, 1494.

These events were closely followed at the Vatican and caused no end of consternation. In the summer of 1493, Alexander had substantially increased the size of the College. Red hats were dutifully doled out to France, England and Spain, hoping to win favor with their powerful monarchs and undermine the influence of the della Rovere cardinals and other enemies within the College. The Duke of Ferrara's fifteen year old son, Ippolito d'Este, was elevated to the purple. Closer to home, Alessandro Farnese, brother of the Bride of Christ, and Cesare were also named cardinals. Probably no man in history was less enthusiastic about receiving a red hat than Cesare, who desired only to be given an army to command (and his younger brother's title and lands).

When Ferrante died, Rodrigo was forced to commit himself. Charles sent an ambassador who demanded that Alexander declare Charles, as successor to the Anjou claim, King of Naples. Alfonso, Duke of Calabria, also sought the Pope's seal. Fearing the unpalatable prospect of a permanent French presence on the Church's southern flank, Alexander endorsed the Spanish claim. He sent the French Ambassador packing with a papal brief threatening Charles with excommunication if he crossed the Alps with his army.

The Vatican went on a war footing. Ascanio Sforza retreated to Milan. Giuliano della Rovere fled to France to press Charles to convene a General Council to depose Alexander. In May, 1494, Alexander sent his nephew, Cardinal Giovanni Borgia, to Naples to formally crown Alfonso and to marry thirteen year old Jofre to seventeen year old Sancia. As part of the transaction, Juan Borgia was named Prince of Tricaria and Count of Claremont, Laurie and Carniole. Jofre, as promised, was made Prince of Squillace, Count of Cariati and Protonotary and Lieutenant of the Kingdom of Naples. Cesare Borgia was granted numerous Neapolitan benefices. Cardinal Borgia and Alfonso witnessed the consummation between Jofre and Sancia (the girl, of rapacious sexual appetite and no moral scruples, had already been scandalously deflowered by her prior fiancé, Onorato Caetani, who had been cast aside by Rodrigo as easily as Lucrezia's Don Gaspare d'Aversa).

In August, Charles departed France with his vast army, enhanced by German, Swiss and Scottish mercenaries, and crossed the Alps to Turin. There, he was greeted and feted for many days by his cousin Bianca, the rich widow of the Duke of Savoy. As Charles was virtually broke (having drained the French treasury to finance his invasion), he "borrowed" some of Bianca's dazzling jewelry and immediately pawned them for 12,000 ducats for traveling money. On September 6, Charles left Turin and journeyed to Chieri, where (his reputation for lechery having proceeded him), he was presented with a collection of Italy's "most beautiful women" for his pleasure. Those rejected by Charles were appropriated by his generals and ranking officers. The common soldiers satisfied their baser urges by purchase or rape of the local girls, depending upon their pocketbooks and personal morality.

From Chieri, Charles' campaign of debauchery proceeded to Asti, where he met with Ludovico and Beatrice, who presented him with Milan's most skilled courtesans. There, Charles fell ill with the French boils and his procession south was delayed until October.

Meanwhile, Alexander was having serious domestic problems. In May, 1494, when Rodrigo finally made his decision in favor of Naples, his son-in-law, Count Giovanni Sforza, went from being an asset to a liability. Sforza suddenly found an urgent need to return home to Pesaro and left Rome in June, accompanied not only by his wife Lucrezia, but the Bride of Christ as well (Alexander habitually sent his beloved women to the country during Rome's summer plague season).

Alexander demanded that Sforza renounce his allegiance to Milan and take command of a Neapolitan brigade. The unscrupulous Count acceded to the pontiff's command, but then provided intelligence on the Neapolitan troop movements to Ludovico. When Rodrigo learned of Sforza's treachery (no secrets were safe from the Borgia and their vast network of spies), he ordered Lucrezia to return immediately to Rome, but Sforza ordered her to stay put in Pesaro. The poor girl was caught between her husband and the Holy Father. I do not know whether the Count's guards prevented her from obeying the Pope, but she stayed where she was.

Rodrigo was having no better luck with his mistress Giulia. In July, the Pope's Whore received word that her brother Angelo was ill and near death's door at the family seat of Capodimonte. Giulia sought Rodrigo's permission to visit her dying brother, but the Pope refused, Capodimonte being uncomfortably close to the fortified castle at Bassanello, where Giulia's cuckolded husband, Orsino Orsini, was ensconced. But the bonds of family proved too strong and Giulia went to Capodimonte in defiance of the Pope's wishes. As Rodrigo expected, Orsino then bade Giulia to join him at Bassanello.

Alexander was furious. He dispatched an intemperate letter to Giulia:

> Thankless and treacherous Giulia, Navarrico has brought us a letter from you in which you signify and declare your intention of not coming here without Orsino's consent. Though we judged the evil of your soul and that of the man that guides you, we could not

> believe that you would act with such perfidy and ingratitude in view of repeated assurances and oaths that you would be faithful to our command and not go near Orsino. But now you are doing the very opposite, risking your life by going to Bassanello with the purpose, no doubt, of surrendering yourself once more to that stallion. We hope you will recognize your error and make suitable penance. Finally, we herewith ordain, upon pain of excommunication and eternal damnation, that you shall not leave Capodimonte or Marta and still less go to Bassanello – this for reasons affecting our State.

I am not an expert on the history of the Church, but I would venture that this is the first time that a Pope threatened to excommunicate a woman if she had relations with her husband instead of the Vicar of Christ. Giulia, appreciating the threat to her body and soul, kept away from Orsino.

I have digressed again. I do not mean to make light of the French invasion. For while Charles was fornicating and Rodrigo was fuming, bloodshed of an unprecedented nature was taking place at Rapallo, just outside of Genoa. A Neapolitan army, under the command of Alfonso's son Ferrantino, had been transported by galley to halt the French advance. The French, supplemented by Swiss mercenaries, surrounded the Neapolitans who broke and scattered. About 300 Neapolitans were killed in the battle, but many were taken prisoner. In an Italian war, the prisoners would have been duly ransomed and permitted to return home. But the barbarian Swiss murdered them all and then sacked Rapallo, killing everyone, including forty sick patients in the hospital. Word of this outrage reached Genoa, whose angry citizens then arose and murdered many Swiss soldiers.

This barbaric bloodshed set the tone of the war. When Charles recovered from the pox sufficiently to travel, he proceeded to Casale, where he borrowed and pawned the jewels of the Marchioness, the mother of the Duchess of Savoy, and then to Pavia, where young Gian Galeazzo Sforza and his wife, Isabella of Aragon, were in exile after fleeing Milan. Isabella got down on her knees before Charles and begged him to protect her husband and to abandon his campaign against Naples. Charles found her amusing. Ludovico, emboldened by Charles indifference to the young Duke, had Gian Galeazzo poisoned and, after his death, arrested Isabella and her four children and imprisoned them in Milan. Ludovico then proclaimed himself the successor Duke of Milan.

Word of Ludovico's atrocity reached Charles at Piacenza. The young monarch was shocked at Ludovico's brazen assassination of a lawful ruler, who was, in addition, a cousin of the French king. Indeed, the house of Valois had its own claim to the Duchy of Milan. With his relation with his chief Italian ally now sour, Charles contemplated returning to France. But my perfidious cousins, Lorenzo and Giovanni di Pierfrancesco de Medici, prevailed upon the King to continue southward through Tuscany and pledged that Florence would rise up against Piero and then ally with France.

So, the French marched to our province's northern border and Charles demanded formal safe passage. My idiot brother, notwithstanding an army of 50,000 men threatening the city, sent ambassadors who expressed regret that Florence was obligated by treaty to support Naples and therefore could not oblige the French. Charles responded by expelling the Medici bank from Lyon and advancing to the Tuscan town of Fivizzano, where every man, woman and child was put to the sword. From there, Charles lay siege to the fortresses at Pietrasanta and Sarzana and threatened to sack Florence.

It was then that a messenger from the Vatican arrived at my palace and informed me that the Pope required my immediate attendance in Rome for urgent consultations. I had no illusions regarding Alexander's demand. He intended to hold me hostage to insure that Piero would not reverse himself and ally with France. I also knew that Piero would not be influenced in the slightest by the danger to my person. I was only eighteen, too young to die, but I had sworn the cardinals' oath of allegiance to the Holy Father and so reluctantly departed for Rome, once again spending the first night at my abbey at Passignano.

I have always believed that men of bullying disposition are cowards at heart and Piero was no exception. In a pale imitation of our father's journey to Naples, Piero sent a letter to the Signoria pledging to treat with Charles and "return to the satisfaction of ourselves and the city, or lose my life in the attempt."

Piero rode to the French camp on horseback, but Charles refused to see him, delegating his chamberlain, Rienne, and his general, Brissonet, to negotiate. When Piero saw first-hand the vast French army laying siege to Sarzana, his manhood deserted him. Brissonet demanded that Sarzana be immediately handed over. Piero agreed. Rienne demanded that the fortresses at Pietrasanta, Sarzanello and Librafratta be handed over. Piero agreed. Amazed at the ease with which Tuscany was being dismembered, Brissonet added the cities of Pisa and Leghorn to the list. Piero agreed. Not to be outdone, Rienne then demanded a 200,000 florin payment to the King. Piero agreed. The envoys could think of nothing else to ask for and hurried to inform Charles that they had both conquered Tuscany and financed the war without firing a shot.

When word of Piero's pathetic performance reached me at Passignano, I immediately recognized that it would be suicidal to continue on to Rome. Fearing that Medici rule was in serious jeopardy, I turned north. I rode directly to the Medici palace, where my idiot brother was serving wine and cakes to the common people and bragging how he had saved Florence from ruin. His wife and children and my brother Giuliano, as useless as a woman, had already fled to Careggi.

While Piero was sojourning in his fantasy world, Savonarola was mustering his supporters to revolt against my family and turn Florence into a theocratic dictatorship. On November 4, the Signoria called a special meeting of the Council of Seventy (normally a stronghold of Medici supporters) to discuss Piero's capitulation to France. We were not invited. At the meeting, Piero Capponi declared: "Piero de Medici is no longer fit to rule the State. It is time to be done with this government of children."

The revolution had begun. The Council selected a committee of five, including Savonarola and Capponi, to negotiate a new treaty with Charles. When Piero heard the news, he indignantly strode to the Signoria to demand a parliament, but was refused admission. Boiling mad, he returned to the Medici palace where he armed himself and returned to the Palazzo, with a company of Paolo Orsini's mercenaries, to take it by force. The gates to the Palazzo had been barred and the alarm bell was rung. A mob quickly assembled, surrounding Piero and taunting him. Boys threw rocks. Piero drew his sword, but his courage again deserted him and he sheathed it and beat a cowardly retreat to our palace.

I was at my own palace near Sant Antonio when I heard the Vacca. Fearing the worst, I mounted my horse and rode alone towards the Via Larga. The streets were teeming with men brought to arms by the bell. It seemed that every working man in Florence was armed with a billhook, stake or dagger and hurrying to the Piazza della Signoria. These common people were the foundation of Medici support in the city and I yelled: "Palle! Palle!" to rally them to our cause. When I reached the Church of San Bartolommeo, I encountered a mob led by Francesco Valori, formerly one of our family's staunchest supporters. I called: "Palle! Palle!" to which the traitor retorted: "Abbasso le palle!"°

Upon hearing this, the mob grew ugly. Had I not been wearing the scarlet robes of my high office, I would likely have been murdered on the spot. Even so, I was subjected to sacrilegious taunts and oaths and more than one chamber pot was emptied towards me from the surrounding apartments.

Ignoring the danger, I rode through the hostile crowds to the Medici palace. To my great surprise, I discovered that Piero, Paolo Orsini and his mercenaries had already fled Florence to seek sanctuary in Bologna. The great palace was deserted except for a small contingent of guards and household staff, who were bravely manning the gate to keep the mob at bay. I knelt and prayed for guidance and protection from our Lord.

° Translator's note: "Down with the balls."

While I was praying, Michelangelo arrived and was granted admission. Together, we quickly assembled as many works of art, antiquities and coin as we and the servants could carry. We armed ourselves and, with the remaining guards, forced our way through the crowd. As we departed, the mob rushed in to ransack what was left.

Our small group traveled the short distance down the Via Larga to San Marco. There, the pusillanimous brothers, under the thumb of Savonarola, barred the door to their benefactor and only reluctantly agreed to take possession of the art for safekeeping. Michelangelo and I then parted company, not to see each other again for many years.

The mood on the streets was violent and I soon determined that not even my red hat would protect me from injury. I hurriedly made my way to Santa Croce, where I exchanged my cardinal's robe for the hooded brown habit of a Franciscan friar. Suitably disguised, I proceeded on foot back to my palace. That night, I borrowed a horse from Pier Antonio Carnesecchi and followed Piero to Bologna.

Giovanni Bentivoglio, the tyrant of Bologna and my father's great friend, gave us temporary shelter at his palace, but nothing more. He angrily excoriated Piero for capitulating to the mob without even the pretence of a fight. He taunted us by bragging: "I would rather have been hacked to pieces than abandon my State in this fashion." This was an empty boast, as later events shall prove. But it unnerved Piero, who quickly left Bologna disguised as a valet and made his way to Venice. To my great delight, my cousin Giulio soon arrived from Pisa to take his place.

Had Piero not fled Bologna like a coward, our rule would likely have been quickly restored. Charles triumphantly entered Florence a week after our departure and was housed at our palace, which had been confiscated by the Signoria. A Florentine delegation, headed by Capponi, informed the King that the concessions made by Piero were null and void. When Charles rejected this effrontery and insisted that Piero's treaty be honored, Capponi declared: "If these be your terms, you may sound your trumpets, and we shall ring our bells."

Charles was now in a difficult position. He was in the center of the city, surrounded by thousands of armed and unfriendly Florentines. His army could not maneuver in the narrow streets, surrounded by fortified houses and palaces. So, the King compromised. The 200,000 ducat payment was reduced to 125,000 ducats and Charles pledged to return the fortresses, Pisa and Leghorn to Florence in not more than two years.

But Charles was privately furious and, of course, was categorically opposed to the concept of republican rule. He dispatched an envoy to Bologna with a letter requesting Piero's immediate return to the French camp, together with a pledge to return Florence to the Medici by force of arms. Piero had already departed when the messenger arrived, so I forwarded the letter to Venice and awaited my brother's response.

Once again, Piero proved himself an idiot. Instead of returning to Bologna immediately upon receipt of the letter, he instead brought it to the Senate of Venice and asked for guidance. Needless to say, the Venetians, who favored a weak and divided Florence and had no love for the French, strongly urged Piero to remain in Venice and posted spies and guards to insure that he followed their advice.

When word of Piero's blunder reached us, Giuliano and I agreed that the time had come to forsake Bentivoglio's begrudging hospitality. Giuliano left for Urbino, where lonely Duchess Elizabetta Gonzaga (the Duke was impotent and often away on military campaigns) had assembled an effete collection of courtiers who ate, drank, played games and wrote poetry each day and ate, drank, played games, read poetry and fornicated each night. Giuliano fit right in.

I traveled from Bologna, accompanied by Giulio, to Pitigliano and then to Castello, where we enjoyed the genuine hospitality of the Vitelli family. After a long stay at Castello, I joined Giuliano at Urbino, where I refrained from the debauchery that was rampant in the palace.

While I was wandering in exile, Charles was marching south. Tuscany offered no resistance, but once the French entered the Papal States, the butchery that had characterized the start of the campaign was renewed with vigor. The army sacked Aquapendente and Viterbo and slaughtered the garrisons of every fortress in its path. The Colonna, allied with Charles, captured Ostia, cutting off Rome's access to the sea. Even the Orsini deserted the Pope, surrendering their fortress at Bracciano to Charles as headquarters for the final attack on Rome.

At first, Alexander remained steadfast in his opposition to Charles. The King dispatched the renegade cardinals della Rovere and Colonna to negotiate safe passage for his army through Rome and Borgia promptly had them arrested and jailed at the Vatican. But then, on November 29, a French reconnaissance squadron happened upon the Bride of Christ and took her prisoner.

Rodrigo was inconsolable. He immediately opened urgent negotiations with Charles for Giulia's safe return. Charles, in a show of good will, had her escorted to the Vatican by a company of 400 French soldiers. It only cost Borgia 3,000 scudi and a promise to treat with Charles at the Vatican. Since the Neapolitan army had been routed and Alexander had no troops of his own after the Orsini defected, it was not difficult for him to agree to Charles' proposal.

Alexander prepared for the upcoming negotiation by moving his bed, belongings, treasury, food and every other moveable item from the Vatican to the impregnable Castel Sant'Angelo. He freed Cardinals della

Rovere and Colonna in his own show of good will and then demanded that Ferrantino of Aragon, King Alfonso's son and commander of the Neapolitan army, quit Rome with his remaining forces.

On December 31, 1494, Charles made his triumphant entrance into Rome. I am told it took six hours for his troops to parade from the Ponte Molle to the Vatican. Thirty thousand Frenchmen now encamped within Rome, plundering, murdering and raping the citizenry at will. Alexander, safe within the Castel, paid no attention to the suffering.

For three weeks, Borgia demonstrated his domineering personality and superior negotiating skills. He easily out-maneuvered Giuliano della Rovere, who unsuccessfully argued for a General Council to depose Alexander. On January 19, 1495, after many sumptuous feasts, lavish entertainments and lengthy private meetings, Charles appeared at public consistory in the Sala Reale, bowed before the Pope and swore allegiance to the Holy See. He kissed Alexander's foot and hand and then Rodrigo rose him up and allowed the King to kiss the papal cheek. In return, Charles received nothing more than a red hat for Brissonet and a vague promise from Alexander to invest him as King of Naples should he prevail in his upcoming battle against King Alfonso.

When Charles and his army left Rome on January 28, he was accompanied by Cardinal Cesare Borgia, ostensibly as legate to Naples, but in realty as hostage to insure that Rodrigo did not betray the French. Cesare, exhibiting the audacity and craftiness that soon would become legend, quickly escaped and returned to Rome. When the angry French commandeered his abandoned baggage train, they discovered the chests and cases filled with rags and garbage.

King Alfonso was a meaner and more vicious bully than Piero and hence, an even greater coward. As soon as Charles left Rome for Naples, Alfonso surreptitiously fled to Sicily, like a thief in the night, purloining the Kingdom's treasury and crown jewels and leaving his family and subjects destitute. Ferrantino immediately declared himself king.

Charles' army met only futile resistance. The fortresses of Montefortino and Monte San Giovanni refused demands to surrender and were leveled by the French siege cannon and their entire garrisons were put to death. General Trivulzio surrendered Capua to Charles without a fight. No Neapolitan troops now stood between the French and Naples, so Ferrantino and his family (including his half-sister Sancia and Jofre Borgia) boarded a ship and escaped to the island of Ischia. The people of Naples, finally freed from the cruel rule of the Aragonese, greeted the French like liberators, but soon discovered that the barbarians from the north were infinitely more disagreeable than their former rulers.

In fact, all Italians were horrified by the carnage wrecked by the French (not to mention the pox being spread by the army) and the fear that the ugly dwarf might soon control the entire peninsula. Ludovico

Sforza, ever the opportunist, organized a meeting of all the Italian states, as well as representatives of King Ferdinand and Emperor Maximilian. Ostensibly, the purpose of the meeting was to organize a defense of Christendom against the Turks (hence the name Holy League), but the real purpose, of course, was to drive France out of Italy. Milan, Venice and the Pope signed onto the League, but Florence, under the spell of Savonarola, refused and proclaimed neutrality. In secret annexes, Ferdinand and Maximilian were to be paid large sums by the Italians to launch military campaigns across France's borders.

When word of the united opposition reached Charles in April, 1495, he had little choice but to return to France with the bulk of his army to protect his homeland. Before he left, however, Charles had unfinished business to attend to. He sent envoys to Alexander with a demand that the Pope (as Borgia had promised) invest him as King of Naples. Charles sweetened the pot with an offer of 150,000 ducats upfront and 4,000 ducats per year tribute thereafter. When Alexander, committed to the Holy League, temporized, Charles crowned himself king.

Four days later, on May 20, Charles departed Naples and headed to Rome, where he intended to force Alexander to honor his promise. When he arrived, Cardinal Pallavicini warmly welcomed him and advised the King that the Pope and remainder of the cardinals had urgently been called to Orvieto. Not wasting time to pillage Rome for a second time, Charles hurried to Orvieto, only to find that the swift-moving pontiff had left the night before for Perugia.

The Holy League's army was gaining strength every day, so Charles gave up the chase and moved north towards France. It was around this time that my brother, with his pathetic sense of timing, slipped out of Venice and offered his services to the French. The idiot was convinced that Charles would restore Florence to the Medici during his march through Tuscany. However, Savonarola, whom Charles held in superstitious awe, met Charles at Poggibonsi and warned the King that if he restored the Medici, God would strike him dead. The terrified monarch then marched around Florence and on to Lombardy.

The two opposing armies finally met at Fornovo on the river Taro. The French, badly outnumbered, fought bravely and well on the first day. But then the Italians abandoned their attack to loot and plunder the massive French baggage train, brimming with loot and plunder from the ten month campaign. As the Italians fought each other over the booty, Charles and his army successfully escaped back to France.

Around this time, I received a letter from Alexander requesting my return to Rome, where the Pope said he would welcome me with great love and affection. Given that Savonarola was becoming an increasing irritant to Rodrigo, it seemed relatively safe and highly prudent to honor his command.

Once back at my Roman palace, I maintained a decidedly low profile. At consistories, I obediently followed the lead of Rodrigo, giving him no cause to treat me ill. I rarely left my palace other than to attend to the duties of my office. I scrupulously avoided most invitations to other cardinals' palaces and refused to engage in political gossip. Instead, I turned my palace into an oasis of culture, inviting artists, writers, poets, philosophers and musicians to enliven my evenings. And, of course, I satisfied my passion for the hunt during the season.

After the battle of Fornovo, Ferrantino launched a successful attack on the remaining French garrison at Naples. To celebrate, he married his fourteen year old aunt (which required a dispensation from the Pope, readily granted) for whom Ferrantino had developed a passion during his time in exile (poor Ferrantino died of excessive marital exertion months after the ceremony). After the wedding, Rodrigo recalled Jofre and Sancia back to Rome. He also recalled Juan, Duke of Gandia, from Spain to lead a military campaign of revenge against the Orsini.

Rome was not big enough to contain the Borgia men, particularly since Rodrigo, Cesare and Juan all lusted after Sancia. The beautiful harlot entertained them all, but settled upon Cesare, whose violent temperament matched her own. Jofre (whose pacific nature caused Rodrigo to occasionally speculate that he was actually the issue of a momentarily unfaithful Vanozza and her cuckolded husband) did not interfere with his older brother's presumption.

My life became more complicated and infinitely more disagreeable when Piero arrived in Rome and moved into my palace. The year before, just after the battle of Fornovo, Piero had paid 10,000 ducats (half of them mine) to Virginio Orsini to turn his idled mercenary army against Florence on our behalf. Our erstwhile friend, Bentivoglio, was supposed to lead a Bolognese army from the east in support. Piero and Orsini had maneuvered to the outskirts of Florence when an envoy arrived from Charles bearing a large payment to induce Orsini to march south to reinforce the French garrison at Naples. Virginio accepted the French commission and deserted Piero (without returning a single ducat of our payment) and Bentivoglio never left Bologna.

Piero's failure accentuated all of his vices. While I have never been an early riser, Piero would lie in bed until just before the dinner hour. If my menu was not to his liking, he would beat my servants and then ride to the palace of Cardinal Sanseverino, a host of exemplary generosity whose daily banquets were legend. After dinner, Piero habitually entertained himself with courtesans. After supper, Piero would depart with an assortment of disreputable associates for a night of drinking, gambling and whoring.

My brother always had a violent streak, but it was now beyond control. He beat both his and my servants with regularity and murdered several in fits of pique. He dared not lay a hand upon me, but often behaved with excessive insolence, even in public. Had he not been the master of the House of Medici, I would have evicted him from my palace. But I could not find it within me to turn upon my elder brother.

Piero's vices and schemes drained away our meager fortune. My plates now made regular journeys to the pawnbrokers, where they paid their respects to my tapestries and jewels. My rate with the banks rose to twenty percent.

But my issues with Piero paled in comparison with Rodrigo's problems with his children. Juan's recall from Spain to lead the Pope's troops against the Orsini sparked dangerous jealousy in Cesare, which even Sancia's charms could not temper. Juan, the newly appointed Captain-General of the Church, together with the Duke of Urbino, whose army had been hired to assist him, departed Rome in October, 1496. They marched north and ten Orsini castles surrendered in quick succession. The Orsini now had only two fortresses left, Trevignano and Bracciano. Trevignano was taken, and its town sacked, in January, 1497, but Duke Montefeltro was wounded. Now in sole command of the papal forces, Juan twice stormed Bracciano (which was commanded by Bartolommea Orsini, sister of Virginio), but was repulsed both times.

The Borgia's war against the Orsini had raised concern among the petty tyrants of the Romagna. Vitelli of Citta di Castello and Baglioni of Perugia marched south towards Bracciano to aid the Orsini, as did Cardinal della Rovere, heading a force of his own financed by the French. Juan lifted the siege at Bracciano and met the opposing armies at Soriano. He sustained a minor wound to his shoulder and immediately retired from the field. Left leaderless, the papal army was routed and the Duke of Urbino, still recovering from his own more serious wounds, was captured.

Alexander was forced to sue for peace. He agreed to return all of the captured fortresses to the Orsini for a 50,000 ducat indemnity. Borgia refused to ransom Montefeltro, who languished in the dungeon of the castle at Soriano until his own family arranged for his release.

Juan's arrogance was not curbed by his unspectacular performance in the field. Indeed, in Rodrigo's eyes, Juan, his favorite, could do no wrong. Not only did Alexander direct the payment of the 50,000 ducat Orsini indemnity to Juan, but he also ceded to him the Holy See's fiefs of Benevento, Terracina and Pontecorvo. At the secret consistory where we cardinals consented to Alexander's grant (only Cardinal Piccolomini protested this nepotistic conversion of valuable Church property) I could see pure rage on Cardinal Cesare's face, although he said not a word. The rage only intensified when Juan began openly consorting with the harlot Sancia. The cuckolder was now himself being cuckolded.

The witches' brew that was simmering in the spring of 1497 included Lucrezia as well. As previously noted, her husband Giovanni Sforza had disgraced himself in the French War and remained in Pesaro, far from his wife and father-in-law. When Juan marched north against the Orsini, Alexander ordered Sforza to join the Duke with a contingent of men. Sforza sent his regrets and the Pope then ordered him back to Rome, where he promised he would be most welcome. The alterative to obedience was the steel of Juan's lances, so the Count reluctantly journeyed to Rome, arriving in January, 1497. Alexander, true to his word, treated Giovanni with dignity and respect, but it was Lucrezia herself who warned her husband that Rodrigo and Cesare were plotting to poison him. On Good Friday, Sforza retreated back to Pesaro as fast as his horse could carry him.

Now, in the interest of an honest accounting, I must temporarily detour from the story of the Borgia and return to my own family and an episode I would just as soon forget. As I previously wrote in my chapter on Savonarola, by 1497 the people of Florence were becoming disenchanted with the Devil's Instrument and the famine, plague and economic collapse that attended his regime. In March, Bernardo del Nero, a staunch supporter of the Medici, was chosen Gonfaloniere for the traditional two month term. Bernardo sent a secret message to Piero promising that Florence would welcome our return and rise up against Savonarola.

I quickly approached Alexander, who declared he had no objection to the Medici returning to rule in Florence. The Venetian Ambassador warmly endorsed our plan and Cardinal Ascanio opined that Milan would abstain from any support for the Republic. Piero and I pledged what little remained of our fortune and retained Bartolommeo d'Alviano and his 1,300 man army to lead our assault. My brother Giuliano took a break from his poetry and fornication in Urbino to join Piero in the field.

We met at my palace with Ludovico da San Miniato, an emissary from our supporters in Florence, to plan a concerted campaign to retake the city. It was agreed that at dawn, on April 29, the San Pier Gattolini Gate was to be opened from within and our troops would pour through and retake the Signoria. At our meeting, San Miniato suggested then establishing a twenty-five man council to assist Piero in his administration of the restored State. Piero, true to his character, responded:

> You ought to know by this time that I don't mean to ask anyone's advice, and prefer rather to manage badly on my own account than well by others' help.

I have often considered ordering those words engraved on Piero's tomb.

Piero, Giuliano and d'Alviano departed Rome on April 20 and stopped at Siena, where its tyrant, Pandolfo Petrucci, offered his best wishes and provided hospitality to the entire army. By the 28th, Piero had advanced to the monastery of San Gaggio, just outside of Florence. According to the plan, the gate would be opened at dawn the next morning. But that night it rained heavily. Piero and Giuliano, not wanting to expose their splendid new uniforms and armor to the elements, remained ensconced at the monastery.

Dawn came and went and the army remained supine. By time the rain let up, local peasants had alerted the Signoria that Piero's army was approaching the city. Our supporters were quickly arrested and armed guards placed atop the walls. When Piero arrived at the gate, it was firmly barred. For four hours, Piero and d'Alviano paced up and down before the walls, debating whether the heavily armed mercenaries should take the city by storm. From time to time, Piero yelled demands that the gates be forthwith opened to Florence's lawful ruler. The guards responded with taunts and jibes.

In the late afternoon, Piero displayed his cowardly nature to all by turning tail and retreating with his large army. Not an ounce of blood had been spilled. The mercenaries, deprived of their promised booty, ransacked several Tuscan villages on the retreat south. Needless to say, this episode did nothing to improve Piero's disposition (or my own). Unfortunately, this comedy was intermixed with tragedy. Five of our most loyal supporters within the city, including Nero, were hung for treason.

When Lucrezia's husband slipped out of his grasp again, Alexander immediately opened negotiations with Ludovico and Ascanio Sforza to have the marriage annulled. Given the political uncertainty prevailing in Italy at the time, the Sforzas were not going to risk alienating the Pope by supporting their errant cousin. It was agreed that Giovanni Sforza have the choice of consenting to one of two grounds for annulment: (1) the marriage was invalid because the pre-existing marital contract with Gaspare d'Aversa had not been properly released or (2) the marriage had never been consummated (which took some gall to propose since Rodrigo himself had witnessed the deflowering).

The Count of Pesaro, safe within the walls of his own castle, rejected both choices and instead publicly insinuated that Rodrigo wanted the marriage annulled so that he could once again carnally possess Lucrezia for himself. This allegation shocked everyone. While nobody exactly believed Sforza's claim, it could also not be rejected out of hand since it was already widely held that Lucrezia had had unnatural relations with both Juan and Cesare. Given Rodrigo's lusty nature and his overwhelming love for his children, it could have been true. If so, he would have been one of the few men in history (and certainly the first Pope) to have had carnal relations with a woman, her two daughters and her granddaughter. Lucrezia was so mortified by the accusations and rumors that she fled the Vatican and took refuge at the Convent of San Sisto.

While the negotiations over the annulment were proceeding, Cardinal Ascanio gave a grand reception at the Vice Chancellor's Palace. I attended, together with all other cardinals then present in Rome. All of

Rodrigo's sons were also present, as was Sancia, who looked ravishing as she flirted with both Juan and Cesare in the presence of Jofre. Juan, who appeared already inebriated when he arrived at the party, drank still more and then, without provocation, grossly insulted Antonio Orsini (a relative of both Cardinal Ascanio and the Bride of Christ) and his two sons. Orsini, himself drunk, responded in kind, calling Juan a coward and common bastard. The Duke of Gandia drew his sword, but then turned on his heel and angrily left the palace. A short time later, a contingent of papal guards arrived, dragged Orsini to the courtyard of Ascanio's palace and hung him dead from an olive tree.

For a week, this outrageous breach of protocol was the only topic of whispered gossip at the Vatican. But then it was swept into insignificance by a most shocking incident. I was at consistory on June 15 when I could not help but notice that Alexander appeared almost beside himself with worry. After the session adjourned, I learned from my colleagues that Rodrigo's three boys had attended a dinner party at their mother's house. Juan and Cesare had departed together, but Cesare claimed that Juan had left him to go whoring in the Ghetto. Juan had not yet returned to the Vatican and Alexander feared the worst.

Papal guards were dispatched to canvass Rome for signs of the missing Duke and they found a boatman who testified that he observed a body being taken off a large white horse and thrown into the Tiber near the sewage outfall. When the mutilated body of Juan's groom was found near that spot, the river was dragged and Juan's body recovered. The corpse, bloated and covered with filth, had its throat cut and eight other stab wounds in the head, body and legs. Juan's money belt, containing thirty ducats, was untouched.

I was not there when the Duke's body was viewed by the Pope and he fell into a swoon. I was present, however, after Rodrigo locked himself in his chamber and refused all entreaties to open the door for sustenance or consolation. For four days and nights, we cardinals took turns at his door, listening to his animal-like moans and sobs which never ceased, even in the darkest hours of the night.

While the Pope was locked away in grief, the Curia launched an investigation. There was no shortage of suspects. Cardinal Ascanio topped the list, given the insult that had just occurred at his palace. The Orsini, kin of the slain man and still smarting over the attacks on their fortifications, were next. Also on the list were the Duke of Urbino, General Gonsalvo of Naples (who had clashed repeatedly with Juan), the Count of Pesaro and Jofre Borgia. Conspicuously absent from the list of suspects was Cardinal Cesare, the last person to see Juan alive and the only nobleman in Rome owning a large white horse.

When Alexander finally emerged from his chamber, he was, for the time-being, a changed man. At consistory on June 19, he announced that he viewed the Duke's death as a "visitation" from the Lord and that he would "attend with all due diligence to the reform of the Church" and "give no further occasion for scandal." To prove his seriousness, he appointed Cardinal Caraffa to chair a five cardinal commission to propose appropriate reforms. Then, he sent Jofre and Sancia away to their principality of Squillace. Cesare was dispatched as papal legate to Naples, where he presided over the investiture of Federico as King of Naples (Ferrantino, his nephew, died without issue). While there, Cesare contracted the Naples' disease (French boils).

Cardinal Caraffa's commission submitted its list of proposed reforms in September, but by then Alexander had recovered his equanimity. He quashed the investigation of Juan's death and filed away the commission's recommendations without further comment.

In November, the Count of Pesaro had finally been convinced by Ludovico and Ascanio to swallow his pride and consent to the annulment, which he did at a ceremony at the Vatican on November 18. As part of the arrangement, he was permitted to retain the 31,000 ducat dowry and Alexander pledged his safety. On December 22, Lucrezia was summoned from the convent to the Vatican to hear the official Bull of Annulment, in which it was confirmed that she remained "virgo intacta". That she remained impassive during this ceremony is testament to her theatrical skills, as she was visibly pregnant. The likely father, Pedro Calderon, Rodrigo's handsome chamberlain who carried messages to the nunnery, was soon murdered by Cesare in the Pope's own apartment. Naturally, rumors abounded that the true father was Cesare (or Juan or Rodrigo). The mysterious *Infans Romanus*, Giovanni Borgia, was born the following April and Sancia was designated to raise him.

That April, Charles VIII of France died suddenly after hitting his head on a door lintel (not an easy task for a dwarf). This accident changed everything in Italy. Because Charles had died childless, the crown went to his older cousin, Louis, Duke of Orleans, who was invested as King Louis XII on May 27, 1498. Like Charles before him, Louis was infatuated with the beauty and land-holdings of Anne of Brittany and was determined to marry his predecessor's widow. Unlike Charles, who was only married by proxy when he pursued Anne, Louis had been married for twenty-two years to his cousin Joan, the daughter of Louis XI. Since divorce was anathema, Louis appealed to the Pope for a Bull of Annulment. Louis chose the only possible grounds available to him – non-consummation. This, of course, enraged Joan, particularly since Louis was known for boasting publicly regarding his sexual endurance.

Louis' petition gave Alexander some much needed leverage with the new King. Louis desired to not only possess Anne, but Naples (through the Anjou claim) and Milan (through the Valois claim). Leaving no doubt as to his intentions, he named himself King of Milan, Naples and Sicily at his coronation. Another French invasion of Italy was on the horizon.

After Juan's death, Alexander refocused his ambition to create a secular state for the Borgia upon Cesare, which was what his son had wanted all along. This, of course, meant that Cesare needed to return his red hat, which he was eager to do. Although unprecedented in Church history, we in the College readily gave our unanimous consent. That same day, Louis (to curry favor for his pending petition) conferred upon Cesare the title Duke of Valence (a small city near Lyon). The former Cardinal of Valencia was now the Duke of Valence. His Italian nickname, "Valentino," could remain unchanged.

Cesare also required an Italian wife and title. For that, Alexander turned to Naples, now the weakest state in Italy. Rodrigo proposed a double marriage to King Federico. His "virgin" daughter Lucrezia would marry Alfonso II, Federico's handsome nephew and Sancia's brother. Cesare would marry Federico's daughter Carlotta, who was being raised at the French Court, and Cesare would receive the title Prince of Tarento. Federico, a man of strong spirit, consented to the Alfonso-Lucrezia match, but rejected out of hand admitting Valentino into his immediate family. He said he would rather die and lose his kingdom than align with the treacherous Borgia son. Carlotta was of like mind.

So, when Louis' annulment petition arrived, Alexander seized the opportunity. He sent Cesare north to France, carrying the Bull of Annulment but under instruction not to deliver it until Carlotta was betrothed to him. Given that Carlotta was essentially a prisoner in Louis' palace, it seemed a strategy sure of success.

After a delay occasioned by a visible outbreak of Cesare's French boils (he took to wearing a black silk mask in public until his death), he proceeded north with a magnificent 100,000 ducat wardrobe and royal-like retinue and was warmly greeted with great pomp by the French.

But Louis had no interest in cementing an alliance between the Borgia and the Aragonese, so he did not lift a finger to force the engagement. Cesare held onto the Bull of Annulment and announced his intention to return home, but Louis opined that it was not convenient for him to leave. The Pope's son was now the hostage of the French King.

After a politically uncomfortable, but highly elegant and luxurious standoff, Louis suggested that Cesare instead marry his cousin Charlotte d'Albret, the sister of the King of Navarre. This would connect the Borgia directly with French royalty. Cesare leapt at the opportunity and, in his enthusiasm, consummated the marriage six times on his wedding night (a feat which Rodrigo told us in consistory broke his own endurance record).

This new alignment had immediate political consequences. Spain and Portugal sent a joint embassy to the Vatican to protest. At a consistory unlike any I have ever attended, the Spanish Ambassador had the temerity to proclaim that Alexander had obtained the papal throne through simony and was thus not the lawful head of the Roman Church. Rodrigo responded by threatening to have the Ambassador thrown into the Tiber.

But no one was more upset by the Borgia's alignment with the French than Ludovico Sforza. The usurper of Milan had no ready allies to help him defend against the upcoming invasion. In an act of desperation, he signed a mutual aid treaty with Florence, pledging to assist the Republic in its unending, unsuccessful war against its former vassal Pisa. This enraged the Venetians, who were Pisa's principal ally. The Venetians retaliated by entering into a treaty with France calling for a joint invasion of Milan and the partition of its possessions in Lombardy. A signature line was added for Alexander. He signed when the French and Venetians promised to conquer and deliver to Cesare the old papal fiefs (now ruled by independent tyrants) of Imola, Forli, Faenza and Pesaro. When Rodrigo inked the treaty, Cardinal Ascanio and his principal allies, Cardinals Colonna and Sanseverino, fled Rome.

This new treaty offered a unique opportunity for the Medici. Piero approached his friends in Venice and proposed a joint attack on Florence, which the Venetians, their own army under heavy pressure at Pisa, readily accepted. Venice dispatched an army under the joint command of the Duke of Urbino and Astorre Baglioni of Perugia. We retained (once again, I pledged nearly all my possessions) our old condottieri Bartolommeo d'Alviano and Carlo Orsini. Piero, Giuliano and Giulio joined the combined armies at Marra in the Val de Lamone. As our armies marched west towards the narrow Apennine passes, the joint Florentine-Milanese army, under the command of the brilliant condottiere Paolo Vitelli, blocked the passes and harassed our supply lines. Unable to get adequate food, our troops began starving and terrible weather bogged them down in the barren district of Casentino. Piero once again displayed his cowardly nature by abandoning our troops in the middle of the night (along with the Venetian commissioners) and fleeing for safety to the town of Bibbiena. Bereft of leadership, our entire army surrendered to Vitelli. Consistent with civilized conduct, our soldiers were permitted to return home.

After Piero's third ignominious defeat, we Medici were at our lowest ebb in 300 years. Our fortune was dissipated, our banks were shuttered, our political influence was nil and Piero was the laughingstock of Italy. Only my multiple benefices provided any source of income. With the political situation in Italy fluctuating wildly on an almost daily basis and a Florentine bounty on my head, this seemed a good time to indulge my curiosity regarding life in the barbarian north.

I carefully approached Alexander for permission to travel abroad, waiting for a day when the pontiff appeared in excellent humor. Since I no longer had any financial or political usefulness, the Pope granted my request and wished me safe journey. As you might imagine, I had no desire for either Piero or Giuliano to accompany me on my expedition and so invited Giulio, who readily accepted. We decided to recruit ten additional friends with compatible temperaments and sensibilities. This would create a group large enough for security and amusement, but not too large so as to excite fear or suspicion as we traveled.

We assembled in Venice, where the Senate extended me gracious hospitality despite my brother's unseemly flight from battle. I decreed that, notwithstanding my exalted rank, each of us would have equal stature on the trip. Each night we would draw lots to determine who would be the unquestioned leader for the following day. I packed away my vestments and we all disguised ourselves as mendicant monks on pilgrimage.

We journeyed north and traversed the high Alpine passes on donkeys. The size and majesty of the mountains surpassed the limits of my imagination. We arrived in Bavaria and it became clear why the barbarians of the north had, for a millennium, turned their eyes and armies south to gentle Italy. The German forests were vast, dark and forbidding. Great marshes and swamps extended for miles. Barren, rock strewn plains, with hard flinty soil provided an inadequate basis for agriculture.

The climate was atrocious. Cold, ice, snow, winds that never ceased and tempests of a severity unknown in our fair land prevailed. Sunny days were confined to summer, but the absence of cooling waters made the heat unbearable.

The harshness of the people of Germany matched the climate. They were a moody people (understandably), roughly clothed, guttural of tongue, living lives more like livestock than humans. Indeed, they lived with their domestic animals in the winter, sharing quarters for warmth, sustenance and perhaps amusement.

And yet I experienced some of the happiest days of my life. For the first time, no one had expectations of me. My companions and I had complete freedom to do as we pleased. No politics or religious duties interfered with the excitement of seeing exotic new places.

We had no money to speak of, but I learned that its absence was not an impediment. The mere mention of the Medici name and a flash of my sapphire ring garnered us instant credit wherever we roamed. I formed the absolute conviction that God would always take care of my financial requirements, which has remained true to this day.

Over several months, we visited the principal towns of Bavaria. The architecture was striking in a gloomy Gothic sort of way, with none of the grace of our modern Italian buildings. At Ulm, the magistrates became suspicious of our little band and we were placed under arrest and sequestered in a most despicable jail. I had no choice but to reveal my true identity and demand that my presence be announced to the Emperor. The magistrates, unnerved by the badges of my office and my universally recognized name, arranged for an immediate escort to Maximilian's seat at Wiener Neustadt.

The Emperor greeted us with great joy. He highly esteemed my father and regaled us with stories about Lorenzo. He complimented me on the magnanimity and patience with which I was bearing the temporary reversal of Medici fortunes and assured me that better days lay ahead. He commended me for my travels. It was far better, he said, for a man, however highly placed, to enlarge his mind by the study of men and manners abroad, then to sulk in luxurious idleness at home.

From that day forward, money was no longer any concern for us. We spent nearly a month of luxurious idleness at his palace and then journeyed west with a plenary passport under Maximilian's personal seal that provided us with instant hospitality throughout the Empire.

We crossed into Flanders, which was ruled by Maximilian's son Philip. There, we were treated with not just hospitality, but magnificence. After dreary Germany, Flanders was a revelation. I had never seen such fertile land and bright, healthy people. The cities of Flanders bustled with commerce and displays of wealth that surpassed anything I had seen outside of Milan.

From Brussels, we journeyed to the Flemish coast where I was intent on crossing the Channel to the legendary kingdom of England. For two weeks, the weather was stormy and the sea raged unlike any I had ever seen. Even though the weather then improved, my companions balked at crossing such forbidding waters. I had a strong urge to overrule them, but remembered my pledge and reluctantly bowed to the consensus of my friends.

Thwarted in my desire to visit England, we turned south to tour France. When we reached Rouen, we were once again arrested. This time, my Medici name excited only increased suspicion and we were kept under lock and key while correspondence was sent to King Louis at Milan seeking instructions as to our fate. Fortunately, Piero was at the French encampment and interceded on our behalf. Louis dispatched a passport assuring our safe passage throughout his kingdom.

From Rouen, we toured Paris, Orleans, Bourges, Lyon, Avignon, Nimes and finally Marseille. As we traveled through this magnificent land, it became obvious to me that Italy would never be able to match the might and wealth of France.

The situation in Italy had stabilized sufficiently since our departure to contemplate a return home. When we left, Alexander was torn between his Aragonese connections (Lucrezia's and Jofre's spouses) and his new French connection (through Cesare's marriage). Lucrezia's Alfonso, not wishing to chance the Pope's continued good will, fled Rome for Naples in July 1499. Lucrezia, once again with child, had been deserted by a husband for the second time.

Alexander was furious. He forbade Lucrezia to follow Alfonso and instead named her governor of Spoleto and dispatched her north to the castle where she remained a virtual prisoner. Rodrigo ordered Jofre to stay with her at Spoleto and deported Sancia back to Naples. The split with the House of Aragon was now complete.

King Louis crossed the Alps with his army in July, 1499 and headed straight for Milan. Ludovico appealed to the Emperor for assistance, but Maximilian was preoccupied battling the Swiss and declined. King Federico, having learned from his nephew's mistake, kept the Neapolitan army close to home. The Sforzas, bowing to the inevitable, fled Milan and Louis' soldiers marched into the city, where they were greeted as liberators. Louis, accompanied by Cesare and Giuliano della Rovere, himself made a triumphant entry on October 6.

As promised, the Venetians were given Cremona and a large body of French troops was placed at Cesare's disposal to enable him to conquer the Romagna. Imola quickly capitulated, but Forli, under the command of the virago, Caterina Sforza, resisted brilliantly until Caterina, not willing to see her followers slaughtered, surrendered to the French commander, Ivo d'Allegri (the same officer who had captured the Bride of Christ). Caterina demanded to be escorted to King Louis, but Cesare intervened and took her prisoner himself (and violated her person at his pleasure in a most ungentlemanly manner).

Cesare was just about to attack Cesena and Pesaro when his push south was interrupted. The Sforza brothers (Ludovico and Ascanio) had earlier fled to the Tyrol from Milan. There, using the vast wealth that they had prudently taken with them, they engaged 7,000 Swiss mercenaries to retake their city. When Louis was called back to France to quell riots at the University of Paris (a play satirizing the marriage of Cesare and Charlotte had been closed by the authorities and 6,000 students took to the streets), Ludovico seized the opportunity and descended upon Milan from the Alps.

The people of Milan, like those of Naples before them, now realized that their home-grown tyrant was preferable to the barbarian French and rose to greet the Sforzas. The gates to the city were thrown open and the French troops retreated to the citadel. But Louis was not about to give up his great prize. D'Allegri was ordered to detach from Cesare and march back to Milan, where he was to link up with 6,000 fresh French troops and 10,000 Swiss mercenaries.

The opposing armies faced each other at Novara. The two Swiss commanders (one on each side) secretly met to discuss the impending battle. Since friendship with King Louis was essential in light of the Swiss' ongoing dispute with the Emperor, the Sforza's Swiss elected to desert and return home. Ludovico, now without an army, fled for his life, but was captured by the French. In the normal course, he would have been ransomed. But Ludovico had behaved so treacherously and caused so much disturbance in European affairs, that neither Louis nor any other ruler in Europe wanted him freed. So Ludovico finally received his just deserts. He was entombed in the lightless dungeon at the castle of Loches in France, where he survived ten years of solitary confinement before he perished, un-mourned but well-remembered.

With Ludovico gone and Louis content to consolidate his gains before pressing on to Naples, this appeared an auspicious moment to return to Rome. We embarked at Marseille for my first sea voyage (and God-willing, my last). I confess that I do not possess a constitution amenable to the rolling motion of the sea. For days, I was violently ill with nausea, vomit and headache. Never before had I fervently wished for my own death, which seemed preferable to my continued misery. The weather gods also conspired against me and our ship was forced to seek safe harbor at Savona.

At Savona, we unexpectedly discovered Cardinal Giuliano della Rovere in residence. Having backed the right horse in the recent war, he was in ebullient spirits. Giulio and I had a pleasant supper with the Cardinal, catching up on news and gossip. At the conclusion of the evening, we pledged to each other our continued affection and support.

From Savona we traveled to Genoa for an extended visit with my sister Maddalena and Franceschetto Cibo, during which time I fully recovered my health. By May, 1500, I was ready in mind and body to renew my acquaintance with Alexander.

Rome was packed with pilgrims for the Jubilee Year and Alexander was in hearty good humor. Lucrezia had given birth to another boy (named Rodrigo) and Alfonso had returned to Rome, with papal blessing, for the christening. Even Sancia had been forgiven and had rejoined Jofre. I had a long private audience with the Pope, at the end of which we pledged to each other our continued affection and support. Alexander then escorted me to the Chapel of the Kings of France where Michelangelo's *Pieta*, commissioned by Cardinal Riario, had recently been installed. It was a most beautiful marble and Rodrigo was very proud of it.

It seemed initially that a new era of good feelings had descended upon the Vatican. But then a series of portents accurately foreshadowed the calamities lying just ahead. On June 28, a great iron chandelier detached itself from the ceiling and fell within inches of Alexander. The next day, the Feast of Sts. Peter and Paul, a sudden tempest blew up on a clear sunny day and a mighty bolt of lightening struck the Vatican, sending three floors of rubble down upon Alexander, who was seated on his throne. The Pope was completely buried and it took his servants half an hour to extricate him from the pile. Miraculously, he was not seriously injured.

Alexander had reconciled with Alfonso, but Cesare detested his brother-in-law and made no attempt to hide it. On July 15, Alfonso was set upon by a group of armed men on the steps of the Vatican and gravely wounded. He was carried up to the Borgia apartments where Rodrigo ordered a heavy guard and Lucrezia and Sancia ministered to the Duke night and day. Gradually, Alfonso began to recover. Opinion in the Curia was divided between those who viewed the Orsini as responsible for the attack and those who suspected Cesare. Cesare did little to divert suspicion. He said in public: "I did not wound the Duke, but if I had it would have been no more than he deserved." It was rumored that he said directly to Alfonso: "What started at noon could be finished by nightfall."

What is beyond doubt is what happened next.   On August 18, Cesare's captain, Don Micheletto Corella, burst into the sickroom, ordered Lucrezia and Sancia out and strangled Alfonso to death. Cesare excused this outrage by telling Alexander that Alfonso had shot an arrow at him while he was walking in the courtyard below. Rodrigo accepted the explanation with equanimity. Lucrezia, heartbroken, departed for Nepi to mourn.

Cesare itched to return to the field to complete his conquest of the Romagna, but Alexander was running short of cash. In September, 1500, he sold twelve new red hats, but the income was not sufficient. So, using the pretext of a new Crusade against the Turks as an excuse, Alexander levied a special tax upon all clergy, including cardinals. I was assessed a tax of 600 ducats upon the 6,000 ducat income from my benefices. I had to visit the pawnbroker to obtain the funds, but defaulting to Rodrigo Borgia was not a sensible option.

Now that the money issue had been solved, Cesare departed Rome on October 1 at the head of a 10,000 man army (with Leonardo da Vinci as his chief military engineer).   Joining him were condottieri from the Orsini, Savelli, Baglioni and Vitelli, who found it more prudent to assist rather than resist their former foe. Cesare first set his sights on Pesaro and Giovanni Sforza (Lucrezia's former husband) fled without a fight, as did Pandolfo Malatesta of Rimini. He next turned to Faenza, but the people rallied around their popular seventeen year old ruler, Astorre Manfredi, forcing a siege.

While Cesare rampaged through the Romagna, King Ferdinand once again betrayed his Aragonese cousins. In November, 1500, he and King Louis entered into a secret pact dividing the Kingdom of Naples between Spain and France. The plan called for Louis to invade Naples, at which point King Federico would naturally call for military assistance from his cousin. Spanish troops would land in Naples, but then join the French to defeat Federico's army. Louis would get the city of Naples, together with the provinces of Lavoro and Abruzzo and Ferdinand would get Calabria and Apulia. For once, a secret remained secret and no one in Rome knew of the perfidy.

When spring came, Cesare renewed his assault on Faenza, forcing Astorre to propose an honorable surrender. Cesare accepted the terms and then dishonored himself by putting Astorre and his brother in chains and sending them to Castel Sant'Angelo, where they were put to death.

Bologna was next. Giovanni Bentivoglio had supported his grandson Astorre's resistance at Faenza and so Cesare turned his army west. The tyrant who had sanctimoniously lectured us in 1494 about courage, now showed his own true color by surrendering Castel Bolognese to Cesare and pledging large annual tributes. Alexander gleefully bestowed the title Duke of Romagna upon his son, turning the Papal States into a hereditary principality of the Borgia.

My idiot brother then conceived the notion that Cesare should take Florence and return it to the Medici. Piero hurried to Cesare's camp and proposed his plan, which Valentino naturally accepted, it being perfectly obvious that Tuscany was his next target (but not for our benefit, of course). Cesare and Piero proceeded to Barberino, in the Mugello just outside of Florence, where the army encamped while Cesare negotiated his demands with the Signoria. He wanted Florence to engage him as its principal condottiere, paying him a stipend of 36,000 ducats per year, in advance, for three years. He wanted a non-aggression pact, pledging no Florentine interference when he attacked Piombino and other towns in southern Tuscany. He wanted six leading Florentine citizens as hostages. He threatened to sack first Campi and then Florence itself if his demands were not met.

While the fine points of the arrangement (which did not include return of the Medici) were being negotiated, Cesare received an urgent brief from his father, ordering him and his army back to Rome. It seems that King Louis had no interest whatsoever in the Borgia extending their empire into Florence and told Alexander, in no uncertain terms, that if Cesare did not withdraw he would order his own army (now marching south towards Naples) to attack Cesare. Cesare abandoned the campaign and Piero had once again been played for a fool.

The advance guard of the French army, under the command of the ubiquitous Ivo d'Allegri, arrived in Rome on June 19 and encamped just beyond the Ponte Molle. Alexander welcomed them with 150 casks of wine, bread, meat, eggs, cheese, fruit and sixteen prostitutes. The main body of the army, under Bernard d'Aubigny, arrived on June 22 and d'Aubigny revealed to Alexander the secret treaty between Louis and Ferdinand. D'Aubigny demanded a papal Bull blessing the treaty and formally deposing Federico. The Pope, having no other viable option, complied.

Cesare was in vile humor when he arrived in Rome at the end of June. He understood exactly the game that Louis was playing. His distemper only intensified when the Emperor, disturbed at the pact between Spain and France, threatened to launch his own invasion to take the Romagna from the Borgia. When Valentino's French boils flared again, everyone with any sense in Rome kept their distance from him.

In late July, Cesare and his troops took Capua. As in the previous French invasion, the city surrendered without a fight. But Cesare, being still ill-tempered, ordered Capua sacked. Three thousand men-at-arms, 200 knights and 3,000 civilians, including priests, monks and nuns were murdered. All the women and girls in the city were raped and many were taken away as booty. Cesare himself took forty Capuan beauties captive for his personal pleasure.

King Federico prudently spared Naples a similar fate. He paid d'Aubigny a tribute of 70,000 ducats to insure good order in the city after surrender. Federico agreed to go into exile, first at Ischia and then in France, where Louis named him Duke of Anjou (thus uniting the Aragon and Anjou claims) and granted the former king a lifetime pension of 30,000 ducats per year.

Now that Spain and France both had strong presences in Italy and Maximilian was threatening invasion, Alexander looked within Italy for ways to strengthen Cesare's hold on the Romagna. He naturally focused his attention on the Este dynasty in Ferrara, the wealthiest and strongest independent duchy in Italy. Through intermediaries, he approached Duke Ercole d'Este regarding a potential match between his eldest son Alfonso and Lucrezia. At first, the Duke was repulsed by the idea of uniting his ancient and honorable family with the Spanish upstarts (not to mention Lucezia's notorious reputation). However, like many other rulers in Italy, he began to think that being the Borgia's friend was better than being their enemy. So Ercole set out to negotiate the best price for the match.

The Duke had the upper hand and extracted handsome concessions from Alexander. The cash dowry was set at 100,000 ducats with another 75,000 ducats in the form of jewels, clothes, plate, tapestries and works of art. Ferrara's annual tribute to the Holy See would be reduced from 4,000 ducats to 100 ducats. Alexander was to detach the castles of Cento and Pieve from the diocese of Bologna and deed them to Ercole. Like compliant sheep, we cardinals unanimously approved the Church-related concessions in secret consistory.

When Lucrezia received the news regarding her third husband, she was ecstatic. The match offered her the opportunity to permanently vacate Rome and live a more normal life at the magnificent and cultured Este court in Ferrara. Alfonso's French boils (which was rotting away his hands) was unfortunate, but it was presently difficult to find any young noble male who had not contracted the vile disease.

In October, Cesare hosted a dinner party at the Vatican to celebrate the upcoming nuptials. Rodrigo, Lucrezia and a select group of cardinals (for reasons unknown, I was among them) were invited. The party began conventionally enough, with a delightful banquet and flowing wine. Then, as the hour grew late, fifty courtesans arrived to dance. They began fully clothed, but removed their garments as they gyrated until all were naked. Cesare and Lucrezia scattered chestnuts onto the floor and everyone laughed merrily as the whores crawled naked on their hands and knees to recover them. Rodrigo, enjoying himself immensely, then announced a contest. Prizes (silken doublets, shoes and hats) would be awarded to the men who copulated with the greatest number of whores. The competition was stiff (given my disinterest in females, I declined participation) and a splendid time was had by all, including Lucrezia, who kept score and offered a running commentary on the performance of her brother and other guests.

Lucrezia was married by proxy at the Vatican in December and then the couple celebrated a face-to-face ceremony in Ferrara in February, 1502. To avoid future allegations regarding non-consummation, both sides to the match insisted upon multiple affiliated and independent witnesses. The bedroom was therefore crowded as Alfonso performed his duty thrice for the observant audience.

When Lucrezia left for Ferrara, the last restraint upon Cesare's nature was removed. He tyrannized all Rome with his increasingly erratic and cruel behavior (possibly a consequence of his French boils, which seemed to be ravaging his mind as well as his body). A man who was overheard insulting Cesare at a tavern had his hand and tongue cut off and nailed together. A Venetian who circulated a pamphlet critical of the Borgia was murdered and his body thrown into the Tiber. When the Ambassador lodged a protest, Alexander sighed: "The Duke is a good-natured man, but he cannot tolerate an insult."

Everyone in Rome breathed a sigh of relief in June, when Cesare left Rome with his army to continue his campaign of conquest. Sancia used the occasion to begin an affair with Lucrezia's new brother-in-law, Cardinal Ippolito d'Este.

Valentino moved his army to Nocera and served notice that he intended to take the city of Camerino from the Varano family. He sent a messenger to Guidobaldo di Montefeltro, the Duke of Urbino, requesting safe passage and a contingent of artillery and foot soldiers to assist in the Camerino campaign. The Duke, one of Alexander's most devoted and honorable condottieri, complied immediately. Cesare, as he marched his army down the Via Flaminia, turned off the main road and treacherously attacked Urbino, now bereft of its artillery and defenders. The Duke barely had time to flee for his life to his brother-in-law, the Marquis of Mantua.

Having conquered Urbino through subterfuge, Valentino moved on to Camerino, his stated target. Giulio da Varano, its ruler, requested a parlay to negotiate a treaty. Cesare agreed and when Varano and his two sons entered his camp, they were imprisoned and executed. Valentino then marched in and claimed Camerino as his own. When news of the conquests reached Rome, Alexander was beside himself with joy.

With the conquest of the Romagna nearly complete, Cesare turned once again to Tuscany. He took Cortona, Anghieri, Borgo San Sepolcro and Arezzo. My idiot brother hurried yet again to his camp to encourage an attack on Florence. Piero Soderini, the Gonfaloniere of Florence, hurried to Milan where King Louis was holding court. Louis, anxious to maintain good relations with Florence, once again ordered Alexander and Cesare to leave Tuscany immediately and return the Tuscan towns to their deposed rulers.

Cesare's treacherous behavior was causing grave consternation throughout Italy. War was a savage business, but in Italy there were certain rules observed by gentlemen and Cesare had broken them all. The condottieri fighting under Cesare's banner, Vitellozzo Vitelli, Francesco and Paolo Orsini, Pandolfo Petrucci, Gianpaolo Baglioni and Oliverotto da Fermo, became convinced that Cesare, deprived of Tuscany, would turn on them and take their lands. So, while Cesare was in Milan pleading the Borgia's case to King Louis, they rebelled and organized a confederacy. Giovanni Bentivoglio joined the confederacy and the Marquis of Mantua, still outraged over the treatment of his brother-in-law, lent his support. The new confederacy immediately liberated Urbino and returned it to Guidobaldo.

Upon hearing of the mutiny, Cesare hurried south and his loyal forces clashed with the rebels at Fossombrone. Cesare's troops were routed and his small army was surrounded at Imola. Alexander was terrified by the turn of events and sent an urgent message to Louis requesting French troops to break the rebels. Louis, needing the Pope's friendship because his treaty with Spain had, to no one's surprise, broken down, dispatched troops to assist Cesare. Alexander, not confident of military success, opened negotiations with Cardinal Orsini to effect reconciliation between Cesare and his former condottieri.

During this period, I lived in terror myself. Cardinal Ferrari of Modena had died of suspicious causes in July and Alexander, consistent with Curial precedent, had claimed his large estate. Rumors were rife within the College that Borgia had decided upon a creative new method for financing Cesare's hugely expensive war – poison. Now that conflict between the Borgia and the Orsini had begun, I was in the unenviable position of having unbreakable links to the Orsini. While my benefices were modest in comparison to my colleagues, there was no telling how desperate Alexander was for cash. So, I rarely left my palace and made every excuse possible to avoid even consistories.

I will never understand why Cardinal Orsini believed a negotiated settlement of the rift would be honored by Rodrigo and Cesare, but he nonetheless facilitated a treaty between the feuding parties. Each of the confederate condottieri would receive an immediate upfront payment of 4,000 ducats. Each would be guaranteed freedom of rule in his respective fief, subject to acknowledging Cesare as sovereign. In exchange, the condottieri would assist Cesare in recapturing Urbino and would pledge their loyalty.

The treaty was inked in early December and Guidobaldo made a more leisurely exit from Urbino as the combined armies moved to retake his duchy. Cesare held a meeting with envoys of his condottieri and they collectively agreed that Sinigaglia, ruled by Francesco Maria della Rovere, should be the next target. The armies moved to attack in late December and Andrea Doria, the commander of the town's fortifications, abandoned his post and fled.

Valentino sent an invitation to his condottieri to join him in ceremoniously entering the now-defenseless town. Unwisely, the two Orsini, Vitellozzo and Oliverotto accepted and personally accompanied their commander into the town hall, where they were immediately seized by Cesare's guards. Cesare's captain, Don Micheletto, who had strangled Lucrezia's husband, repeated his specialty on the unfortunate dupes.

Alexander and Cesare must have jointly planned this treachery because at the same time that the mutineers were being murdered, Alexander arrested Cardinal Orsini, Rinaldo Orsini (the Archbishop of Florence) and various other Orsini adherents in the clergy. I thanked God that I was not on Rodrigo's list because Cardinal Orsini shortly thereafter met his death by poison.

Cesare now marched his troops in pursuit of Baglioni and Petrucci, raping, looting and pillaging along the way. Baglioni fled Perugia and Cesare captured it without a fight. Petrucci likewise fled Siena, but before Cesare could capture that great city, Rodrigo recalled him to Rome owing to rumors that the Orsini Duke of Bracciano was about to attack the Vatican.

Cardinal Ippolito, Sancia's latest lover, prudently left for Ferrara as Cesare rode towards Rome. Cardinal Michiel, whose only vulnerability was a large fortune, imprudently remained in Rome and was poisoned by Borgia in April. Meanwhile, a Spanish army under General Gonsalvo drove the French out of Naples. To satisfy Valentino's insatiable appetite for money, Alexander sold nine new red hats in May (recognizing the new political reality, five went to Spaniards) and eighty new lesser offices.

As summer approached, Rome became too hot for me, both in temperature and politically. I received permission from the pontiff to visit my brother Giuliano in Mantua and rode north in June. It is fortunate that I did, for as Alexander said himself of that August: "this month is a bad one for fat people."

Alexander made that remark at the funeral of his nephew, Cardinal Juan Borgia, who had just died of malarial fever, which was even more deadly than usual that summer. On August 5, Rodrigo and Cesare attended a dinner given by Cardinal Adrian di Corneto, at his country villa. Within days, all who attended the dinner had fallen ill, including Corneto and both Borgia. Cesare was initially more violently affected by the fever, but his constitution was stronger than that of his seventy-three year old father. Rodrigo was bled of thirteen ounces and rallied, but then a new bout of fever struck and he expired on August 18. Cesare, still gravely ill, sent Don Michelotto to strip Alexander's apartment of all valuables (some 200,000 ducats worth of coin, plate, tapestries and art). According to Burchard,° Alexander's body turned black and swelled up hideously, giving off a noxious stench. It took many strong men, wearing pegs on their noses, to cram the corpse into its wooden coffin. I am told that only four cardinals attended his funeral and his body was quickly interred at the Chapel of Santa Maria della Febbre.

Rumors naturally abounded that the Borgia had been poisoned. Some even suggested that Cesare had poisoned Rodrigo and took a small dose himself to divert suspicion. I prefer to believe that God had just grown tired of the blasphemous pontiff and dispatched him to his just reward in the Ninth Circle of Hell.

° Translator's note: The Pope's Master of Ceremonies.

POPE JULIUS II

Rodrigo Borgia and Giuliano della Rovere were like two sides of the same coin. At their centers, the rivals were identically intelligent, ambitious, ruthless and violent. But they presented two different faces to the world. Rodrigo, a lawyer by training and nature, was crafty, duplicitous and flexible. He was like a river, inexorable in its journey to the sea, but continuously twisting, turning and sometimes even doubling back on itself. Giuliano, a soldier at heart, was overbearing and confrontational, but you always knew exactly where he stood. He was like a massive boulder descending in an avalanche, obliterating everything in its path as it rolled arrow-straight down the slope.

When I received word of Alexander's death, I confess I said a prayer of thanksgiving, to which I added a humble request for the Lord to protect me. Papal interregnums were always a time of violence and uncertainty, but none in centuries rivaled the death and destruction that Borgia's unexpected demise had triggered.

I had traveled from Florence to the last conclave accompanied by a large contingent of soldiers commanded by Paolo Orsini. This time, I journeyed incognito with only a handful of servants and guards. As I moved south through the Romagna, armed men were on the move everywhere. Within days of Alexander's death, the displaced tyrants had summoned their supporters to retake their cities – Perugia, Castello, Urbino, Pesaro, Camerino, Rimini, Piombino and Sinigaglia. Closer to Rome, the Orsini and the Colonna put aside their own feud to take joint vengeance upon the supporters of the Borgia. Over 200 homes of Borgia adherents (including Cardinal Cusa's palace) were sacked and burned.

Cesare was still quite ill, but Don Michelotto and his men provided security for him within the Vatican. Cesare's army, camped just outside the city gate, was still a formidable force, although many had deserted upon Alexander's death. The French army marched south towards Rome from Viterbo to support Louis' choice for pontiff and the Spanish army marched north from Naples to support Ferdinand's. Rome was on the precipice of becoming a killing field.

We cardinals were caught in the middle. We decided to assemble for our own protection within the impregnable walls of Castel Sant'Angelo. Cesare had earlier attempted to commandeer the castle, but its governor, Francesco Roccamura, God bless him, had fulfilled his obligation to the Sacred College and barred the gate. The College had been newly bolstered with Spanish appointments, but we were united in our desire to force Cesare out of the city and keep the opposing armies away from Rome.

Delicate negotiations were begun with all of the contending parties on August 25 and final agreement was not reached for several weeks. Cesare was permitted to retain his title as Captain-General of the Church and all parties guaranteed him safe passage through the Papal States, provided he vacated Rome within three days. The College agreed to send a letter to Venice requesting the Republic not to advance against the few remaining Borgia holdings in the Romagna. The Orsini and Colonna pledged to withdraw their troops to not less than eight miles from Rome and the French and Spanish commanders pledged to remain at least ten miles from the city.

Once the Vatican was safe from organized violence (disorganized mayhem of course remained unchecked but that was inevitable during such periods), we set about our holy task. The unanimity of purpose that had characterized our efforts to get rid of Cesare immediately disintegrated.

Valentino rode to King Louis' camp at Nepi and pledged to support the King's choice for Pope, Cardinal Amboise of Rouen. Cesare thought he could deliver the votes of the Spanish cardinals, but had seriously overestimated his influence over his countrymen. The last thing King Ferdinand wanted was a French pope, so the eleven Spanish cardinals unanimously gave their support to Cardinal Carvajal. The only thing we Italian cardinals could agree upon was that there was no way that any of us were going to vote for another Spaniard.

As was customary in Italian politics, both ecclesiastic and temporal, every man looked strictly after his own interests. Ascanio Sforza had been released from prison (he and Ludovico were arrested together years before) to attend the conclave upon his promise to King Louis that he would support Cardinal Amboise. But honoring a pledge was impossible for any Sforza and Ascanio immediately began efforts to secure his own election. Giuliano della Rovere had broken with the French after Louis embraced the Borgia, but the Spanish were deeply distrustful of the headstrong cardinal, who rivaled Alexander for ambition and ruthlessness. Cardinals Caraffa and Riario mounted their own bids for the throne.

I, as usual, was hampered by my family ties. Piero and Giuliano were present at the French camp (Giuliano had developed an intimate friendship with King Louis) and it would have been extremely awkward for me to support anyone but Amboise. In a private meeting with della Rovere, I explained my predicament and pledged that I would vote for him if my vote would deliver him the papacy, but not otherwise. He understood my dilemma and accepted my promise.

The first scrutiny established beyond doubt that no candidate was close to receiving the two-thirds majority required for elevation to the supreme dignity. Della Rovere led with fifteen votes, but close behind him were Caraffa (fourteen), Amboise (thirteen), Carvajal (twelve) and Riario (eight).

So the search began for a compromise candidate and, as is the tradition in such cases, attention focused upon the most elderly and infirm cardinals. Ascanio and I proposed Cardinal Piccolomini, who was both. He was sixty-four years old; his gout had crippled him and a recent operation on an ulcer upon his leg had not been successful. It was clear he was not long destined for this world. Cardinal Amboise, recognizing that his own candidacy was doomed, joined us, as did the Spanish cardinals, who were most intent upon denying della Rovere the throne. On September 22, Piccolomini was unanimously elected and took the name Pius III (his uncle was Pius II).

Everyone in Rome was overjoyed when the announcement was made. Pius was the antithesis of Alexander. He was modest, pious, abstemious and dedicated to true reform of the Church. The floodtide of fear that had swept over the Curia for a decade seemed to recede overnight. It was too good to last and of course it did not.

Pius' rule began auspiciously. He announced plans for a General Council of the Church to ratify sweeping new reforms. He decreed immediate improvements in the governance of the Papal States. His activism defied his age.

But it was business as usual outside of the Vatican. Louis marched his army south in his quest to retake Naples from Spain and refused to take Cesare along. The Orsini and Bartolomeo d'Alviano marched towards Cesare's diminished army (only 650 men remained). Cesare, about to be trapped, sent a message to Pius asserting he was fatally ill and begging the Pope for sanctuary so that he could die at peace in Rome. Pius, a true Christian at heart, agreed.

Cesare quickly returned to the Vatican, looking no worse than normal and occupied Castel Sant'Angelo. There was great consternation and anger within the College. Pius apologized and said: "I am neither a saint nor an angel, but only a man, and liable to err. I have been deceived." I doubt a statement of such humility was ever made before by a pontiff and doubt it will ever be made again. But Pius refused to revoke the protection he had granted to that child of the devil.

I do not know whether Pius was poisoned as a result of his decision to protect Cesare (rumor attributes the deed to Pandolfo Petrucci) or died of natural causes (which is more likely). In either case, Pius died on October 18, just twenty-six days after his election. One can only wonder why our merciful Lord gave Alexander eleven years as pontiff and Pius less than a month.

Giuliano della Rovere had used the month of Pius' reign to build upon his already formidable support for the papacy. He concentrated upon the Spanish cardinals, who were impressed by the enmity shown to della Rovere by the French during the just completed conclave. Their votes were for sale and Giuliano was prepared to pay their price. Giuliano was also willing to treat with Cesare, the son of his sworn enemy. In addition to the influence Valentino still had with the Spanish and a handful of Italian cardinals, della Rovere was also concerned about the aggression exhibited by Venice since Alexander's death. Venice had seized or threatened numerous cities, towns and fortresses in the north of the Romagna. For the short term, Giuliano needed to prop up the remaining Borgia forces and promised Cesare that he would continue as Captain-General of the Church, be protected from his enemies and be confirmed as the hereditary ruler of the Romagna. Personally, I doubt that Cesare believed any of this, but he was now a virtual prisoner at the Castel and had no option but to agree with the next pope.

I had my own meeting with Giuliano and of course pledged him my unconditional support. I refused his offer of compensation, just as I had previously turned down Rodrigo's offer eleven years before. On November 1, 1503, in the shortest conclave in the history of the Church, della Rovere was elected pontiff. Where Rodrigo Borgia had taken the name of the Greek conqueror of the world, Giuliano assumed the name of the Roman conqueror of the world – Julius II.

The name was fitting as Julius inspired both admiration and fear. There is an Italian word used to describe men like Julius, "terribilita," which has no precise translation to Latin. Although he was sixty years of age when he assumed the papacy, Julius had the constitution and energy of a man half his age. He was restless, and ever in motion, ceaselessly active and perpetually occupied with some great design, self-willed and passionate to the highest degree. He had no patience and took counsel from no one. Indeed, he was argumentative to the point of violence in his discourse. His orders had to be initiated immediately, although he was prone to changing his mind without reflection. His volcanic temper was legend. But he was not a mean or greedy man and drove himself as hard as he drove others. He had indomitable courage, perseverance and strategic purpose. Only one man I have ever known had the same "terribilita" personality – my old friend Michelangelo. It is no surprise that the two men engaged in a decade-long battle of titanic wills.

As I have previously described, I had a reasonably warm relationship with Rovere from the time I first arrived in Rome, notwithstanding the enmity that existed between his uncle and my father. In virtually all respects, I was his opposite. Where he was loud, I was subdued. He was a talker, I was a listener. He was short of temper, I was genial. He was impetuous, I was deliberative. He relished feuds, while I did all in my power to avoid dissension. He loved arms and battle, I despised them.

The ancients said that opposites attract and our friendship evidenced that truth. I also believe that Julius, without ever admitting it, recognized that I could leaven the more intemperate elements of his personality. As will be told, I played a far greater role in his papacy than I would ever have predicted in November, 1503.

Upon his elevation, Julius first addressed himself to re-establishing the rule of law in Rome and the Campagna. During Alexander's reign, the city had been neglected, brigands and murderers ruled the streets, and the Orsini and Colonna conducted their bloody feuds with impunity.

Every criminal act (other than directly against the Borgia) could be expunged with a bribe. That changed even before the coronation. Romans, fearing the wrath of the warlike pontiff-to-be, remained in their houses during the brief interregnum. For the first time in memory, there were no riots or sacking during the conclave.

Julius pressured the Orsini and Colonna to maintain the truce that had come into effect upon Alexander's death. Order was ruthlessly, but honestly, restored to the streets by the arms of Niccolo de Fieschi, Julius' Captain of the Watch. The great Roman roads became safe to travel again. And Julius launched a massive program of public works, rebuilding the crumbling infrastructure of the city. Hopes ran high that a new age of peace and prosperity had begun.

The coronation occurred with great pomp on November 28 and Julius held his first consistory the next day. He gave out four red hats, two of which went to his relatives, his second cousin, Clemente Grosso della Rovere, and his nephew, Galeotto della Rovere. Unlike many of the "nephews" of prior popes, Galeotto was genuine (the son of Giuliano's sister Luccina).

Galeotto was the Pope's favorite relative and Julius bestowed upon him his now-vacated title of S. Pietro in Vincoli. He was a few years older than me and came from a noble family in Lucca, so he was a fellow Tuscan. At first, I struck a friendship with him for political purposes. But soon, for the first time in my life, I experienced the emotion of love.

I recognize that, by convention, one should feel love towards one's parents and siblings, but I confess I never did. I have previously alluded to my less than satisfactory relationship with my mother. If Clarice had maternal instincts, they were limited to her daughters. She displayed the same haughty aloofness to her sons that she displayed to the world. I felt more warmth towards my nursemaids than I did to her. And, of course, she died when I was just twelve.

I have no doubt that Lorenzo loved us, but I suspect that it was as extensions of himself. From our earliest days, he made his expectations clear and our lives were molded to advance his goals for the Medici. I, in turn, only respected my father. From the time I was a toddler, I cannot recall a single conversation in which I did not receive instruction, criticism or commands from The Magnificent.

There is hardly any need to further elucidate my feelings towards my two brothers. Piero was a fool, a bully, a coward and incompetent in all respects. Giuliano was all shiny surfaces, but no depth. Everyone admired him. He was handsome, cultured and a skillful courtier. But he was useless as a compatriot in my quest to restore the Medici to our rightful position of greatness. We always got along (both of us were adept at getting along), but there was no particular love between us.

I probably felt closest to my sisters. But like us boys, they were in constant training for their future duties as Medici and our interactions were rarely spontaneous and always supervised. There was a sense of melancholy about my sisters. It was if, even as children, they understood that they would one day be bartered to men they did not know for political or financial gain; men who would freely partake the charms of others while maintaining my sisters like birds in gilded cages.

Of course I knew carnal love, but chiefly as a physical act. My principal teacher, Bibbiena, was motivated only by subjugation and conquest. Others have been more chivalrous, but my feelings towards them never rose above the commonplace.

Galeotto transported me to a wondrous new place. I was transfixed by his beauty; the softness of his hands and the fullness of his lips. I tremble even now as I recall his tender caresses and gentle coupling. Our love transcended the mere physical. We delighted in the same pursuits – art, literature, music, hunting and hawking. With his large fortune, he was a generous patron and my palace (where he spent all his non-working hours), resonated with culture and amusement as we surrounded ourselves with the leading artists and intellectuals of our time.

At no time in my life was I so content. Lying together in the warm summer sun in a meadow in the Compagna, alone save for a flask of Tuscan wine for company, I experienced the closest approximation of heaven on this earth. It pains me to write about Galeotto, so I shall race ahead for the short number of years we had left and bring his story to its tragic conclusion.

Ascanio Sforza finally died in May, 1505 and Julius elevated Galeotto to Vice Chancellor of the Church. The old Pope loved his nephew almost as much as I did (although, thank God, not carnally since Galeotto was far too old for Julius' taste) and heaped responsibility upon him; responsibility which Galeotto was more than competent to assume. My own stature within the Curia grew commensurately. It was a foregone conclusion that my friend was destined to ascend to the Seat of St. Peter upon his uncle's death.

During the Roman summer, men with any sense leave the city for malarial fever and plague run rampant. I have already written of many deaths caused by pestilence. But there was too much going on in the summer of 1507 and Galeotto's duties precluded a long sojourn in more healthy climes. I, of course, remained with my friend. In early September, Galeotto became ill with fever. It attacked his body with such rapidity and intensity that poison was immediately suspected.

Oblivious to the danger to my own person, I remained constantly by his side to sponge his brow and offer what comfort I could. Within days, he fell into a terrible swoon, screaming from pain, and then lay still, unconscious to the world, barely breathing. The doctors offered no hope. His face and body burst out in bloody blotches, spots which Paris de Grassis° opined were consistent with poison. And then, with one last horrible rattle of breath, he died before my eyes. Julius ordered an autopsy and the surgeons judged that he had died of a superfluity of blood.

All of Rome mourned the passing of this celestial being, but none more than me. A shadow descended upon my own world. Never again would the sky seem so blue, the forest so green or the sun so bright. Perpetual joy was replaced by oppressive melancholy. Not since have I experienced genuine passion and coupling gives me little pleasure. My work, of course, continues to motivate me, but only out of a sense of duty. I have forbidden my servants and friends to mention Galeotto's name in my presence. When others do, I must turn my head to hide my tears.

A second life-altering event occurred just after Julius' coronation. Piero had continued on with the French army as Louis made his ill-fated effort to recover Naples from Spain. On December 29, he was camped by the Garigliano River when the Spanish forces secretly maneuvered around the French and attacked in force at dawn from the rear. Piero, ever the coward, fled the field and drowned in the river. His body was not recovered for several days. I ordered his corpse interred at my abbey at Monte Casino. I did not commission any monument since there was nothing suitable to be engraved.

Piero's son Lorenzo was only eleven years old, so I was now the undisputed master of the House of Medici. I immediately resolved to reverse Piero's disastrous policies. I sent word to the Signoria pledging an end to all Medici attempts to reinstate our rule by force. As evidence of my new policy, I opened my palace to all visitors from Florence, regardless of their party affiliation. Everyone was entertained and indulgently feted. I sent gifts to brides upon their weddings and provided pensions to widows upon their bereavement. I used my connections in the Vatican to promote Florentine business. Former enemies began seeking audiences and young Florentines, uncaring about past history, flocked to my palace.

This new policy required significant additional expenditures, which stretched my meager resources beyond their limits. Bibbiena and Giulio, who shared my palace and handled my accounts, urged restraint. But they could not fully appreciate the strategic purpose of my liberality. As I learned on my adventure in the north, as long as men believe you have money and power, you do. Great men are the handiwork of providence and I believed nothing would be wanting to me if I were not wanting to

---

° Translator's note: Burchard's successor as Papal Master of Ceremonies.

myself. And so I ignored my friends' earnest advice and sent my plate and valuable possessions to the pawnbroker whenever the occasion required.

Julius did not confirm Cesare as the Captain-General of the Church as he had promised prior to his election. Valentino remained in residence at the Vatican and the two men warily negotiated Borgia's future, with neither giving ground. When Cesare, who feared Julius, proposed leading his greatly diminished army against the tyrants who had retaken their old fiefs, Julius readily gave his consent. As far as the Pope was concerned, the farther Borgia was from the Vatican, the better. And he saw little chance that Valentino would succeed in his efforts.

No sooner had Cesare departed for Ostia when word arrived that Venice had seized Faenza from Cesare's officers and had also taken possession of Rimini in the north of the Romagna. Julius was furious and summoned the Venetian ambassador, who coolly informed the pontiff that Venice was acting only against Borgia, not the Church.

To undercut the Venetian argument, Julius dispatched Cardinals Soderini and Remolino to Ostia, where they met Cesare at the residence of Cardinal Carvajal and demanded the keys to the remaining Borgia-controlled fortresses in the Romagna. When Valentino refused, he was immediately arrested and returned to Rome.

Needless to say, many in Rome urged Julius to put Borgia to death. But Julius, who did not easily break a pledge, allowed Cesare to occupy the Torre Borgia at the Vatican (the same apartment where Cesare had his brother-in-law strangled) while the two men continued negotiations. The negotiations dragged on until January, 1504, when Cesare pledged that the fortresses at Cesena, Bertinoro and Forli would be surrendered to the Church within forty days. Julius allowed Cesare to return to Ostia and pledged that if the fortresses were returned, Cesare could have safe passage to a destination of his choice.

The three fortresses were surrendered in April. Cardinal Carvajal, upholding the Pope's end of the bargain, arranged for Valentino to be received in Naples, where General Gonsalvo de Cordoba now ruled the city. Gonsalvo received him cordially and Jofre and Sancia, who had fled to Naples after Alexander's death, received him warmly.

Cesare, never one to quit, immediately began planning a new invasion of the Romagna and asked Gonsalvo for help. Gonsalvo sought instructions from King Ferdinand. Ferdinand astutely recognized that Borgia represented the past and Julius the future. He ordered Gonsalvo to arrest Cesare and transport him immediately to Spain for safekeeping.

This pleased Julius immensely. He had permanently disposed of Borgia without having to break his pledge.°

With Borgia finally gone, Julius turned his full attention to Venice, which refused to surrender the cities and fortresses it had seized after Alexander's death. The Committee of Ten mistakenly believed that because the Venetian cardinals had unanimously supported della Rovere in the last two conclaves, they could ignore the Pope's clear warnings. They misunderstood the nature of the man.

However, when Alexander died, Don Michelotto had stripped the papal treasury, so the Vatican was virtually bankrupt when Julius assumed his office. Consequently, he was unable to mount a credible military attack on Venice, so an uneasy standoff prevailed.

The years 1504 and 1505 were wonderful years for me. The world was at peace (notwithstanding the posturing between Julius and Venice) and my relationship with Galeotto was at its zenith. But the restless Pope required a project of enormous scope and ambition upon which to concentrate his surfeit of energy. He decided upon a grand burial mausoleum for himself – a collection of marble statuary and bronze friezes that would dwarf the monuments of the other popes buried at St. Peter's and surpass the tombs of Augustus and Hadrian in magnificence.

Julius discussed his idea with the papal architect, Giuliano da Sangallo, a Florentine, who immediately recommended his friend Michelangelo as the only sculptor in the world with sufficient vision and skill to undertake such a massive commission. Julius was familiar with Michelangelo's *Pieta* and immediately ordered the sculptor to Rome from Florence.

Michelangelo had recently finished a giant statue of the Bible's David and was currently in the middle of a contest with Leonardo for a commission to paint the main hall of the Palazzo della Signoria. But a command from the Pope took precedence over everything and Gonfaloniere Soderini suspended his obligation to the Republic.

Upon his arrival in Rome, Michelangelo naturally first visited my palace to pay his respects. It had been more than a decade since that terrible day when he and I rescued the treasures of the Medici palace from the mob. Michelangelo had little changed. He still dressed indifferently and smelled in need of a bath. His eyes had the same burning intensity and his demeanor continued gruff and unpolished. I

° Translator's note: Cesare escaped from his Spanish prison in 1506 and fled to his brother-in-law, the King of Navarre. In 1507, he died honorably in battle during an uprising against the King.

asked him whether the rumors were true that his giant *David* symbolized the people of Florence overthrowing the Medici. He responded that nothing was farther from the truth and that enemies of the Medici were responsible for this slander. He assured me that he continued to hold my family in the highest regard, because without us he would have been nothing but a stone cutter. He asked me the nature of the project the Pope was considering and I honestly replied that I did not know.

Michelangelo was pleased by the scope of the Pope's commission and set upon the project with his usual zealotry. His sketches matched the grandiosity of Julius' vision, with huge statues of Moses and St. Paul anchoring the tomb. Julius was pleased and approved a 10,000 ducat budget. Michelangelo then departed Rome for Carrara to personally supervise the selection and transport of the massive marble blocks required for the tomb. That was a mistake.

Donato Bramante was an architect from Urbino who had worked for Ludovico Sforza in Milan. He fled to Rome after the French invasion and attached himself to Cardinal Riario. Julius gave him some minor public works commissions around Rome. But Bramante had great ambition and was as skillful at intrigue as the most devious Curia functionary. As soon as Michelangelo departed for Carrara, Bramante began insinuating to Julius that his tomb deserved a setting more magnificent than the ancient, gloomy and structurally unsound Basilica of St. Peter. Why not raze the crumbling building and construct a colossal new home for Christendom?

This idea seized Julius' mind and all other projects, including his tomb, were immediately forgotten. What better legacy could he have than the largest and most magnificent cathedral in the world? We in the College were aghast. While we all agreed that St. Peter's was in dire need of substantial repairs (it had nearly killed Alexander), it was sacrilegious to destroy 1,200 years of Church history and disturb the resting place of scores of popes, starting with St. Peter himself. Nor did we want to work at a construction site for the rest of our lives. Nor did the Vatican have the money for such an enormous project.

Naturally, Julius was not deterred in the slightest by our objections. Naturally, we were submissive to the Holy Father's desire and authorized a competition for designs; a competition which Bramante was fore-destined to win. As soon as his contract for the new St. Peter's was sealed, the wily Bramante whispered to the Pope that it was bad luck to construct one's own tomb; it could even hasten his death. Besides, he added, Julius would be long dead before his new basilica would be complete to the point where Michelangelo's monument could be installed.

Michelangelo returned to Rome in the spring of 1506 to supervise the unloading of the marbles he had purchased in Carrara. But when he requested additional ducats to pay the boatmen, there was no response from the papal treasurer. He tried on several occasions to obtain an audience with the Pope, but each request was denied. Michelangelo was beside himself. He came to my palace and ranted about the Pope's insolence, having just learned from Sangallo that Julius no longer desired a tomb. I cautioned Michelangelo against commencing a feud with a pope every bit as "terribilita" as him.

The cornerstone of the new basilica was laid on April 18, 1506. The procession was led by the Cross, followed by the Holy Father and the entire Sacred College. The excavation for the cornerstone was twenty-five feet deep, but Julius would not be deterred and scrambled down the ladder to its base. There, he personally placed the marble stone over twelve medals, two of gold and ten of bronze, each depicting his profile on one face and a rendering of the new basilica on the other. The inscription on the cornerstone read: "Pope Julius II, of Liguria, in the year 1506, the third of his reign, restored this basilica, which had fallen into decay."

The Pope blessed the cornerstone and climbed out of the pit. He then offered the papal benediction and granted a plenary indulgence for anyone who contributed towards St. Peter's construction. We all returned to the Sala Reale where a functionary informed the Pope that Michelangelo had just left Rome, with the parting message: "Tell the Pope that if he wants me any more he will have to find me wherever he can."

Julius was furious and dispatched envoys to bring the errant sculptor back to Rome. But Michelangelo reached the safety of Florentine territory before Julius' deputies caught up with him. He refused their entreaties and sent them back with a letter addressed to Julius:

> For the good service which I have rendered to your Holiness, I have not deserved to have been turned out of your Palace as if I were a worthless lackey. Since your Holiness no longer requires the monument, I am freed from my obligation, and I will not contract any new one.

The battle between the two towering personalities was joined.

But a new battle now occupied the Pope's mind, so the conflict with Michelangelo was temporarily set aside. Julius did not possess the military strength to attack Venice, but he calculated that he could return Perugia and Bologna to papal control. While both cities were technically fiefs of the Holy See, their tyrants, Gianpaolo Baglioni and Giovanni Bentivoglio (our old family friend) ruled them independently in defiance of the commands of the Pope. Baglioni, a man of epic cruelty and low moral character, was despised by his subjects. Julius and Bentivoglio had clashed repeatedly during the period that Julius was legate to Bologna under his uncle, Pope Sixtus IV.

At a secret consistory in August, 1506, Julius announced that he going to launch a military campaign to depose the two tyrants. This did not surprise us since he had been threatening to do so since assuming the supreme dignity. What did surprise us was that he intended to lead the papal army himself. What surprised us even more was that he ordered all cardinals resident in Rome to accompany him (eight cardinals were later excused on account of age or infirmity).

We left Rome on August 26, before dawn in order to avoid traveling in the heat of the day. Julius, dressed in armor and mounted upon a battle charger, led our army. We cardinals (twenty-four in all) rode next upon our mules, followed by our attendants and baggage train. We were accompanied on our expedition by a paltry 500 knights. Our little group would have appeared comical – an old man dressed in white robes and silver armor, two dozen unshapely mule riders decked out like gaudy birds in scarlet robes and tasseled hats, dozens of wagons loaded with gold, silver, plate and jewels – were it not for the fact that we were going into battle against two of the most venal, treacherous and violent despots in Italy.

In the first days of our expedition, our only enemy was the mosquito and we were completely vanquished. Every man's exposed skin was covered in angry red bites. For me, the most difficult effort was rising before dawn each day, a task that was completely foreign to my constitution. But the Pope was insistent, pushing himself (gout-ridden as he was) and us forward.

On the third night, we stopped at Civita Castellana and spent the next day there as it was the Feast of St. John the Baptist. We were joined there by Niccolo Machiavelli, the envoy from Florence, who delivered the message that the Republic would support the Pope in his campaign against Bologna (Machiavelli had previously been envoy to Cesare Borgia, where he apparently developed an infatuation with the monster).

After Civita Castellana, we traveled to Viterbo and then to Montefiascone (where Julius' favorite wine was pressed, the Pope being inordinately fond of fine wine). At each stop, Julius dispatched fiery briefs to Baglioni and Bentivoglio ordering the tyrants to surrender and issued pointed briefs to other rulers demanding military assistance.

We were met at Orvieto by the Duke of Urbino, who had favorably responded to the Pope's request for arms. And then Antonio Ferreri, the legate to Perugia, arrived with welcome news that Baglioni had bowed to the papal will and would peacefully deliver Perugia to Julius. He pledged his two sons as hostages and even offered to lead 150 Perugian knights against Bentivoglio. By sheer force of character alone, Julius had accomplished the first goal of his crusade.

We made our triumphant entry into Perugia on Sunday, September 13. The eight Priori met us at the Porta San Pietro and delivered to Julius the keys to the city. All the bells were rung; the streets were thronged with cheering crowds and triumphal arches. The Marquis of

Mantua and several Roman barons now joined us, so our army now resembled a respectable military force with 2,500 men-at-arms. At the Cathedral, the papal choir sang the *Te Deum* and Julius gave his benediction and proclaimed an indulgence. That night, after imbibing much good wine, Julius informed us that after restoring the Papal States to the Church, he would personally lead us against Constantinople and Jerusalem. We were less than thrilled about that prospect.

After eight days of rest and recuperation, we departed Perugia for Bologna. We crossed the Apennines at the Furlo Pass and stopped at Urbino, where the Duke presented Julius with the keys to the City. After lingering for a few days at the Duke's magnificent palace, the impatient Pope pushed us on towards our goal. We departed on September 29 and immediately encountered horrible weather. It snowed at night and torrential cold rain drenched us during the days. We were now high in the mountains, the roads had dwindled to narrow tracks, even our mules were slipping and our wagons were up to their axles in mud. But nothing would deter Julius and he relentlessly forced a grueling pace.

We received wonderful news at Imola. Bentivoglio, who had supported France during the last two invasions, had urgently petitioned King Louis for assistance. The King, in residence at Milan, had promptly dispatched a strong force of 8,000 infantry and 600 knights. Julius sent daily briefs to Louis requesting him to desist. Now, word arrived that the King had ordered his generals to desert Bentivoglio and fight on the side of the Church.

Bentivoglio was trapped between two mighty armies. He understood resistance was futile and so negotiated safe-passage through the French lines to Milan, where his betrayer Louis received him cordially. We made our entrance into Bologna on November 11. I could describe the procession myself, but a pamphlet was recently published,° attributed to my friend Erasmus (which he denies), which wonderfully captures the spirit of the moment:

> Carriages and horses, troops under arms, generals prancing and galloping, handsome pages, torches flaming, dishes steaming, pomp of bishops, glory of cardinals, trophies, spoils, shouts that rent the heavens, trumpets blaring, cannon thundering, largess scattered among the mob.

Julius had not forgotten Michelangelo's insolence. Now that the campaign against Perugia and Bologna had been brought to a successful conclusion, he returned his attention to my friend. The Pope dispatched Cardinal Soderini to Florence with a blunt message to Soderini's brother, the Gonfaloniere: either send Michelangelo to me in Bologna or Florence

---

° Translator's note: Julius Exclusus.

114

will be next on my itinerary. The errant sculptor was called before the Signoria and ordered to surrender to the Pope; Florence would not go to war on his behalf.

We were all having dinner when Michelangelo made his entrance and bowed before the Pope. It was quite a dramatic scene. Julius observed the prostrate sculptor for an inordinately long time and finally spoke:

> It was your business to have come to seek us, whereas you have waited till we come to see you.

Michelangelo remained upon his knees, but raised his head. He apologized for his flight, but then added: "I did not deserve the treatment I received in Rome." There were gasps of astonishment from the assembled company. Julius remained still, but his face turned crimson. He was like a caldron about to boil over. The Bishop of Lucca, who had been deputized by Cardinal Soderini to accompany Michelangelo from Florence, intervened:

> Your Holiness should not be so hard on this fault of Michelangelo; he is a man who has never been taught good manners, these artists do not know how to behave, they understand nothing but their art.

With the speed of a man half his age, Julius rose from his chair and struck the Bishop a heavy blow with his staff. He thundered:

> You venture to say about this man things that I should not have dreamt of saying. It is you who has no manners. Get out of my sight you miserable, ignorant clown.

The Pope's guards immediately seized the poor Bishop and roughly dragged him from the dining hall. Julius, his rage now dissipated, gave his benediction and permitted Michelangelo to kiss the holy ring. He then immediately commissioned the sculptor to cast a giant commemorative bronze of himself (7 cubits high)° to grace the niche over the entry to the Cathedral of St. Petronius in Bologna. Although Michelangelo had never before worked in bronze, he wisely accepted the commission without further remonstrance.

King Louis now demanded compensation for his support of the Pope. Naturally, he wanted money (over and above the 8,000 ducat bribe Julius gave to his generals and 10,000 ducat bribe to his soldiers to keep Bologna from being sacked), but he also wanted the right to make all clerical appointments in Lombardy and three more red hats for

---

° Translator's note: About fourteen feet.

115

Frenchmen. This last demand caused us Italian cardinals great consternation and infuriated Julius, but there was little choice as the French army remained camped just outside the city. So the Archbishops of Auch and Alby and the Bishop of Bayeux were elevated to the purple.

We departed Bologna in February, 1507 and retraced our steps in a more leisurely fashion, arriving back in Rome in late March. The construction of the new St. Peter's was proceeding, but the slow pace infuriated the Pope. Since Julius could not magically speed up this colossal project, he took it into his head that he would no longer occupy Alexander's apartments and embarked upon a new campaign to redecorate the Apostolic Palace, obliterating as much of the Borgia influences as possible.

Naturally, Julius wanted Michelangelo back in Rome as soon as his bronze was completed, but Bramante had an antipathy towards my bad-tempered friend. So Bramante convinced the Pope to assign Michelangelo an impossible commission – to paint the barrel-vaulted ceiling of the chapel constructed by Julius' uncle Sixtus. The Sistine Chapel already had two cycles of paintings on its side walls – the Life of Moses and the Life of Christ, commissioned by Sixtus himself and painted by Ghirlandaio, Botticelli and Perugino. But the ceiling was just plain blue with gold stars.

Bramante assumed that because of the extreme height, curved surfaces and vast area of the ceiling, it would take Michelangelo years of toil to accomplish a mediocre result. This was exactly what Bramante wanted, because he had his own choice of artist for the more lucrative and visible commission of the papal apartments – his distant relative and co-citizen of Urbino, Raphael Sanzio.

Raphael was different in every way from Michelangelo. He was beautiful in appearance, immaculate and fashionable in dress, cultured in speech, genial and accommodating in personality. Julius was smitten by the young artist at first sight (as was I). He immediately awarded Raphael the prime rooms in the Palace, displacing Piero della Francesca, Luca da Cortona and other lesser artists.

Michelangelo wanted no part of the Sistine commission. Only marble carving excited his soul and he understood the game that Bramante was playing. But the more Michelangelo resisted, the more implacable Julius became. It was a test of wills and the pontiff was not about to be bested by the artist.

When my beloved Galeotto died in 1507, his place in the Pope's heart was taken by Francesco Alidosi. Alidosi had been Julius' catamite when Cardinal della Rovere was legate to Avignon. While Alidosi was now too old for the Pope's carnal interest, he remained a favorite. Alidosi was elevated to the purple in 1505, over the objection of virtually all of us in the Sacred College. He was a cruel, vicious, greedy and corrupt man, but Julius was blind to his faults. The Pope used Alidosi as an intermediary to negotiate most of his artistic commissions and the Cardinal always drove a hard bargain. Michelangelo was eventually forced to take just a 3,000 ducat commission for what turned out to be four years of back-breaking toil (Raphael, whom Julius loved and personally commissioned, received 12,000 ducats for each of the three rooms he painted).

As you might expect, Michelangelo despised Raphael. The young artist had left Siena for Florence to study first hand Michelangelo's cartoon of the *Battle of Cascina* and had changed his own style to mimic that of the master. But Michelangelo was neither flattered by the imitation nor impressed by Raphael's own work. He also suspected that Raphael was in league with Bramante in planting the Sistine commission within the Pope's mind.

Michelangelo refused to have any discourse with his fellow artist. One day, I observed Michelangelo crossing the Borgo – alone, his face and clothes smattered with paint, his spine bent, a large goiter upon his neck, all from years working on his back – when he spied Raphael. As always, the young artist was elegantly dressed and surrounded by disciples and admirers. Michelangelo uncharacteristically approached Raphael, but it was only to deliver an insult: "You go about your business like a general with his staff," Michelangelo sneered. "And you, all solitary like the hangman," was Raphael's prompt retort.

Julius' restless mind could not be contained by projects of decoration alone. He remained intent upon his goal of reuniting the Romagna under the direct control of the Vatican, but progress remained elusive. In Bologna, the French were not so secretly assisting Bentivoglio in numerous intrigues to regain control of the city. When Julius discovered that his legate in the city, Cardinal Ferreri, was embezzling Church revenues, he imprisoned the Cardinal at Castel Sant'Angelo (where he soon died in captivity) and replaced him with Cardinal Alidosi. We in Rome were happy to see him go. Alidosi continued the embezzlement (but on a grander scale) and supplemented it with violence. Upon his arrival in Bologna, he had four leading citizens strangled to death for alleged conspiracy with Bentivoglio.

But the primary irritant to the Pope continued to be Venice. Not only did the Republic refuse to release Faenza and Rimini to the Holy See, but its Senate appropriated to itself the appointment of bishops within its territory. Julius attempted to negotiate, but the haughty Venetians gave no ground. He threatened to reduce Venice "to a little fishing village again," but the Ambassador just laughed.

But Venice's power, riches and arrogance had angered Europe's principal monarchs as well. Envoys of Maximilian, Louis and Ferdinand met at Cambria in December, 1508 to form a League to dismember Venice's empire and distribute it amongst themselves. Julius was promised Venice's holdings in the Romagna in exchange for placing the

Republic under papal interdict. The Pope had little interest in seeing France, Germany and Spain increase their influence in Italy, but the insolent Venetians still refused to return the purloined cities, so the Bull of Excommunication was issued in April, 1509.

When Venice's belated effort to buy its way out of its predicament failed, it prepared its army and fleet for battle. Venice assembled a mammoth army of 50,000 men and easily subdued the Emperor's troops, but Julius' nephew, Francesco Maria della Rovere, the new Duke of Urbino (Guidobaldo di Montefeltro, being impotent, had died without an heir) captured Faenza, Rimini and Brisinghalla, where he put 2,000 civilians to death. The Marquis of Mantua attacked Verona in force.

Louis himself led the French army of over 40,000 infantry and knights and he was joined by his principal Italian ally, the Duke of Ferrara. The opposing armies faced each other at Agnadello in May. In less than three hours, 10,000 soldiers were dead and countless others wounded. The Venetians were routed. The Senate quickly ordered all Venetian troops in its empire to retreat to defend Venice itself. The keys to all of Venice's former conquests in the Romagna were delivered to Cardinal Alidosi and five envoys were sent to Rome to beg Julius for forgiveness.

Once Julius recovered the Romagna, he turned on his French ally. Julius had not forgotten the manner in which Louis had extorted concessions from him at Bologna or forgiven numerous other slights over the years. Julius could not abide France controlling the entire north of Italy, so he set out to dismember the League he had joined just a few months before. "These French," he said, "are trying to reduce me to being nothing but their King's Chaplain, but I mean to be Pope, as they will find out to their discomfiture."

In February, 1510, Julius signed a treaty with Venice, with both powers pledging to drive the French from Italy. The Pope also tried to detach Ferrara from its alliance with Louis. Alfonso d'Este, its Duke, was Captain-General of the Church and his brother, Ippolito, a Cardinal. Alfonso's sister, Isabella, was married to Francesco Gonzaga, the Marquis of Mantua, with whom Alfonso's wife, Lucrezia Borgia, was having an intimate affair.

Gonzaga had been captured by the Venetians during the war and was held in severe confinement. Isabella's pleas for his release had fallen on deaf ears and the Venetians would not even entertain negotiation of the traditional ransom. Isabella begged Louis, Maximilian and Ferdinand to intervene on her behalf and all politely refused. In desperation, she turned to the Pope. She knew there was a terrible price to pay for his assistance, but she was out of options and was prepared to pay it.

Julius, whose coarse and violent demeanor terrified men, turned to trembling jelly in the presence of a beautiful young boy. The old man was helpless around them and Isabella's beautiful ten year old son,

Federico, had been an object of Julius' desire for some years. Julius demanded, as the price for his assistance, that Federico be sent to Rome to live with him as hostage to insure the Marquis' faithful service to the Church. Like any mother, Isabella was reluctant to give up her son, but she recognized the political advantages which flowed from her boy being the Pope's new catamite (her husband had been a former lover, as had my brother Giuliano). So Isabella delivered Federico to the Pope and Gonzaga was duly released. The golden haired, intelligent and happy child became a regular fixture at the Vatican and Julius fawned over the boy as if he were his own.

Julius calculated that the combination of the Gonzagas, Lucrezia and the Holy See would be sufficient to detach Alfonso from Louis. But he was wrong. The Duke not only refused, but continued his military siege against the Venetian stronghold of Lignano. Julius flew into a rage. He stripped Alfonso of his title of Captain-General of the Church and awarded it to the newly freed Marquis of Mantua. And then he excommunicated the entire Este family and their supporters (which arguably included Louis and Maximilian).

French Cardinal Auch protested the excommunication, but Julius threw him into the dungeon at Castel Sant'Angelo, where he joined Cardinal Clermont (who had previously attempted to flee to France without papal sanction). When the remaining French cardinals protested this insult to the College, he threatened to send them to the Castel as well.

Louis, exasperated by Julius' conduct, called a conclave of all French ranking clerics at Orleans and put to them the question as to whether the King had the right to oppose the Pope by force of arms. The clerics, surrounded by French soldiers, answered in the affirmative. The King then issued an invitation to his sometimes foe, Maximilian, to co-sponsor a General Council to depose Julius. The Emperor, who entertained pretensions to himself assuming the Seat of St. Peter, concurred.

Battle lines were now drawn. Julius retained 15,000 Swiss mercenaries to attack the French in Milan. In Genoa, the Fregosi would rise up against the French, supported by Venetian galleys. Julius' nephew, the Duke of Urbino, would attack Ferrara with support of the Venetian army (he was the new Captain-General of the Church; the Marquis of Mantua, perhaps feeling conflicted by the order to attack his brother-in-law and his lover, took to his bed with a supposed relapse of French boils).

In August, 1510, Julius decided to take residence in Bologna, where he would be closer to the front lines. Once again, he commanded his cardinals to accompany him. Once again, we were plagued by miserable weather. As our train slogged its way through the deep mud, the local people laughed at our folly rather than pay proper respect to their pontiff. Because of the weather, we did not arrive in Bologna until September 22.

There, we discovered the true extent of Cardinal Alidosi's misrule as legate (he had just fled the city for Modena). No one had a good word to say and many terrible stories of his cruelty and corruption were whispered to us. Some went so far to say that Alidosi had been secretly conspiring with Louis. Julius then fell ill with fever and melancholy. My brother Giuliano rode from Mantua to pay his respects to me, but the Pope, aware of his intimate friendship with Louis, arrested Giuliano as a French spy. I attribute this act of madness to Julius' illness. It took all of my persuasive powers to convince the Holy Father of his error, which fortunately he acknowledged and ordered Giuliano's immediate release.

The mood grew even more somber when the French cardinals who remained at liberty, together with Cardinals Carvajal and Borgia, defected from the Pope and took sanctuary at the French camp in Milan. Word also arrived that the revolt in Genoa had failed and the Swiss mercenaries had never left the Tyrol.

Next, the Duke of Urbino took it upon himself to arrest Alidosi for treason and return him to Bologna in chains. It was quite a scene at the palace when the Pope's former catamite and the Pope's own nephew argued their respective cases. Alidosi knew his lover well and lied through his teeth with a silken tongue and aggrieved manner. The young Duke, a true della Rovere, spoke violently and argumentatively. Julius ruled immediately in the Cardinal's favor and even named him Bishop of Bologna, an act which further soured the mood of the Bolognese.

By late December, Julius recovered his health (ignoring his doctors' advice, he limited his diet to just wine and plums and refused all other remedies). He was deeply distressed by the lack of progress at the war front. The Duke of Urbino's troops had laid siege to Mirandola and Concordia, key towns on the road to Ferrara. Concordia capitulated, but Mirandola stubbornly refused to yield. Unable to contain himself, Julius put on his armor, mounted his horse and rode to the front in one of Italy's worst snowstorms. Yet again, I was ordered to accompany him, although I had no military skills.

The weather was the worst I had ever encountered. Violent snow squalls caused drifts half the height of a horse. The cold was fierce. But Julius was possessed like a madman. "Let us see who has the bigger balls, the King of France or I," the Pope shouted to us as we approached the front. He took residence in a farmhouse within range of Mirandola's artillery. The house was demolished by a cannonball that killed two servants but spared the pontiff (he kept the ball as a souvenir and later donated it to the Shrine of Loreto). He then moved to the Convent of St. Giustina, where he lived in the kitchen and we cardinals were relegated to the open stables.

Julius took control of the army from his nephew, redirected the artillery and coordinated the attacks. Under the Pope's generalship, the wall was breached and the flag of surrender appeared over the battlements. Not content to wait for a formal ceremony, Julius, with his sword drawn, mounted a scaling ladder and entered the city through the breach in the wall. I confess I was at the convent during this dramatic scene, but numerous participants have verified the accuracy of this account.

The Pope now moved to Ravenna to prepare the final attack on Ferrara. But Duke Alfonso was a skilled condottiere and checked the papal forces. Then word arrived that the Emperor and Kings Louis and Ferdinand desired a conference to discuss peace. A temporary cease-fire was declared and we all returned to Bologna. Julius parlayed with envoys of the monarchs for four weeks, but was implacable in his demand that the French relinquish Milan and quit Italy. Needless to say, the French rejected the Pope's ultimatum and dispatched a large force from Milan in early May.

Julius was no coward, but he was also not a fool. He appreciated that the Bolognese, chaffing under the misrule of Alidosi, might turn against the papal retinue at any time. So, on May 15, 1511, we left the city for Ravenna. Julius left Alidosi in charge of the city and his nephew camped with his army outside the wall. Neither would talk with the other.

As soon as we departed, the Bolognese, incited by partisans of Bentivoglio, took to the streets. Alidosi, fearing for his life, fled the city in disguise for the safety of Castel Rio near Imola. The Duke of Urbino did not distinguish himself either. When word arrived of riots within the city, he ordered his army to retreat, which soon disintegrated into a headlong flight. All of the artillery, and most of the baggage and colors, fell into the hands of the enemy. The French army marched unopposed into Bologna on May 23 and returned the government to Bentivoglio. The only casualty was Michelangelo's statue of Julius, which was unceremoniously dislodged from its niche above the Cathedral door. It was cut into pieces and delivered to the Duke of Ferrara, who melted it down and forged a cannon from the bronze. He named the gun "Julius."

Julius, furious at the cowardly conduct of Alidosi and Francesco Maria at Bologna, summoned both to Ravenna to explain themselves. The Duke arrived first and argued his case in public consistory at the Monastery of Saint Vitale. He placed the blame fully on Alidosi, whom he once again reviled as a traitor. The Pope reproached his nephew severely, with violent oaths, foul invective and threats of execution. But he withheld final judgment until after hearing from the Cardinal, who was on route to the consistory. But Alidosi never arrived.

As the angry young Duke rode from Saint Vitale, his path crossed with Alidosi, who was proceeding to his audience. The confident cleric smiled at Francesco Maria and raised his hand in mock salute. The Duke, his impetuous della Rovere blood boiling, drew his sword, cried: "Traitor, art thou here at last! Receive thy reward!" and ran Alidosi through. Mortally wounded, Alidosi fell from his mule. He died an hour later, mumbling: "I reap the reward of my misdeeds."

We were still in consistory, awaiting the cardinal, when word arrived of the Duke's sacrilegious murder. We were, of course, shocked and outraged by the deed; but, truth be told, none of the cardinals present were terribly unhappy that Alidosi would be among us no more. The Pope was another story. He reacted just as Alexander had upon the murder of his son Juan. The old man crumpled on his throne, beat his breast and demanded the immediate departure from accursed Ravenna. He ordered the capture and execution of his nephew and heir, who had prudently already fled the city. That night, Julius lay in his curtained litter as we made our way to Rimini. From within, we could hear loud cries of impotent rage and deep groans of sorrow.

The calamities continued at Rimini. There, we learned that the French cardinals, together with Carvajal, Borgia, Ippolito d'Este, King Louis and Emperor Maximilian, had just issued a proclamation for a new General Council to depose Julius and reform the Church. The Council was to commence on September 1, 1511 in Pisa. For me, this was good news since Florence (which had finally recaptured Pisa after the rout of the Venetians) had given the schismatic clerics permission to hold the Council. Julius now resolved to punish Florence and pledged to me his support in effecting the return of the Medici. In return, he asked me to serve as president of a four cardinal commission to investigate the murder of Alidosi and recommend the proper punishment for the Duke.

This was obviously an assignment of great delicacy. To recommend the execution of the Pope's own blood relation was out of the question, but so was excusing the murder of a prince of the Church (even if that prince was venal, corrupt and cruel). I resolved to myself that the investigation by my commission would be exceedingly thorough, taking many years to complete.

The Pope's health, which had not fully recovered from his previous fever, deteriorated once again. His chronic gout became inflamed, making all movement painful. The military and political situations were equally bleak and he ordered a return to the relative safety of the Vatican.

Our return to Rome brought no respite from bad times. The Vatican treasury was empty. Julius had sold eight red hats while we were at Ravenna, but the demands of the condottieri were insatiable and the papal army had scattered to the four winds when money ran out. The Pope was reduced to the indignity of pledging the papal tiara itself for a 40,000 ducat loan from the Sienese banker Agostino Chigi.

It is a tribute to the iron constitution and will of Julius that, despite all the recent calamities, he began to rally in the summer of 1511. On July 18, he issued a Bull proclaiming his own General Council of the Church, to commence at the Lateran in Rome on April 19, 1512. In an instant, the schismatic Council at Pisa had been rendered impotent. Half a dozen cardinals who previously endorsed Pisa (including Ippolito d'Este) now declared their allegiance to Julius.

He also conducted intense diplomacy with King Ferdinand of Spain. Ferdinand was almost as worried as Julius over the unchecked power of France in Italy. He sent his Ambassador to Julius carrying a pledge to defend the Holy See against French attack. He offered Julius use of his army to restore Bologna and the Romagna to the Church. And he pledged to enlist his young son-in-law, Henry VIII of England, and Emperor Maximilian into a new Holy League.

Julius was wary of substituting one over-bearing barbarian occupier with another. But he had no other choice and intense diplomacy was initiated between the Vatican (in which I played a major role) and the Kings and Emperor.

By August, the heat in Rome had become unbearable and we were worn out from our labors. Julius invited me to hunt at La Magliana, his lodge near Ostia. The air at La Magliana is dangerous during the fever season, but the marshes and fields teem with birds and game and cooling breezes from the nearby sea make the heat tolerable. Putting aside all caution (hunting being my one obsession), I accepted the invitation. Once again, the weather gods did not cooperate and we were lashed by gales. But we were oblivious to the elements and enjoyed tramping through the fields, all of our cares being blown off by the incessant winds.

Our gamble with malarial fever was ill-considered, as Julius was stricken on August 17. The old man, already weakened by the tribulations of the campaign, sank quickly. We transported him by litter back to the Vatican, where his physicians pronounced his case hopeless. I remained by his side, just as I had with Galeotto four years earlier.

The news spread like lightening throughout Italy that Julius was dying. Cardinals hastened to Rome for the expected conclave, rioting erupted in the streets and, in a disgraceful repeat of the past, the papal apartments were looted and stripped of all valuables.

The night of August 23 was the worst. The Pope's breathing became shallow and raspy, his color blanched. I remarked to the Venetian Ambassador that he would most likely expire before dawn. But the tough old warrior survived the night. The next morning, he was given the Holy Viaticum, which perversely appeared to revive him. Little Federico Gonzaga arrived to pay his respects and fed Julius some broth. He begged for the Pope to forgive his brother-in-law, the Duke of Urbino, which Julius accommodated by lifting the interdict and restoring to Francesco Maria his dignities. Julius, proving he was in full control of his faculties, said that his absolution was "not by process of justice, for that would be too lengthy, but by Apostolic grace." This brought joy to my heart, because my investigatory commission was now moot. The Pope also lifted the bans on Bologna and Ferrara and made his will, leaving his servants to Cardinal Riario with 34,000 ducats to divide amongst them.

These exertions exhausted the Pope and he fell unconscious, remaining in a near-dead state for four days, taking no nourishment. During this period, the situation in Rome worsened considerably and civil disorder reigned. The Governor and Minister of Police both abandoned their posts and took refuge in Castel Sant'Angelo. The Sacred College met at the Castel and ordered Paris de Grassis to make the necessary arrangements for the funeral.

I was heartbroken, since I had come to love the fierce old man. I spoke with Paris and we resolved to dismiss the Pope's doctors and replace him with my own, Bonet de Lattes (a Jew). He immediately ceased all remedies and offered the Pope whatever he wanted for nourishment. Julius requested wine, peaches, plums and nuts; substances which medical wisdom calculated would kill him within hours. Instead, Julius rallied and, by the end of August, had convalesced.

By late fall, our diplomatic efforts bore fruit and the new Holy League was organized. Venice committed all of her forces to drive France from Italy. Ferdinand contributed 12,000 soldiers under the command of Ramon de Cardona, the Viceroy of Naples. Julius hired Marc-Antonio Colonna and Fabrizio Colonna as condottieri for the Church. He once again engaged Swiss mercenaries to invade Milan. King Henry pledged to invade Normandy.

Julius recognized that his frail body was not up leading the forces of the League into battle. He entrusted that great responsibility to me, naming me legate to both the League and Bologna. Although I had no military experience or aptitude, I had earned the Pope's love and respect.

I confess I felt trepidation at the enormity of my assignment and prayed for wisdom and strength in fulfilling my holy mission. In late December, 1511, I departed Rome at the head of the papal army. But before I left, I called Michelangelo to my palace. Julius had pledged that, once the French had been vanquished, I could use the League's forces to restore Florence to the Medici. Michelangelo was highly esteemed in Florence and I wanted him by my side. The sculptor reiterated his love for the Medici, but then made excuses – the ceiling of the Sistine Chapel required his full attention; Soderini was also a beloved friend, etc. – and refused my request. I vowed that Michelangelo's disloyalty would not go unpunished.

My army arrived at Bologna in January, 1512 and lay siege to the city. Unfortunately, due to procrastination by Cardona, we arrived too late to coordinate with the Swiss attack on Milan. This enabled the French to bribe the Swiss commanders to return home until springtime. The Venetians, in the meantime, had driven the French from Brescia with the assistance of the grateful citizenry.

The French garrison at Bologna was commanded by the ubiquitous Yves d'Allegre, who stubbornly resisted our efforts to breach the walls.

The Spanish engineer, Pedro Navarro, laid explosives below the wall by a small chapel dedicated to the Virgin. I watched the large explosion lift a segment of the wall and chapel high into the air and my delight turned to horror when the stones fell back, leaving both wall and chapel intact. This "miracle" discouraged my troops and emboldened the French defenders.

In February, a 16,000 man French army, under command of Louis' young nephew, Gaston de Foix, and the renegade Cardinal Sanseverino, arrived to relieve the siege. I desired to confront the French, since our army was of similar strength, but Cardona determined that our tactical position was inferior and ordered a withdrawal to the strong fortifications of Imola. I castigated him severely for his excess of caution and warned him that Julius would not be pleased by his timidity. He not so politely suggested that I leave military matters to the experts and noted that the Pope was not paying his salary. From his arrogant demeanor, I conjured that perhaps Ferdinand had ordered his commander not to unduly risk Spanish lives in support of the League.

Once Bologna was secured, Gaston de Foix proceeded by rapid march to Brescia, where his army recaptured the city and engaged in a bloody week-long sack. Ten thousand Italians were murdered. Bergamo surrendered without a fight, paying a 60,000 florin indemnity to avoid Brescia's fate.

From there, the French returned to the Romagna and, now joined by the Duke of Ferrara and his artillery, besieged Ravenna. The coward Cardona moved the Spanish army to the mountains by Faenza, sending out just small raiding parties to harass the French lines of supply. In the spirit of the indomitable Julius, I dispatched Marc-Antonio Colonna to support Ravenna. In a fierce battle upon the ramparts, Colonna lost 1,500 men in just four hours, but succeeded in repelling the French.

I was now successful in shaming Cardona into supporting my Italian troops. We marched from the mountains and made entrenchments by the Basilica of St. Apollinare in Classe, about three miles from Ravenna. The French entrenched about a mile away, between the Monte and Ronco rivers.

The sky dawned blood-red on the morning of April 11, Easter Sunday. My superstitious soldiers took this as a bad omen. Dressed in my scarlet robes and tasseled hat, I rode on my white palfrey up and down the lines offering prayers and words of encouragement to our soldiers. Because of my deficient eyesight, I was useless as a field commander, but as prince of the Roman Church and legate of the Holy Father, I elevated the spirits and determination of the men.

In the late morning, the advance guard of the French crossed the Ronco towards our camp. Fabrizio Colonna urged an attack before the crossing could be completed, but Cardona overruled him and the enemy army crossed unmolested. The French rolled their artillery to the front of the line and commenced firing. But Pedro Navarro ordered the Spanish soldiers to lie flat upon the ground, their faces in the dirt. This strategy was cowardly, but effective. The French shot passed harmlessly over the Spanish lines. The bombardment continued for two hours.

Then, without warning, mayhem descended upon the field. The Duke of Ferrara had surreptitiously wheeled his superior guns to the woods along our flank and opened fire on the Italian cavalry.   The heavy balls harvested horses and knights like a scythe through wheat.   Shattered limbs, decapitated heads, disgorged entrails and mutilated horses lay in an ocean of blood where once a line of cavalrymen had stood. Colonna, seeing his men cut down by the hundreds, ordered the survivors forward into the French lines.

The Spaniards, inspired by the courage of the Italians, rose from their bellies and joined the charge. In an instant, a great wave of 20,000 bodies rolled towards the French lines. I was swept up by that wave. I cannot explain my motivation (I was unarmed and virtually blind), but I ordered Giulio to remain with Cardona and spurred my horse forward.

The French did not break, but advanced as well. Now two great waves, 50,000 men and horses, rushed towards each other and crashed with ferocity unknown in our times. Madness ruled the field. Men fought as if possessed by Satan; lunging, thrusting, opening skulls with maces. I was caught in the epicenter of the maelstrom. All around me, corpses piled like cordwood, three, four and even five deep. My horse had nowhere to go. The ground had disappeared under bodies and blood. Fighting raged in all directions.

I sat upon my horse, unmoving as if in a trance. Whether it was the insignia of my office or the protection of the Lord I shall never know, but no man lifted a sword or lance against me. Then I heard a thunderous noise to the east. My eyesight prevented me from discerning its source, but I later learned it was the entire reserve of French cavalry, their polished armor reflecting in the afternoon sun as they galloped into the lines, their lances at the ready.

The overwhelmed Spanish then broke and the papal army scattered in headless flight. I did not. I remained upon my horse and saw young Gaston de Foix himself charge past me, his sword drawn in impetuous pursuit of the fleeing Spaniards while his generals rode behind imploring their young commander to desist from his reckless action.

The cacophony of battle was now replaced by the haunting moans and cries of thousands of dying men and horses.   For every man or boy crying out to Christ, five were begging for water and ten were calling for their mothers. I remember wondering to myself whether I would call for Clarice on such an occasion.

I confess that I have never devoted sufficient attention to the spiritual obligations of my office, but on this terrible afternoon I was possessed, without consideration of the consequences, to render solace to the injured and sacraments to the dying faithful, be they Italian, French, Spanish or German.

I was on my knees, in blood the color of my robe, giving comfort to a dying Italian boy who had been disemboweled, when I was thrown forward into his entrails by a mighty blow to my shoulder. My glass was pitched from my hand, but I could discern two mounted French knights looming above me. One of them had struck me with the flat of his sword. I lay helpless as the other aimed his lance to run me through.

But God was with me. A Bolognese knight named Piatese, in the employ of the French, observed the impending sacrilege and set upon his allies, killing one and wounding the other. He begged absolution for his sin of opposing the army of the Church, which I readily granted. He asked forgiveness for having to discharge his duty to the King by taking me prisoner, which I granted as well.

At Ravenna's field of death, I lost sovereignty over my mind. I have previously written how Galeotto's death introduced melancholy to my disposition. But Ravenna holds my mind hostage. During a perfectly ordinary day, I may smell a smoky fire, or hear a horse whinny in the stable or see a flash of distant lightening and suddenly, I am back at Ravenna. It is impossible to explain this to one who has not experienced it, but I become prisoner to these thoughts which I am helpless to banish from my mind. I become unable to function, my body wracked with real, not imagined, pain. Many people have criticized my employ of jesters and buffoons, my lavish banquets and entertainments, my devotion to the hunt, but they do not understand that without constant distraction, Ravenna comes unbidden. Quiet unnerves me. My life is no longer my own.

Piatese escorted me to Federigo Gonzaga di Bozzolo, who in turn brought me to the French headquarters and released me into the custody of Cardinal Sanseverino. Sanseverino was a giant bear of a man, standing well over six feet tall. He was cast in the mold of Julius and was still dressed in his armor, his massive forearm and shield stained red with fresh blood. The Cardinal and Julius were long-time opponents and Sanseverino was one of the organizers of the schismatic Council at Pisa. But he and I had always gotten along (as I did with everyone) and he welcomed me with the attention and collegiality due a fellow prince of the Church (although Sanseverino had been stripped of his red hat and excommunicated by Julius for his sponsorship of the Council).

Sanseverino briefed me on the outcome of the battle. The victory belonged to France. Almost 10,000 soldiers of the Holy League lay dead on the field and all of our artillery, banners and baggage had been captured. I was not alone among the illustrious prisoners. Fabrizio

Colonna, the Marquis of Pescara and Pedro Navarro had also been captured.

But the French victory was not without substantial cost. More than 10,000 Frenchman had died. It shocked and grieved me that for every two men who entered the battle, one did not survive the day. How this barbarian warfare differed from civilized Italian warfare. Impetuous Gaston de Foix had galloped straight into the retreating Spanish line where a ball knocked him from his horse and the enraged Spaniards hacked his body to pieces. The ubiquitous Ivo d'Allegri would be ubiquitous no more and his two sons died with him. Marshal Lautrec, second in command of the French army, was badly wounded. The Duke of Ferrara, sickened by the carnage, left for home.

Command of the remaining French forces fell to Jacques de la Palice, who was held in low esteem by Sanseverino. During dinner, I observed first hand a near violent argument between the two men. Sanseverino wanted to press the advantage by marching down the Via Flaminia, taking Rome and deposing Julius. Palice wanted to take Ravenna and then retire his decimated army to Milan. Naturally, the French general prevailed over the Italian prelate.

The surviving French army marched upon Ravenna, forcing Marc Antonio Colonna to surrender to the superior force. The city was then brutally sacked. Imola, Forli, Cesena and Rimini all sent delegations to Palice, pledging obedience to Louis in exchange for avoiding similar carnage.

I worried that all of the Romagna, and perhaps Rome herself, would surrender unless the intelligence I had gleaned from my presence at the French headquarters could be conveyed to Julius. I inquired of Sanseverino regarding the fate of Giulio and was informed that he was safe at the camp of Cardona. I humbly requested the Cardinal to arrange for his return to me, as I was virtually helpless without him. Sanseverino, believing this to be true, issued a safe-conduct pass and I had a joyful reunion with my faithful cousin. After secretly passing on my intelligence, I pressed Sanseverino to permit Giulio to travel to Rome, to arrange for my ransom and to suggest to the Pope negotiations with the King. Once again, the accommodating cardinal agreed.

I did not know it at the time, but my subterfuge likely saved the Church. The only news that had previously reached Rome was of the destruction of the papal army. Gaston de Foix had earlier threatened to sack Rome and put Julius and his loyal cardinals to death, so panic gripped the streets and Vatican (it not being known that Foix was dead). Both the Colonna and Orsini declared their support for France. Julius locked himself in the Castel Sant'Angelo and was seriously considering the advice of the Spanish Ambassador to flee Rome for sanctuary in Spain.

Giulio's arrival changed everything. Once Julius was made aware of the gravity of the French losses and the dissension within its ranks, his characteristic courage returned and he reasserted his authority. Pledging all of the Vatican's precious jewels, Julius raised 100,000 ducats for recruit of a new army. He forced the Orsini and Colonna into renewed obedience. He rallied his European allies. And, most important, he opened the Fifth Ecumenical Council at the Lateran on May 3, 1512. The Emperor, the rulers of every Italian state and all but one of the Kings of Europe sent envoys to the Council, pledging loyalty to the Church and its pontiff. Louis was now completely isolated, militarily, politically and religiously.

Louis opened diplomatic discussions with Julius to resolve their differences, but Julius negotiated solely to buy time to complete his military preparations. He had no intention of any resolution short of expulsion of the hated French from Italian soil.

Meanwhile, I continued as a prisoner of France. Cardinal Sanseverino escorted me to Bologna, where the people greeted me with open hostility, but Bentivoglio treated me with great respect. From there, I was transported to Modena, where Giovanni Bentivoglio's daughter, Bianca Rangone, gave me her jewels so that I would not suffer deprivation in my captivity.

Finally, I arrived at Milan, seat of the French occupation and the new home of the heretic Council which, reflecting the new political reality, had been evicted from Pisa. I resided in great splendor at Sanseverino's palace (he was Milanese) and was permitted free travel within the city upon my own recognizance. I was prisoner in name only. Giulio arrived carrying a commission from Julius granting me plenary power to absolve those who had taken up arms against the Church. Thereafter, I became the most sought after man in Milan. General Trivulzio, the Marshal of France and Governor of Milan, and hundreds of lesser soldiers begged me for absolution, which I magnanimously granted without reciprocal demands.

By the end of May, the long-delayed Swiss finally made their entrance into Italy and threatened Milan. Although Julius had contracted for 7,000 soldiers, over 18,000 men marched south, motivated by the anticipated plunder of the richest city in Europe. The Swiss were reinforced by Venetian troops under Gianpaolo Baglioni and papal troops under the Duke of Urbino (now fully restored to Julius' good graces).

The military situation was now hopeless for the French and Palice ordered a general evacuation from Italy. Unfortunately, I was ordered to accompany the army to France to be held as a hostage by King Louis. I resolved to thwart this plan.

I was placed under close guard among the schismatic cardinals who were also fleeing Italy. When we reached the Po River by Bassignano, I feigned illness and was sent to the home of the parish priest to rest while the remainder of the party was ferried across the river. While there, I dispatched Bengallo, a priest in my service who hailed from Piedmont, to raise a party of liberators.

Bengallo went to his relative, Rinaldo Zazzi, a wealthy landowner and begged for assistance. Zazzi offered support, but conditioned upon the approval of his overlord, Ottaviano Isimbardi. One of Bianca's jewels purchased Isimbardi's support and the two noblemen raised a gang of peasants from their estates.

I had contrived to delay my crossing of the Po until the entire army had crossed, but for my handful of guards. Just as I stepped onto the barge, Zazzi, Isimbardi and their men burst onto the scene and drove off my startled and outnumbered captors. I donned a military uniform as disguise and made my escape.

The French were furious and organized a canvass of the countryside. Isimbardi brought me to the castle of his relation, Bernardo Malespina. Malespina, a partisan of France who no doubt expected a handsome reward for betraying me, locked me in his dirty pigeon house. He sent word to General Trivulzio of my capture. But Trivulzio, grateful for the absolution I had recently bestowed upon his soul, ordered Malespina to release me unharmed. Thus I made my way, still in disguise, first to Voghiera and then to Mantua, where the Marquis and Isabella entertained me hospitably.

Once the French withdrew, Italy reverted to its normal state of every man for his own interest. The Milanese rose up against the French sympathizers remaining in the city and 1,500 were murdered. Ottaviano Sforza, Bishop of Lodi, claimed the city for the Holy See. Genoa also rose against the French and installed Ottaviano Fregosi as Doge. The cities of the Romagna quickly reaffirmed their allegiance to Julius. The Duke of Urbino was dispatched with his army to Bologna. He carried orders from his uncle to remove its inhabitants to Cento and then raze the entire city to the ground as revenge for its disloyalty to Julius and destruction of his statue.

As you may recall, I was papal legate to Bologna and was aghast at the Pope's rash order. Destroying one of the richest cities in Italy would hardly insure to the credit or treasury of the Church. I dispatched an urgent message to the Pope from Mantua and he relented and authorized me to take residence in Bologna and restore the faith of its citizens. The Duke was not pleased by the countermand of his orders and he developed an antipathy towards me that was to have later consequences.

I entered Bologna in June and took residence at the Bentivoglio palace, which had been vacated by the fleeing tyrant. Unlike my predecessor Alidosi, I ruled with justice and good will towards all. I bore no grudges and sought no revenge. The apprehensions of the populace were assuaged, tranquility restored and the entire city sounded with acclamations and applause for my performance.

No ruler in Italy now felt more alone than Alfonso d'Este. The Duke of Ferrara had been Louis' principal ally in Italy and his artillery had killed thousands of his countrymen. He now sought reconciliation with the Pope. At Ravenna, Fabrizio Colonna had also been captured. Unlike me, he was delivered to Alfonso who took him to Ferrara, refusing Louis' command to deliver him to Palice. He treated Colonna with the respect his noble name and military skills merited and released him without ransom or conditions upon the withdrawal of the French from Italy.

Alfonso now asked Fabrizio to serve as intermediary with the Pope, a role which the grateful condottiere was happy to assume. Colonna arranged for safe conduct pledges from the Pope and Spanish Ambassador and Alfonso arrived in Rome in early July. His first visit was to his young nephew, Federico Gonzaga, who had more influence over Julius than any cardinal.

The Duke appeared in public consistory, dressed in the coarse robe of a penitent, and tearfully begged for forgiveness. Julius accepted his obeisance and lifted the interdict on the Estes and Ferrara. Alfonso's joy at being reunited with the Church was short lived. The next day, he was informed that his act of contrition was to renounce the duchy of Ferrara and deliver it to the Holy See.° He also learned that the Duke of Urbino was rampaging through his duchy, already having captured Cento, Brescello, Carpi, Finale and Reggio.

Alfonso prepared to leave Rome to take control of his army and expel the Pope's nephew. But Julius refused to allow his departure. Outraged, Fabrizio Colonna and the Spanish Ambassador protested this violation of the safe conduct, but their protests fell on deaf ears. Julius raged that Alfonso was lucky not to be in the dungeon of the Castel.

Fabrizio, his honor impugned, arranged with his family to rescue Alfonso and abet his escape. A large contingent of Fabrizio's soldiers conveyed Alfonso to the Colonna family fortress at Marino (where Julius had often taken refuge during the reign of Alexander), where Prospero Colonna welcomed him. Like me, the Duke disguised himself as a soldier (as well as a cook, hunter and monk) and eventually made his way back home to Ferrara.

Meanwhile, Maximilian and Ferdinand were growing concerned about the resurgent pontiff. Julius had conquered the Romagna, but Germany and Spain had little to show for their efforts on his behalf. They

---

° Translator's note: Julius offered Asti in return, a minor fief of the Valois.

announced a Congress to be held at Mantua to "secure the peace" of Italy. In essence, the monarchs were proposing to sell their endorsements to the highest bidders. Julius was invited to send an envoy and, in deference to my recent invaluable service, deputized my secretary Bibbiena.

Three rich prizes were in play – Milan, Ferrara and Florence. Maximilian Sforza and Alfonso d'Este had ample financial resources and no opponents prepared to pay more (Julius' claim had no merit and the Duke of Urbino was ordered to return the conquered towns to Alfonso). So the Congress quickly devolved into a bidding war for Florence between the Medici and the Republic, which was represented by the Gonfaloniere's brother, Gian-Vittorio Soderini. I had become seriously ill in Bologna (which I shall explain shortly) and dispatched Giuliano and Giulio to serve as my proxies. Julius, true to his promise, named me legate to Tuscany (the same title given me by his uncle Sixtus in 1492).

Matthew Lang, Bishop of Gurck, representing Maximilian, and Viceroy Cardona, representing Ferdinand, made it clear that they wanted large sums of money, both for their masters and themselves. I authorized Giuliano to pledge any amount necessary to secure the monarchs' approval and arms. As always, I cared not that I did not possess the funds being promised. Prior experience had consistently proven that my financial requirements would always be satisfied by divine providence.

Lang and Cardona believed that as well. I was already ruler of Bologna and would shortly rule Florence. My coffers would soon be overflowing. The necessary arrangements for down payments were completed and the Congress obediently declared the Republic an enemy of the Holy League for its support of France and the schismatic Council at Pisa.

I was still the papal legate to the army of the Holy League, so I sent orders to Cardona and the Duke of Urbino to march their armies towards Florence to enforce the writ of the Congress. Cardona, who had already been well compensated, obeyed, but Francesco Maria della Rovere, Captain-General of the Church, smarting over the nullification of his triumphs in Ferrara and still bearing personal animosity towards me, refused my order. He denied me his army and his artillery.

I previously alluded to my illness. From my youth, I have suffered from fistula surrounding my most private orifice, which Bonet de Lattes attributes to a surfeit of amorous penetrations. These superfluous passageways have always been irritating, often painful and sometimes embarrassing, but never worrisome. However, when I arrived at Bologna, the largest fistula suddenly grew ulcerous and suppurating. It became engorged with pus and filth from my body leaked constantly, emitting odors most foul. The pain made it impossible to mount a horse and difficult to sit on anything but the softest of cushions. Moving my bowels became excruciating penance for sins I could not fathom.

A simultaneous stomach disturbance made my life even more unbearable. Eating meat and other heavy foods (which formerly gave me great delight) now caused me misery and uncontrollable flatulence. Bonet prescribed poultices and salves for the fistula and fasting thrice a week for the stomach. He could not attribute a cause to these inflammations, but suggested that my recent martial adventures had unbalanced my humors. At the time, I considered my illnesses the handiwork of Satan, but, as will soon be explained, they turned out to be gifts from God.

Cardona marched his army, 5,000 strong, towards Florence. But the unscrupulous Spaniard had pocketed most of my retainer for his personal enrichment and deprived his soldiers of adequate provisions. His quartermaster was forced to haggle with the most disreputable of vendors and naturally received moldy grain and rancid meat in return. Hundreds of men became violently ill and the rest were on the verge of starvation as they crossed the barren Apennines.

I was carried from Bologna on a litter to Cardona's camp. Having heard of the Francesco Maria's treason, I procured two cannon from Bologna's fortifications, which traveled in my train. I caught up with Cardona at Barberino, near our villa at Cafaggiolo. There, I found him treating with a delegation of Florentine envoys. To my horror, I discovered that he had agreed in principle to a treaty consisting of an affirmation by Florence of its allegiance to the Holy League, a 30,000 florin bribe to Cardona and food for his men. There were no requirements for the disbandment of the current government and the return of the Medici.

My late brother Piero had been similarly betrayed in Barberino by Cesare Borgia, but I am not cut from the same cloth. I took Cardona aside and informed him that, if he persisted in ignoring the mandate of the Congress and my orders as papal legate, I would have my guards immediately arrest him and hang him from the nearest tree.

It will never be known whether I could have successfully carried out my threat. Cardona, not wanting to risk an open breach with Julius, acquiesced to my demand and withdrew his agreement (my promise of additional gratuity did not hurt my cause either).

I then assured the Florentines that the Medici did not demand to rule Florence, but merely to be guaranteed our right to return to our birthplace in safety and repurchase our confiscated property. This request was beyond the authority of the delegates, so they retired to Florence. It appeared that a military conflict was inevitable.

During the war against France, Cardona and I had repeatedly clashed over what I believed to be his cowardly excess of caution. It is safe to assume that his opinion of me was equally unfavorable. The familiar argument now repeated itself. Cardona submitted that there was no way that 5,000 starving soldiers could subdue the Republic of Florence. I conceded the point, but argued that Prato, just twelve miles north of the city, was an easy target and ample provisions could be obtained there for the troops.

Cardona retorted that Prato had been recently reinforced by thousands of Florentine militiamen. These "citizen-soldiers", conscripted by Machiavelli in his silly scheme to avoid the expense of condottieri, had no military experience. Cardona's troops, starving though they may be, were veterans of Ravenna. I replied to Cardona that while an Italian would defend his own home to the death, he would never risk his life for his neighbor's house. This argument appealed to the Spaniard's native prejudice and he agreed to attack Prato.

Owing to the excruciating pain of my maladies, I remained in Barberino temporarily while the army marched to Prato. I soon learned that my prediction was entirely correct. The first assault on Prato's wall had been repulsed. But then my cannon arrived and blasted a small breach in the wall. As soon as the Spanish soldiers moved into the breach, the Florentine militiamen disgracefully threw down their weapons and fled. The Spaniards entered unopposed and set about to feed their bellies.

I was carried into the town a day later and was sickened by what I observed. The Spaniards were behaving worse than animals in their sack of the town. Men, women and children, priests and nuns, were being indiscriminately tortured, raped, mutilated and murdered. The streets and public wells were overflowing with naked corpses. The carnage at Ravenna had shocked my sensibilities; Prato shocked my very soul. It was inconceivable to me that human beings could treat each other in this manner, but I was witnessing it before my own eyes.

I was carried to the Cathedral, where many women and children had taken shelter. Lesser churches, convents and monasteries had already been burned to the ground. I posted my own Italian guards at the entrances to hold the barbarians at bay. When I observed a Moor in the employ of the Spaniards desecrate the Host, I ordered him hung. I confess it was very difficult to function because the sights and sounds of the sack triggered Ravenna in my mind and I was paralyzed by the pain of my mental and physical ailments. I lay on my litter in the sacristy, wishing (as I had on my sea voyage) that I were dead.

When Cardona responded to my summons, I implored him, in the name of Christ, to rein in his men. He agreed and over the course of the next day, calm was restored to the ravaged town. I dispatched a letter to Julius on August 29:

This day, at four o'clock in the afternoon, the town of Prato was sacked, not without some bloodshed such as could not be avoided. The capture of Prato, so speedily and cruelly achieved, although it has given me some pain, will at least have the good effect of serving as an example and a deterrent to the others.

Once again, I was correct in my predictions. When news of the brutality at Prato reached Florence, a general panic ensued. Thirty of my supporters (drawn from nearly every noble family in Florence) entered the Signoria and threatened to hang the Gonfaloniere if Soderini did not immediately abdicate his position and go into exile. He agreed on the spot and left Florence that night with his family.

Cardona dictated his non-negotiable terms for Florence's peaceful surrender – 40,000 ducats to Maximilian, 80,000 ducats to Ferdinand, 20,000 ducats to himself, submission to the Holy League and readmission of the Medici. The Priori agreed.

I was physically unable to make the short journey to Florence, so I sent Giuliano on September 1, with instructions to take control of the government. I lay upon my sickbed, eagerly awaiting news of his accomplishments. Unfortunately, my brother remained true to his useless self.

Upon arriving in Florence, instead of reclaiming the Medici palace, he took residence with his intimate friend, Francesco degli Albizzi. Instead of remaking the government, he ate, drank, wrote poetry and fornicated, just as he had during his exile in Urbino. My confidants reported he was telling everyone that he was perfectly content to remain just a private citizen.

The anger that welled up within me had a salutary effect upon my ailments and I resolved to make the painful journey and reassert the authority of the Medici. I was carried upon my litter to the Faenza Gate, dressed in the full regalia of my high office and accompanied by 400 Spanish lances and 1,000 infantry under the command of Captain Ramazotto. There, notwithstanding the pain, I transferred to my mule, traditional conveyance for a cardinal and made my triumphant reentry into the city of my ancestors. Thousands of Florentines jammed the streets, cheering and shouting: "palle, palle." I rode directly to our palace on Via Larga, which I reclaimed in the name of the Medici.

I wasted no time in demonstrating my resolve. Upon my command, my partisans took to the streets demanding a parliament. The Priori bowed to the will of the people and the parliament authorized a forty-five member Balia, all to be chosen by me. The government was now firmly within my grip.

However, I knew my Florentines well and exercised my power in a manner designed to enamor the population to my rule. The first "suggestion" I made, which the new Priori and Gonfaloniere (being loyal partisans) immediately enacted, was a new law granting reprieves to all men exiled or deprived of office or property on account of sodomy convictions. I followed this with restoration of the sensible sodomy laws prevailing before Savonarola bewitched Florence. And, of course, I reinstituted the masquerades, pageants, festivals and feasts that were the hallmark of Medici rule before being suppressed by Savonarola.

Everyone in Florence now celebrated the Medici and I was cheered wherever I went. I dismissed my bodyguards, which could have proved a fatal mistake had not providence favored me once again. Two young disciples of Savonarola, Pietro Paolo Boscoli and Agostino Capponi, fomented a plot to assassinate me and Giuliano. Fortunately, a letter with the details of the plot fell from Capponi's cloak at the house of Lorenzo Pucci and was recovered and sent to my magistrates. Boscoli and Capponi were immediately arrested, together with another dozen leading opponents of my family, all of whom were named in the letter. These co-conspirators included Cosmo de Pazzi, Archbishop of Florence, Nicolo Valori, my father's biographer and Niccolo Machiavelli, the Borgia-loving envoy.

Boscoli and Capponi immediately confessed their conspiracy (they flattered themselves as Brutus to my Caesar) and pleaded that the others named in the letter were unaware of the plot and listed just as possible sympathizers. Nonetheless, to show my resolve I ordered the other men to be tortured, but only lightly to show my compassion. As for Boscoli and Capponi, I ordered them beheaded. Any lesser sentence would not be sufficient deterrent for such a heinous crime.

And then, on February 23, 1513, I received an urgent message from Rome. Julius was dead.

POPE LEO X

Until now, I have been just a minor character in this tale. Now I move to center stage. From my perspective, Julius' death (which was not unexpected given the accumulation of ailments affecting the old man) could not have happened at a less propitious moment. I was just getting my hands firmly upon the reins of Florence's government, the full extent of the assassination plot was not yet clear and my health was extremely precarious. However, the conclave would wait for no cardinal and so I ordered myself carried by litter to Rome. While on route, I received a charming letter from Isabella d'Este predicting that I would be elected pontiff and backing that prediction with a 500 ducat wager. I immediately accepted, since it was a wager I could not lose. If she was right, the prize was infinitely more valuable than 500 ducats and if she was wrong, I would have some small consolation. I arrived on March 6, two days after the start of the conclave.

After my excruciating trip, I was brought to the Sistine Chapel, where the conclave was taking place. As is customary, the windows had been temporarily bricked over and the doors barred to prevent news of the conclave from leaking out. The dim light and my feverish mind could not diminish the beauty of Michelangelo's newly finished ceiling. Bramante's scheme to marginalize Michelangelo's place in the firmament of artists had utterly failed. No work of art anywhere could compare with that ceiling. But, nonetheless, I could neither forget nor forgive Michelangelo for the disloyalty he had recently shown to me.

Temporary cells for each cardinal had been constructed on either side of the Chapel. Owing to my infirmities, mine was somewhat larger than the others. When I arrived, the politicking was in full force. Cardinal Grimani of Venice was making a strong bid for the Seat of St. Peter, but his candidacy was opposed by Ferdinand and Maximilian. Other candidates seeking support included Cardinals Riario, Bakocz and Alborese. The younger cardinals of noble houses, including Louis of Aragon, Gonzaga of Mantua, Ippolito d'Este of Ferrara and Alfonso Petrucci of Siena were plotting for one of their own to ascend to the supreme dignity. They were tired of violent old men like Alexander and Julius squandering the wealth of the Church on endless wars (and threatening their own principalities).

I should have been actively politicking myself, but my condition had been severely aggravated by my long journey and my infected fistula had abscessed dangerously. I could only lie upon my stomach on my cot. By coincidence, the eminent surgeon, Giacomo of Brescia, happened to be in Rome and was recruited by Paris de Grassis to operate upon my posterior. I believe this may have been the first time a medical operation was performed during a conclave within the Sistine Chapel. If the degree of pain is any measure of an operation's success, then Giacomo was indeed a master surgeon. I have never experienced pain so excruciating, but my fever did begin to recede.

While I was lying in agony, the conclave became deadlocked. After seven fruitless days, no candidate had emerged as a favorite. Paris de

Grassis ordered that only one simple meal of bread, water and meat be provided to the cardinals each day. In addition, the stale, stifling air of the sealed-up Chapel had become loathsome, with the stench from the latrines mingling with that from my abscess.

As I wrote earlier, when conclaves become deadlocked, old and infirm cardinals traditionally emerge as compromise candidates. I was only thirty-eight, but the consensus (supported by my physician) was that my physical maladies made a lengthy reign unlikely. So, the cabal of younger cardinals selected me as their champion. Since I was prostrate on my cot, my conclavist Bibbiena represented my interests.

My years of amiable geniality paid off. Nobody except Cardinal Soderini (whose brother I had just forced into exile) had a bad opinion of me. Bibbiena won Soderini over with a pledge that Lorenzo (Piero's son) would marry one of the Soderini girls. As the senior Cardinal Deacon, it was my privilege to remove the ballots from the urn. On March 11, 1513, I had recovered sufficiently to leave my cot and preside over the second scrutiny. Thus, I was able to announce my own elevation to the supreme dignity. I did so with no trace of triumph or pleasure. With perfect calm, I received the proffered homage from my former peers.

When asked what title I would assume, I deferred to the Sacred College, but I was pressed to make my own decision. I announced that, if it were acceptable to the College, I would like to be known as Leo X (in honor of both my native city and my mother's prescient dream). The gratifying response I received was that my choice was ideal, one which they would have chosen themselves.

As the final ballots were being burned, Cardinal Farnese broke open one of the Chapel windows and shouted to the expectant crowd:

> I bring you tidings of great joy! We have a pope, the most Reverend Lord, Giovanni de Medici, Cardinal Deacon of Santa Maria in Domenica, who is called Leo X!

News of my elevation was received with universal acclaim. Maximilian was ecstatic, having shown me great hospitality during my sojourn in his realm. Ferdinand stated that the birth of his heir, the conquest of Granada and my elevation were the three happiest events in his life. Even Louis conceded that I was: "a good man from whom nothing but good is to be expected."

The Romans were delighted since I already was a generous patron of Roman causes and an advocate for peace. But nowhere was there greater joy than in my native city. I was the first son of Florence ever to assume the papacy and the pride of the people knew no bounds. All the bells in the city were rung; fireworks were exploded; artillery was fired; and in all the streets bonfires were raised. It is ironic that, just a few short months before, Giuliano and I had bounties upon our heads.

On March 15, I was ordained a priest (my earlier ordination was as a deacon); on March 17, I was consecrated a bishop; and on March 19, I was formally enthroned as pope. Cardinals Farnese and Louis of Aragon placed the triple tiara upon my head. The ceremony was held under a make-shift pavilion on the steps of the old basilica (which was being torn down). The inscription above my head read:

> Leo the Tenth, Supreme Pontiff, Protector of the Arts and Patron of Good Works.

I decreed April 11 to be the date of my official coronation procession. This was the first anniversary of the battle of Ravenna and my fortuitous capture and would give additional time for my posterior to heal and a ceremony unlike any since ancient times to be planned. It was also a propitious date according to Luca da Borgo, my astrologer.

Although Julius had to pawn the papal tiara to fund the war against France, reparations, indemnities and taxes had flooded the papal treasury since our victory in the Romagna. There were a quarter million ducats in the treasury on the date of his death. Christ taught that hoarding gold is sinful. I determined to spend the surplus on good works and helping the needy. After years of privation, I resolved to indulge myself as well. As I said to Giuliano on the eve of my coronation: "God has given us the papacy; let us enjoy it."

Of course, my former colleagues were also aware that the Vatican was awash in cash. There is an ancient tradition that cardinals assisting at a papal coronation may present petitions to the new pontiff. The cardinals, aware of my generosity and dislike of refusal, presented me with demands which even I found shocking. At my first consistory, I said to them (only half in jest):

> Take my tiara and act as if each one of you were pope himself! Agree among yourselves on what you desire, and take your fill.

I would have preferred to have spent the weeks between my election and coronation attending solely to the spiritual duties of my new office. Holy Week required my presence at many ceremonies, including Maundy Thursday (where, unlike my predecessors, I actually washed the feet of the poor), Good Friday and Easter Sunday. Unfortunately, politics also demanded a significant share of my attention.

As soon as news of my elevation reached Louis in France, he dispatched a letter of congratulations to his intimate friend, my brother Giuliano, in which he stated his intent to re-conquer Milan. He assured Giuliano that his territorial ambitions extended no farther into Italy and sought my blessing. Giuliano, who was in Florence at the time, sent me a copy of the letter to which I responded, quite directly, that I opposed reintroduction of French troops anywhere in Italy.

Louis was not deterred from his plan of conquest and entered into a one-year non-aggression pact with Ferdinand and a new alliance with his old enemy Venice. Venice, in the treaty made at Blois on March 23, pledged a 12,000 man army to assist the French army attack Milan. Venice, in turn, would recover all the lands it lost in the last war.

To counter this new aggression, I sought help from my old friend Maximilian, Henry VIII of England and Cardinal Schinner, the Swiss cardinal who had recruited mercenaries for Julius. All of these machinations were in play when the glorious day of April 11 arrived.

It was a perfect Roman spring morning, with a bright sunny sky and warm, but not unbearable, temperature. The procession assembled in the courtyard of St. Peter's. First in line were 200 mounted lancers, followed by bands of musicians wearing the papal livery of white, red and green, with the Medici badge on their breasts. Then came the standard bearers for Rome, the University, the Orders of Knights (Giulio carried the standard for the Knights of Rhodes) and the Captain-General of the Church. They were followed by the Papal Marshal, leading nine white horses and three white mules, with red trappings embroidered in gold. Next was the Papal Master of the Horse, clad in red, and the chamberlains of honor, carrying the jewel encrusted papal mitre and tiara.

One hundred Roman barons followed. Fabrizio Colonna and Giulio Orsini rode side-by-side, their hands clasped together symbolizing the termination of their ancient rivalry. The leading families of Florence followed the Romans and they, in turn, were followed by the entire diplomatic corps of the Italian states and European nations. The Duke of Urbino, clad in mourning black for his late uncle, and his sizeable entourage, ended the secular section of the procession.

The ecclesiastical procession started with the apostolic sub-deacons, carrying the great gold Cross, followed by white palfreys which carried on their backs the Tabernacle carrying the Most Holy Sacrament, over which a canopy of gold cloth was carried by four Roman citizens, surrounded by twenty-five grooms with wax torches. The papal choir marched next, followed by hundreds of lesser Curial functionaries. They were followed by 250 abbots, bishops and archbishops, and then the cardinals, in order of rank, each with eight chamberlains.

Two hundred of Julius' personal Swiss Guards, armed with halberds and wearing the dazzling green, white and yellow uniforms designed by Michelangelo, marched next. I followed, mounted upon the same white palfrey I rode at Ravenna, while eight Roman citizens of noble birth carried the embroidered silk canopy that shielded my head from the sun. My chamberlains walked immediately behind me, throwing handfuls of gold and silver coins to the cheering crowds (50,000 ducats in all). The Curia's lawyers walked behind my chamberlains and 400 mounted knights ended the procession.

It took several hours for the marchers who preceded me to exit the Vatican for the two and a half mile parade to the Lateran. At the Castel Sant'Angelo, an area had been reserved for Rome's Jews. In accordance with ancient tradition, I stopped and the Chief Rabbi approached me with his Hebrew Testament. He handed it to me and begged for permission for his people to remain in Rome. I pretended to read a few lines from the Testament and then dropped the book to the ground. "We confirm your privileges," I intoned as custom demanded, "but we reject your faith."

The first ceremonial arch was erected on the far side of the bridge across the Tiber. It read: "To Leo X, the promoter of ecclesiastical unity and peace among Christian nations" (The inscriptions were read to me by my attendants as I did not have my glass for the procession). As we proceeded down the Via Papale, every house was decked with wreaths of laurel and ilex and every window casement displayed rich brocades of silk, gold or velvet. People lined every street and window and chanted: "Leone" or "palle, palle," as I rode by, offering waves and benedictions to the adoring faithful.

As we slowly wound our way to the Lateran, we passed many triumphant arches, trophies and obelisks. In many of the public fountains, water had been replaced by wine. The banker Chigi erected a magnificent eight-columned arch with priceless antique statues of gods and goddesses in its niches. The inscription, in gold letters, read: "Venus has fled, and now Mars' arms at last have yielded to Minerva's charms." The goldsmith, Antonio da San Marco, erected a statue of Aphrodite, with the chiseled inscription: "Mars is fled, and Pallas reigns. Yet Venus still our queen remains." The arch at the Genoese banker Sauli's palace read: "Not for slain victims nor for shedding blood; we rear these trophies but for future peace."

Upon arriving at the Lateran, I was escorted by three cardinals to a marble throne under the portico. I sat upon the chair and the cardinals raised me from my seat chanting: "He raiseth the poor from the dust." I entered the church, prostrated myself before the high alter and then received the insignia of my office. We next retired to the chapel of St. Silvestre, where the nobility was admitted for the honor of kissing my feet. The prelates were then admitted to kiss my hand. I handed each bishop a silver medal and each cardinal two silver medals and one of gold. Following that ceremony, we went to the Great Hall of Constantine for a magnificent banquet.

The sun was already setting when we made the journey back to the Vatican. As it grew dark, torchlight illuminated our way through the crowds. I confess I was exhausted by the proceedings (and my posterior ached mercilessly) and elected to spend the night at Castel Sant'Angelo rather than climb the hill back to the Apostolic Palace. It was a spectacle, everyone agreed, unmatched since the glorious pageants of ancient Rome.

The success of my coronation was soon matched by the success of my initial diplomatic and military initiatives as pope. I have previously written regarding the alliance between France and Venice to reclaim Milan for Louis and my counter-effort with Henry and Maximilian. My efforts were successful and a treaty was signed at Mechlin for a new League. Henry invaded France, supported by Maximilian, and captured Calais. Schinner's Swiss mercenaries, under contract with me, engaged and defeated the French army at Novara, killing 8,000 (the Swiss lost 5,000 men). The French retreated from Italy and the Venetians marched back home. While Henry was engaged in France, his treacherous brother-in-law, King James IV of Scotland, invaded England from the north. But Henry's commander in England, the Earl of Surrey, met the Scots at Flodden and roundly defeated them. James and 10,000 of his soldiers lay dead on the field.

The victory of my troops and allies was complete, although it grieved me deeply that so much Christian blood was spilled in the course of the short but brutal war. I then quickly moved to consolidate my spiritual, as well as temporal, authority. I took residence at the Lateran and opened the Sixth Session of the Lateran Council on April 27. After the *Veni Creator* hymn, I delivered my first pastoral oration and exhorted the assembled delegates to use their utmost endeavors for the benefit of the Church. I declared that it was my intention to establish a general peace among all the princes of Christendom, so that the full might of Christian arms could be brought down upon the Mohammedans.

The most pressing issue before me was what to do about the schismatic former cardinals, Carvajal and Sanseverino, the prime sponsors of the heretical councils at Pisa and Milan, who had so forcefully supported France and opposed Julius. After the French defeat at Novara, both had left Lyon and journeyed to Florence, where they sent envoys with messages begging to be readmitted to the Church and vowing their love and support for me.

I could not forget the cordiality of both during my early years as cardinal and, of course, the generous hospitality and protection afforded me by Sanseverino when I was taken prisoner at Ravenna. However, there was still great animosity towards them among some key cardinals, most particularly Schinner and Bainbridge. I sent word to Florence that they should remain there until the groundwork for their return had been laid.

The discussion of this issue at consistory and within the Lateran Council was spirited, but I carried the day (as well I should as Christ's Vicar). On June 27, Carvajal and Sanseverino entered the Vatican in the black habits and bonnets of simple priests. They were led through the most public parts of the Vatican, where their humiliation was witnessed by a great concourse of people, who acknowledged that by this act of penance they had made a sufficient atonement for the errors of their past conduct. They were introduced to the full consistory (only Riario, who was ill, and Schinner and Bainbridge, who remained obstinate in their opposition, were absent). There, they prostrated themselves and begged forgiveness. This submission profoundly affected the proud Spaniard, whose body shook visibly as he knelt before me. In accordance with the script I had prepared, they acknowledged their errors, approved all acts done by Julius (including their own excommunication), disavowed the councils at Pisa and Milan as schismatical and detestable and implored me, as God's Representative on earth, to intercede with the Almighty on their behalf.

At the end of their confession, I bade them to rise, salute and make obeisance to the College, which they did. The cardinals did not rise from their seats in return. When this mortifying ceremony came to its conclusion, I restored Carvajal and Sanseverino to the Church and their former rank and privileges. However, I could not restore their benefices and ecclesiastical revenues, as these had been sold to others upon their excommunication.

In the time-honored tradition of my predecessors, I nominated my first cardinals in September. Naturally, I elevated my faithful cousin Giulio to the purple. First, of course, I had to legitimize his birth. I appointed a commission which determined that his mother, Fioretta Gorini, had secretly agreed to marry my uncle Giuliano before his assassination. Since, but for this unfortunate event, the lovers would have been married before Giulio's birth, the Curia's lawyers pronounced this adequate. I conferred upon my cousin my former title of Santa Maria in Domenica.

My second nomination was my tutor, secretary, intimate friend and advisor, Bibbiena. His political skills and love of luxury made him a perfect fit for the College. Next was my Florentine friend, Lorenzo Pucci, the Apostolic Datary° under Julius. Upon my elevation, I had requested Pucci to implement Julius' Bull prohibiting simony and other practices that might bring dishonor upon the Church. He responded: "Holy Father, you have assigned to me the task of financing this international business. My first obligation is to keep it solvent." Finally, I nominated my young nephew, Innocenzio Cibo, the son of Maddalena and grandson of Innocent VIII. As I said at the time: "That which I received from Innocent, to Innocent I restore." The College, as would be expected, obediently confirmed my nominees.

In these early days of my reign, I had to divert my attention once again to Florence. After nearly twenty years fighting to regain control of our city, Giuliano was allowing Medici power to be dissipated. While I loved my brother deeply, he was useless as a politician. His life revolved around amusement, luxury, entertainment and debauchery. He was perfectly content to allow the Signoria to make important decisions that

---

° Translator's note: Treasurer/Comptroller.

should have been the province of the Medici. I resolved to remove him from Florence, but in a manner that would not bring disgrace upon him.

I prevailed upon Gian-Giorgio Cesarini, Gonfalionere of the Roman Senate and People, to have the Senate declare Giuliano an honorary Baron of Rome. I simultaneously named Giuliano the Captain-General of the Church (and prayed that the Vatican's troops would never be led into battle by him).

A most lavish ceremony was held in Rome in September to celebrate these two great honors. It was held at the Palace of the Capitol, where a temporary theater was erected in the square, decorated with a series of paintings by Baldassare Peruzzi illustrating the historical connections between Florence and Rome. It commenced with a procession from the Vatican to the Capitol, followed by addresses of welcome from all of Rome's notables, Latin orations by Italy's most distinguished poets and a six hour banquet.

After dinner, there was a pastoral eclogue in which the actors bestowed the most gratifying praise upon me and then a series of allegorical scenes. In one, a beautiful woman, robed in golden cloth and representing the city of Rome, was borne on the shoulders of a giant to Giuliano's chair to thank him for the gracious condescension wherewith he had accepted the homage of the imperial city. In another, a beautiful woman, representing Florence, wept for the loss of her ruler and was comforted by Cybele, the mother of all gods, who united the two women and suggested that henceforth both Rome and Florence should dwell in mutual concord and happiness under the rule of the Medici, who loved each with equal devotion.

The festivities continued the next day when Plautus' Latin comedy, the *Poenulus*, was presented in the outdoor theater for the amusement of the population. To show my gratitude to the people of Rome for the honor bestowed upon my brother, I lowered the rate of the papal tax on salt. In turn, the Senate commissioned a statue of me, carved by Michelangelo's gifted student, Giacomo del Duca, which stands today at the Capitol.

I dispatched my nephew Lorenzo to replace Giuliano as ruler of Florence. Like his father Piero, the boy (now twenty) was handsome, athletic and full of life. Unfortunately, he was somewhat lacking in intelligence and wholly devoid of ambition, a deficiency more than compensated for by the raging ambition of his Orsini mother Alfonsina. He was reluctant to leave the dissolute and luxurious society of Rome for the mercantile and political drudgery of Florence. But he was obedient to my command and I sent him off with a lengthy letter of instructions on how to rule Florence without exciting the republican sentiments of its citizens.

Before I resume the history of my papacy, let me dwell for a moment upon my daily routine as pontiff. As my father's letter noted, I have never been an early riser and this preference was not altered by my elevation to the supreme dignity. The sun would be high when two servants would enter my chamber to help me out of bed (my medical ailments, combined with my increasing obesity, made this maneuver difficult to perform on my own).

After my ablutions, my secretary, Gian Matteo Giberti, would enter my chamber to discuss the schedule for the day. He would be followed by the datary, to discuss benefices, and then my chamberlains. I next attended Mass and then the consistory (or other audiences). In late afternoon, I would have my only meal of the day. In accordance with doctor's orders, I ate only bread, vegetables and fruit three times a week and more substantial meals on the other days. After my meal, I would rest in order to give my digestion an opportunity to do its work without the additional stress of exertion. I then would ride through the Vatican's gardens for exercise. This would be followed by a second round of official audiences.

After nightfall, I would relax with friends, playing chess or cards (I paid my gambling losses promptly, but customarily flung my winnings over my shoulder to my lackeys), listening to music or poetry or discussing literature or philosophy (and, of course, writing this memoir). On many evenings I gave or attended banquets or theatricals.

Even I could not grow accustomed to the profligacy of banquets in Rome. Members of the Sacred College vied with each other to present the most extravagant tables. At one banquet at Cardinal Cornaro's palace, sixty-five courses were served, with each course consisting of three different dishes, all served upon an endless supply of silver plate.

The most memorable meal was served in my honor by the Sienese banker, Agostino Chigi, whose fabulous wealth, in part, derived from charging me up to forty percent on my frequent borrowings. It was held in an elegant new hall (bigger than any at the Apostolic Palace), completely enclosed by exquisite tapestries. In front of each guest was a golden table service embossed with his personal crest.

At the conclusion of each of the endless courses, the servants tossed the silverware into the Tiber (I later learned that Chigi had prudently hidden nets at the river bottom to retrieve his precious utensils). When the feast finally concluded, I rose and offered my blessing and gratitude to the host, complimenting him on the beauty of his new banquet room. With a mischievous smile and a signal to his servants, Chigi rose and replied: "Your Holiness, this is not my dining-hall. It is merely my stable." The servants then raised the tapestries, revealing the stalls.

I, of course, entertained as well. Many hours of planning (and countless ducats) were spent to insure memorable evenings. Novelty and humor were the hallmarks of my banquets. Rare delicacies, such as peacocks' tongues, regularly graced my tables. Jests, such as blackbirds flying out of pies or naked little children emerging from puddings, were a frequent occurrence. I employed a small army of dwarfs, jesters and buffoons to entertain my guests. They were led by the Dominican friar, Fra Mariano Fetti, who could consume forty eggs and twenty capons in a single sitting (I named Fra Mariano, who gave me hours of innocent pleasure, the Keeper of the Papal Seals, a lucrative sinecure).

Paris de Grassis once cautioned that such jests were beneath the dignity of my office. I reminded him that they were a time-honored Florentine tradition and I would not abandon my heritage. I did not add that I also needed ever-increasing distraction to keep the memories of Ravenna at bay.

I do not desire to leave the impression that I devoted myself and the papal treasury merely to frivolity. No pope ever spent more for the edification of Rome and its citizens. I built new roads, drained pestilential swamps, renovated churches (St. Peter's first among them) and constructed public buildings. I restored the University of Rome to greatness, supported the Roman Academy, purchased thousands of rare and ancient manuscripts and patronized the most talented artists, scholars, poets and dramatists in Europe. I exponentially expanded the charitable generosity, both public and private, that was the hallmark of the Medici.

When I recalled Giuliano from Florence, he brought Leonardo da Vinci with him to Rome. Leonardo was now an old man, with a white flowing beard, but his beautiful catamite, Salai, remained loyal to him. Salai had served the artist since the age of ten, and was among the most arrogant, impudent, greedy and corrupt young men I have ever encountered. Nevertheless, his golden ringlets and sensuous physique revived passions which had lay dormant since the death of my beloved Galeotto.

Giuliano prevailed upon me to grant a painting commission to Leonardo, whom I housed at the Belvedere°. Months passed with no result. I stopped by his quarters on one of my rides through the gardens and discovered his workshop strewn with strange devices, experiments and inventions, but no art. When I inquired, Leonardo told me that he was preoccupied with formulating a new varnish for preserving the painting, which he had yet to start.

At the next consistory, I remarked to the cardinals: "Alas, Leonardo is never going to do anything, for he starts to think about finishing the work before it is even begun!" When word of this absolutely true

---

° Translator's note: The summer residence constructed by Pope Innocent VIII on the hillside above the Apostolic Palace.

comment reached the temperamental artist, he resolved to not paint my commission. I would not brook insubordination from this artist any more than Julius had tolerated Michelangelo's antics. When word of my displeasure reached Leonardo, he fled the Vatican and hid in the swamps outside the city, where he promptly became ill with fever.

I have digressed enough on trivial matters. After his crushing defeat, Louis sought to reestablish good relations with me. He was still under the stigma of excommunication and his wife, Anne of Brittany, a pious and obedient Catholic, was withholding her favors from him. Ferdinand, Henry and Maximilian had renewed their own alliance against France; only winter weather prevented a resumption of hostilities. For my part, I was amenable to reconciliation, provided it was on my terms. Spain was rapidly moving to fill the vacuum left by the French departure and my spies informed me that Ferdinand was plotting to take Milan (weak Maximilian Sforza, with Cardona's army camped just outside the city, was already little more than a pawn of Spain) and that Emperor Maximilian still entertained pretensions for my tiara.

Secret negotiations with Louis proceeded, ably assisted by Cardinal Sanseverino, the Protector of France. They came to fruition on the last day of the first year of my reign. Envoys of Louis appeared at the Eighth Session of the Lateran Council and, in his name, renounced the heretic councils at Pisa and Milan and pledged complete adherence to the proclamations of the Lateran. Louis also agreed that I would peacefully arbitrate the claims of the parties contending to rule Milan. In return, I granted full absolution for all past offences against the Holy See.

Before I close this chapter of my life, I must report an amusing anecdote. Shortly after my elevation, I graciously pardoned those Florentines named in the Boscoli-Capponi conspiracy against my life (too late for the two principal conspirators who had already been beheaded). In December, Giuliano reported to me that one of them, Niccolo Machiavelli, had written a book offering us advice on how the Medici should rule Italy. I understand he based his ideas on the campaigns of Cesare Borgia. I could only chuckle at his misplaced effort. Borgia had fled Italy in defeat and disgrace; Machiavelli's citizen militia had retreated from Prato like cowards; and the Medici were in firm control of both Florence and the Vatican without his advice. I ordered that no one was to entertain Machiavelli's pathetic attempt to ingratiate himself to us.

HANNO

If I can title a chapter after Savonarola, the man I despised above all others, then I certainly can name a chapter after Hanno, the creature I loved above all others (save, of course, Galeotto). More on Hanno will follow shortly.

The year 1514 began as auspiciously as 1513 had ended. No sooner had I welcomed Louis back to the Church than I received wonderful news that the Christian Kings of Hungary and Poland had achieved substantial victories over the Mohammedan Turks. News also arrived that Vasco da Gama, King Manuel of Portugal's intrepid explorer, had discovered new lands in the east. These propitious events prompted me to proclaim a public celebration of thanksgiving in Rome. I led a great procession to the churches of Santa Maria del Popolo and Sant Agostino and provided feasts and pageants for the people.

Unfortunately, the glad tidings did not last long, for I soon received word from my spies of duplicitous treachery by the ungrateful Louis. In the war of 1513, the Swiss, in addition to driving the French from Italy, had also captured the French city of Dijon. The Duke de la Tremouille had negotiated a treaty, in Louis' name but without his knowledge, for return of the city in exchange for a monumental indemnity of 600,000 crowns, a sum that Louis could not and would not pay. The Swiss were threatening to re-invade France and Henry was also preparing to cross the Channel again with his army.

In desperation, Louis turned to his sometime friend, sometime enemy, Ferdinand and made a most remarkable proposal. In exchange for an alliance against Henry and the Swiss, Louis offered his four year old daughter, Renee, to Ferdinand's thirteen year old grandson and likely heir, Charles, who was also the grandson and likely heir of Emperor Maximilian. Louis pledged Milan and Genoa as dowry, together with recognizing Ferdinand's exclusive claim to Naples. This arrangement was anathema to me. It would one day unite Naples, Milan, Genoa, Spain, France, Flanders, Burgundy and Germany under Charles' rule. Italy would become no more than an outpost of the new empire and the pope the Emperor's parish priest. I resolved to oppose this union with every ounce of my intellect and God-given authority.

However, the anxiety provoked by this shocking development had nearly paralyzed me. Recollections of Ravenna intruded constantly in my mind and I was unable to concentrate upon the difficult task ahead of me. I consulted Bonet de Lattes and he wisely advised immediate diversion and exercise. Specifically, knowing me well, he recommended a hunt.

Upon my elevation, I had reluctantly given up my passion, as canon law is quite clear on the subject (at King Manuel's request, I had even issued a Bull prohibiting Portuguese clerics from engaging in their beloved sport of bull baiting). However, the emergency confronting me and the orders of my physician prompted a reevaluation of my decision.

Paris de Grassis objected strongly, noting the injunction prohibiting the activity and the fact that my hunting costume was undignified and my high riding boots would hinder the kissing of my feet. I pointed out to him that Julius hunted and he responded that Julius was no model of appropriate papal decorum. At this impertinent remark, I had to chastise Paris, which I did with a smile. I reminded him that popes conferred regularly with the Holy Spirit and that their decisions were infallible and not subject to dispute by their employees. Paris wisely withdrew his objections.

I left Rome with eighteen cardinals, several dozen noblemen and an assortment of servants, literati, musicians, buffoons and actors, about 140 men in total. One hundred sixty Swiss Guards accompanied us as security and to assist with the hunt. We traveled to Cardinal Farnese's estate in the Campagna, which abounded with game. Along the way, peasants cheered me and I stopped often to bless them and distribute coins. My Huntsman-in-Chief, Domenico Boccamazzo, preceded us and had enclosed a vast area of the estate with canvas sailcloth to keep the game from escaping. Upon arrival, a sizeable contingent of my bodyguard was dispatched to watch over the fence.

The hunt commenced the next morning (I could always rise early for a hunt). It was quite a spectacle. Cardinal Cornaro looked dashing in a short scarlet doublet and floppy Spanish hat. Cardinal Sanseverino, a giant of a man, dressed as Hercules with a great lion skin across his bare shoulder. Fra Mariano, my buffoon, wrestled with a mule and Paolo Giovio, my historian, fell into a ditch and floundered in the oozy slime.

I mounted my favorite white palfrey and positioned myself near the opening in the sailcloth fence. Upon my command, Boccamazzo released seventy dogs at the back of the enclosure to drive the game towards us. As the frightened beasts rushed through the narrow opening in the fence, my guests fell upon the prey with swords, lances, spears and maces. My confidential chamberlain, Serapica, who attends to my most intimate needs, bravely stood his ground in front of a charging boar and slew it. My servants brought me a netted deer, which I dispatched with a borrowed lance. When the earth reeked from the blood of the slaughtered game, we adjourned for dinner. I excoriated those whose efforts had fallen short and granted petitions and distributed purses of ducats to those guests who had distinguished themselves. The next day, we hawked, fished and fowled.

Bonet was right. My mind cleared and I returned to the Vatican determined to thwart the designs of Louis and Ferdinand. I recognized that Louis would never voluntarily relinquish the Angevin and Valois claims to Milan and his offer to Ferdinand was a desperate attempt to counteract the hostile intentions of the Swiss. Thus, I immediately commenced negotiations with the Swiss to facilitate an accommodation with Louis. I also strove to bring the hostilities between the Emperor and Venice to a conclusion, which would then separate Venice from France. As part of this strategy, I purchased from Maximilian (who, like me, was perpetually short of money) the city of Modena for 40,000 ducats.

Finally, I went to work on both Henry, with whom I had developed a close relationship, and Louis to end the enmity that existed between England and France. I was assisted in this regard by the timely death of the long-suffering Anne of Brittany. I could now propose a royal match uniting these two great nations, which achieved fruition when Henry gave his sister, the beautiful young Mary Tutor, to Louis as Anne's replacement.

These diplomatic machinations occupied virtually all of my time. I was growing increasingly vexed by the interminable length of sermons and homilies at my daily Mass. It seemed like every cleric granted the honor of preaching before the Holy Father felt it necessary to demonstrate his vast learning and brilliant intellect. As I sat perspiring in my heavy regalia, they droned on and on. I finally ordered the Master of the Palace to limit all sermons to not more than one half hour, on pain of excommunication.

There were, however, a number of bright spots in those early days of 1514. The brightest star in the firmament was Raphael, who put the lie to the notion that great artists had to be moody and conceited. Unlike Michelangelo and Leonardo, Raphael was always accommodating. No request was ever refused or even delayed. He was endowed by Nature with modesty and goodness, with a gracious and sweet disposition. Yet his skills equaled those of the two haughty geniuses.

When Julius died, Raphael had completed the Sala della Segnatura at the Apostolic Palace and was in the midst of decorating the Sala di Eliodoro. I immediately ordered completion of all work commissioned by Julius. The principal fresco in the Sala di Eliodoro was the half-completed *March of Attila upon Rome*, in which my namesake, Leo I, forbids the Huns to enter the Holy City. Raphael had already painted me, sitting upon my mule, as one of the cardinals accompanying the pope. Now, to show his gratitude, he painted me again, sitting upon my white palfrey, as Leo and Louis XII as Attila. Raphael painted himself as the cross-bearer who gazes at me with rapturous awe. Thus, the *March of Attila* has been transformed into an allegory for my triumph over Louis at Novara. He also transformed the *Deliverance of St. Peter* into an allegory for my miraculous escape from the French after Ravenna.

After Raphael's mentor Bramante died in March, 1514, I named Raphael to replace him as architect for St. Peter's. He had previously designed the charming portico for my titular church of Santa Maria in Domenica and I was certain that he could carry out this important assignment without the histrionics and drama that characterized the other potential candidates. Despite a workload that was far more than any man could bear, Raphael accepted the appointment cheerfully and gratefully. I rewarded him (in addition to a sizeable salary) by naming him a Groom of the Chamber and a knight of the Order of the Golden Spur.

However, the most wonderful moment of 1514 was the arrival of Hanno. Of all of Europe's monarchs, the pious Manuel of Portugal was the only one who took seriously his Christian duty to subdue the Moors and Turks and convert the heathen of Africa and the east to the one true faith. He was also one of the few monarchs who did not have territorial designs upon Italy. Thus, I was favorably predisposed towards him.

It is an ancient tradition that secular rulers send missions of obedience upon the elevation of a new pontiff (my brother Piero had led the Florentine delegation to Alexander). In my case, the Florentines were naturally first. They sent twelve representatives of the city's leading families, followed by fifty chariots and 200 horsemen attired in crimson velvet. Poland, Siena, Mantua, Avignon, Milan and the Emperor all sent elaborate missions and gifts shortly thereafter.

I set March 12, the first Sunday of Lent, as the date for my reception of the Portuguese mission and on March 8 issued the Bull *Orthodoxe Fidel Nostre*, in which I commanded all the Portuguese people to support Manuel in his crusade against the Moors in Africa.

On March 12, Cardinal Medici (Giulio) and I walked the Corridore from the Vatican to Castel Sant'Angelo to witness the mission's procession from the best vantage in Rome. My cardinals led the procession, mounted on their mules, which were draped in purple. They were followed by their footmen and chamberlains. Next were my cavalry, followed by trumpeters, pipers and drummers.

The Portuguese clerics marched behind the musicians, all dressed in crimson and scarlet, with gold collars around their necks. They were followed by Manuel's three principal envoys: the great explorer Tristao da Cunha, his ambassador to the Vatican, Nicolau de Faria, and the eminent jurist, Diego Pacheco. My archers and Swiss Guards marched next.

The most exciting part of the procession came last – my gifts. A Nubian slave rode upon a magnificent white Persian horse, upon which clung a trained cheetah. Two leopards, many parrots and some rare Indian dogs and fowl followed. A Saracen boy walked behind, guiding a large white elephant (Hanno). Hanno's back was covered by a cloth of crimson velvet and his head was decorated with gold brocade. An elegantly dressed Moor rode upon his neck. A silver tower with many turrets was placed upon Hanno's back, enclosing a silver coffer bearing additional gifts for me.

After crossing the Tiber over the ancient bridge, Hanno came to a stop under my window. To my great amazement, he knelt upon his front knees and bowed his great head in obeisance to me. He did this three times. Then he saluted me with three trumpeting barks. Then he drank with his trunk from a barrel of water and sprayed the water up, soaking me and my guests in a fine mist. I laughed until tears rolled down my cheeks. I immediately sent for Raphael and ordered him to recreate the scene in the lower cupola of the Vatican. As was his custom, he accepted the commission and soon set to work.

On the following Monday, I received the Portuguese envoys in public consistory. Each kissed my feet and the Curia's lawyers presented their diplomatic credentials. Pacheco then delivered the oration of obedience, a noble speech, delivered in Latin, praising me with eloquent words. I responded, also in Latin, praising Manuel's devotion to the Church and urging peace among all the Christian princes so that they might unite their arms against the infidels.

The next day, the cardinals and I went to the Belvedere to inspect Manuel's astonishing gifts. His craftsmen had assembled the rarest textiles, gold, silver and precious gems into articles of radiant beauty. There was a chalice wrought of purest gold, a golden tabernacle to hold the Holy Sacrament, an alter cloth of brocade sown with pearls and precious stones. He also gave me vestments made of gold cloth with pearls and rubies and embroidered images of Christ and the Apostles. Paris estimated the total cost of these gifts at more than 80,000 ducats.

We then examined the living gifts. I ordered several animals to be brought from my menagerie and released in the Belvedere's garden. The cheetah was then let loose and demonstrated its hunting prowess by chasing down and tearing apart its prey.

Hanno, of course, was the primary fascination for the entire Sacred College. He once again performed his obeisance to me and, on my command, sprayed my cardinals. I ordered the elephant housed at the Belvedere until suitable quarters could be constructed closer to the Vatican.

It gave me endless pleasure watching and speaking to the always gentle and obedient pachyderm. I believe the world be a far better place if humans possessed the nobility and equanimity of some of the species over which God gave man dominion. I ordered that the public be admitted to the Vatican to view the elephant every Sunday so that the common people could share in my delight.

At the public consistory, King Manuel's envoys had presented several petitions on behalf of their king. I was only too pleased to grant them. I authorized Manuel to appoint Portuguese explorers and military commanders who had distinguished themselves in the service of Christendom as Knights of the Order of Christ.° I permitted Manuel to retain a tenth of the papal levy upon the Portuguese clergy, provided the funds were used to prosecute the war against the Moors in Africa. I granted Portugal ecclesiastical preferment over all unknown lands and territories which Portuguese explorers might discover in the future and over all lands that Portuguese commanders might acquire in conquests over the infidels. I also presented Manuel with the Golden Rose, the greatest honor a pope can bestow.

I do not wish to leave the false impression that these petitions were granted because of the magnificence of Manuel's gifts or my love for Hanno. Rather, Manuel was one of the few European leaders who recognized, as I did, the grave threat to humanity posed by the followers of Mohammed and the only one who was actively waging war upon the infidels. There is no reason why a monarch who battles infidels (instead of his fellow Christians) should not be rewarded for such efforts. Moreover, Alexander, to further his own ambitions, had favored Spain over Portugal in his Bull *Inter Caetera*, which gave an indefensible share of the New World to Ferdinand. My Bulls merely restored fairness to the division of the heathen world.

In June, 1514, I was placed upon the horns of a dilemma. My nephew Lorenzo, to whom I had entrusted Florence, was planning a magnificent spectacle and pageant on the Festival of St. John the Baptist to celebrate the return of the Medici to Florence and my elevation to the supreme dignity. He requested that I send Hanno to Florence to participate in the festivities. On the one hand, I very much wanted to assist my nephew in his endeavor. However, Hanno's mahout insisted that the long journey to Florence would inflame the elephant's tender feet and put his health in grave danger. In addition, the elephant could not safely walk the distance in less than a month and the festival was just two weeks away.

I therefore had to deny Lorenzo, but I dispatched two wolves from my menagerie with the courier to serve as an inadequate substitute for the divine Hanno. My brother Giuliano, who was going to attend the festival himself, entreated me to allow the cheetah and two leopards to accompany him to Florence. I agreed to his request.

In any case, I already had my own plan for a spectacle involving Hanno. Giacomo Baraballo, the Abbot of Gaeta, whose family was wealthy and respectable, had been imprisoned by Alexander at the Castel Sant'Angelo for suspected forgery of papal briefs. Upon Alexander's death, I ordered him released from the dungeon after payment by his

---

° Translator's note: The military papal order which Pope John XXII established to replace the suppressed Knights Templar.

family of a significant fine. Unfortunately, Baraballo had lost much of his faculty of reason during his confinement. He now fancied himself a poet on par with Petrarch. However, his verse was execrable and the source of no end of amusement at my court.

Bibbiena conceived the idea of crowning Baraballo as the Arch-Poet of Rome at a magnificent ceremony followed by a triumphal procession. I endorsed my cardinal's wicked scheme and proposed that Baraballo be paraded through Rome atop Hanno. I set the date for the Feast Day of St. Cosimo, the patron saint of the Medici. Preparations were immediately undertaken for a festival that would be remembered through history.

When Baraballo's kinsmen in Gaeta learned of the farce, they immediately traveled to Rome to dissuade the old cleric from participating. But Baraballo would not be swayed and accused his family of jealous envy over the great honor about to be bestowed upon him.

On the appointed day, all of Rome turned out – cardinals, bishops, senators, ambassadors, noblemen and other assorted dignitaries, all costumed in their most elaborate vestments and uniforms. Tens of thousands of Romans lined the parade route to the Capitoline Hill.

The great day commenced with a solemn Mass officiated by Cardinal Riario. I pronounced a plenary indulgence for the occasion. Mass was followed by a banquet. A fanfare of trumpets and bagpipes announced the entry of the guest of honor. Baraballo was splendidly dressed in an ancient Roman toga of green velvet with a surplice of crimson satin adorned with ermine and a cape of gold and purple. I invited him to recite some verses to the assembled party, which he willingly did to general applause and laughter.

Then, each of the poets at my court presented accolades to their new champion. Accolti remarked that Dante and Petrarch must be lamenting because Baraballo had stolen from them their glory of language and beauty of poetry. Baraballo beamed with delight.

The accolades were followed by a presentation of the Latin comedy, the *Carminum*. At the conclusion of the play, the time had arrived for the coronation of the Arch-Poet. The dignity of my office prevented me from personally conducting the ceremony, so I nominated Cardinal Lang, the imperious representative of the Emperor, to crown Baraballo. Lang was not pleased by this honor, but was in no position to refuse.

Lang placed a large hat with a triple crown upon Baraballo's bald head and urged the poet to place his lyrics at the service of the Church. With a fanfare of trumpets, Baraballo was escorted through the Vatican to the piazza, where Hanno awaited. The patient pachyderm was draped in a purple saddle robe embroidered with the words *Poeta Barabal*. Atop his back was a high throne with arms terminating in gilded griffins. We all tried to conceal our mirth as Baraballo vainly attempted to mount the elephant. After many unsuccessful efforts, I ordered Hanno's mahout to assist the old man onto his seat. Once enthroned, Baraballo was handed a large laurel branch to hold as a scepter.

The procession then left St. Peter's and I hurried along the Corridore to Castel Sant'Angelo to observe the remainder of the farce. I arrived at my vantage point in time to see an immense gathering upon the bridge. The noise from the musicians and crowd was deafening and poor Hanno balked at walking into the sea of raucous humanity. His mahout urged him on but, for the first time ever, the elephant refused a command and gave his body a mighty shake. Off flew the throne and the Arch-Poet; right onto the muddy bank of the Tiber.

Fortunately, Baraballo was not injured and made his escape into the crowd. With the guest of honor now absconded, there was no point in continuing the entertainment and Hanno was led back to the peace and quiet of the Vatican. Although our plans had been interrupted, it had been a wonderfully amusing day.

Now I must return to the drudgery of politics. In August, 1514, the official treaty between England and France was signed in London, finally bringing peace between the perpetually warring nations. As part of the arrangement, Louis pledged to pay one million crowns to Henry, of which Henry agreed to return about half to Louis in the form of Mary Tutor's dowry.

Ferdinand had been effectively checked in his ambition. Now wary of the English-French combination, he approached me secretly and offered a non-aggression pact pursuant to which neither of us would attack the Italian possessions of the other during our lifetimes. Given that I am a peaceful man, I saw no problem with this arrangement and a secret treaty between Spain and the Holy See was signed in September.

Louis was very grateful for the role I had played in effectuating his reconciliation with Henry and he and I entered into our own secret negotiations regarding a matter close to my own heart.

The Medici had been one of Europe's leading families for nearly two centuries, but no royal blood coursed through our veins. We had no official position, even in Florence. Now Louis proposed a marriage between my brother Giuliano and Filiberta, daughter of the Duke of Savoy and aunt of Francis, heir apparent to the French throne. Giuliano would be confirmed as the Duke of Nemours. As dowry, Louis would renounce French claims to Parma, Piacenza and Reggio and I would then gift the towns, together with Modena, to the couple. The offspring of this Medici marriage would be French royalty.

In exchange, Louis demanded my recognition of the Anjou and Valois claims to Milan. As this was very difficult for me, he also pledged that

France would help drive the Spanish from Naples, which, in turn, would also be given to Giuliano. While these concessions could not, for obvious reasons, be reduced to a formal treaty, it nonetheless favorably disposed me towards my old adversary.

December, 1514, was a difficult month for me (although not as trying as 1515 would commence). Raphael, my new architect for St. Peter's, gave me the highly distressing news that one million ducats would be required to complete construction of the basilica. This monstrous sum was well beyond my ability to fund from conventional sources of papal revenue. Working closely with Cardinal Pucci, I devised a rather elegant method for raising the necessary funds.

I had just invested Albert of Hohenzollern (the Elector of Mainz and brother of the Elector of Brandenburg) with the archbishopric of Mainz (the year before, I had sold him the bishoprics of Magdeburg and Halberstadt). Albert had borrowed the 21,000 ducat fee for the pallium from Jacob Fugger and requested that I allow him to grant dispensations to repay the loan. Instead, I issued a Bull which authorized indulgences for the souls of departed relatives to those faithful who contributed to the building fund for St. Peter's. Since there was an endless supply of deceased relatives (many of them no doubt suffering eternal torment in Purgatory), this had the potential for raising a floodtide of new capital. I gave Albert authority to dispense the indulgences within Germany and agreed that one-half of the revenues collected could be remitted to Fugger to reduce his loan balance.

In December, I also received a most charming, but uninvited, visitor. Isabella d'Este, Marchioness of Mantua arrived in Rome, ostensibly to visit her son, Federico (the hostage and catamite of Julius, who had stayed on in Rome after the old pope's death), but in reality to press her own family's hereditary claims to the towns destined for Giuliano (nothing ever remained secret within Italy). Her nephew, Maximilian Sforza, Duke of Milan, claimed Parma and Piacenza and her brother Alfonso, Duke of Ferrara, claimed Reggio and Modena.

The Marquis and Marchioness had, of course, provided extended hospitality to Giuliano and me during our years of exile. This I could never forget. On the other hand, family blood trumps all other affinities within Italy. I dispatched Bibbiena, with whom Isabella was intimate, to the city gate to greet her and renew their friendship. He immediately presented her with a purse containing 500 ducats – the money I owed her from our friendly wager in the days preceding my elevation. He then escorted her to Cardinal Cornaro's palace, where she was installed in luxurious apartments and feasted at a banquet attended by virtually the entire College.

I received her at consistory. When she bowed before me, I rose her up and bade her to sit beside me. She was the Pope's queen for the day. We talked of trifles and then I sent her off to Cardinal Riario's palace for another banquet.

For the next month, I made sure Isabella was fully occupied all of the time. Bibbiena and Bembo gallantly attended to her physical desires and Raphael was instructed to be her tutor on the art and architecture of the Imperial City. One evening, Baldissare Castiglione presented a performance of Bibbiena's splendid comedy, *Calandria*.

Since it was Carnival time, there were many amusements to divert Isabella's attention from politics. I took her myself to the crest of Monte Testaccio, where, in an annual tradition, fat squealing pigs were stuffed into huge wooden barrels and then rolled down the steep hillside. At the bottom, mobs of peasants armed with axes and daggers fought each other like wild beasts for the gift of pork. I also sponsored for her amusement a regatta on the Tiber, followed by a mock naval battle in which my lackeys pummeled each other with oranges. My nephew Lorenzo also assisted, inviting Isabella to a banquet at his palace, followed by a bull fight during which four bulls were killed.

From time to time, the exhausted Marchionese would delicately make inquiry of me regarding the disputed towns. I would smile benignly and change the subject. One of the best things about being pope is that no one dares engage in unwelcome conversation. After six weeks, she finally gave up and moved on to Naples.

As if all of this was not enough, officers of the Inquisition arrived in December to inform me of an outbreak of witchcraft in Como. Three hundred witches had been burned, but the infection continued to spread. I instructed the inquisitors to use every means at their disposal to rid our country of this satanic scourge.

On New Year's Day, 1515, all of my careful plans for peace in Europe came to naught when Louis XII died in Paris. According to Bibbiena, the marital demands of Mary Tutor exhausted the monarch, who was in poor health to begin with. Francis I, Louis' nephew (and nephew of Giuliano's fiancé), assumed the throne. Like Louis, he was crowned Duke of Milan, King of Naples and Lord of Genoa as well as King of France. I did not personally know the boy (he was only twenty-one), but Bibbiena tells me he is highly educated and idolizes his late cousin, Gaston de Foix, the hero of Ravenna.

I immediately opened confidential communications with the new king, who confirmed his intention to invade Milan within the year. He expressed no opposition to the upcoming marriage between Giuliano and Filiberta, but would not commit to releasing French claims to Parma, Piacenza and Reggio or even confirming the royal title upon my brother.

Ferdinand, of course, wasted no time in renewing the League that was formed at Mechlin to oppose the last French attack on Milan. Henry declined to participate after Francis confirmed the million crown French obligation to England under the August, 1514 treaty negotiated by Louis. Maximilian joined the League, as did the Swiss, who were still outraged at the dishonor of the Dijon indemnity (Ferdinand guaranteed 40,000 crowns per month to the Swiss).

I was now in an extremely delicate position. The Spanish army under Cardona was still camped at Milan, where Maximilian Sforza ruled as Ferdinand's puppet. My old friend Emperor Maximilian was still warring with Venice, which once again united with France. It was fully expected that I would renew my prior membership in the League. However, I did not want to do anything to upset Giuliano's impending marriage; nor did I want to antagonize France's new ruler, particularly since I soon expected the Empire and Spain to unite in the person of Archduke Charles upon the deaths of the two old monarchs.

In February, I sent Giuliano off to France to consummate the marriage and provide me intelligence on the young king. I cannot even estimate the cost of his wardrobe, retinue and gifts for Francis and his royal court. I do know the cost of the palace I purchased in Rome for my brother and his new bride exceeded 100,000 ducats.

Giuliano proved himself virtually worthless as a spy. Weeks passed without correspondence and when it did arrive, it was replete with praise for the good taste and depth of learning of the young monarch, but nary a word regarding the political situation. At least the marriage ceremony proceeded without disaster, but I prayed daily that Giuliano would not fail in his principal duty to produce a legitimate male Medici heir (he has a young bastard son, Ippolito).

In March, Giuliano and Filiberta arrived in Ostia by galley. Cardinal Medici led a delegation of cardinals and noblemen to escort the couple to Rome. Of course, I organized a grand reception for them. Triumphal arches were erected along the parade route. Fifty Roman noblemen greeted them at the Porta del Popolo and the procession to the Campidoglio, led by pipers, drummers and trumpeters, extended for miles.

Against my better judgment, I had authorized Hanno to join in the parade. After the near disaster with Baraballo, a genuine disaster had occurred when I bowed to the popular demand for a public display of my pet's genius. I sent Hanno for a performance at the ancient Baths of Diocletion, which could accommodate thousands, but tens of thousands jammed the ruins for the show. Many Roman nobles arrived on horseback and spurred their horses through the crowd for better views. In the riot that ensued, thirteen Romans were trampled to death and Hanno became extremely distraught.

My concerns were realized when Hanno was frightened by a thunderous salute to Giuliano from the cannon of the Castel. He was carrying a mock castle upon his back in which several soldiers were concealed. The poor pachyderm once again shook his body and catapulted the castle and soldiers into the crowd, causing many serious injuries. I resolved to never again allow Hanno to be taken from the Vatican.

With Giuliano and Filiberta now safely married and ensconced in Rome, I had more freedom in my dealings with Francis, who was already marching south with his army. I gave him my final terms for consenting to French rule of Milan: (i) renunciation of French claims to Parma and Piacenza, (ii) negotiation of a permanent peace between France and Spain, with both committed to a new Christian League to attack the Turks and (iii) renunciation of French claims to Naples in favor of the Holy See (or mutually acceptable third party). When Francis refused my terms, I had no alternative but to reluctantly join the Mechlin League.

Giuliano, the Captain-General of the Church, would now have the opportunity to prove himself more than a useless courtier. I appointed Cardinal Medici as the papal legate to the League and Bologna (my old position) and instructed Giulio to keep close watch upon Giuliano and report to me regularly. I commanded Giuliano to deploy his 3,000 papal troops in defense of Parma and Piacenza, leaving Milan to Cardona and the Swiss. He was also instructed to stop in Urbino on the march north and secure the person and arms of the Duke of Urbino for the upcoming battle.

I had not forgotten the treachery of Francesco Maria della Rovere after Ravenna, when he refused Julius' order to support me in the conquest of Florence. But Giuliano and Giulio reported that the Duke had agreed to raise an army and so I sent several thousand ducats to Urbino to pay for the troops.

Everyone expected that Francis would follow the invasion route of his uncle Louis and so the Swiss heavily fortified the passes. But the canny young king instead took the route to the south, through the Simplon Pass, a journey deemed impossible by military engineers. His army arrived at Embrun, rather than Susa where he was expected. The surprise achieved by the French maneuver was total.

As the great battle approached, Giuliano became ill with fever (or so he and Giulio reported) and departed for Florence to recuperate. My worst fears concerning Giuliano had been confirmed. I had no alternative but to appoint my young nephew Lorenzo as the new Captain-General of the Church. Upon hearing this news, the Duke of Urbino withdrew from the field, refusing to serve under the inexperienced boy. I dispatched a brief to the Duke, reminding him that he held Urbino as a vassal of the Holy See and had sworn obedience to the Holy Father (and had taken my money as well). I ordered him to proceed with his troops forthwith, upon pain of excommunication. Incredibly, he once again refused my direct command.

I renewed with Lorenzo my instructions to Giuliano that papal troops were not to be committed to battle until a successful outcome was assured. From my own direct experience, I had little faith in Cardona's martial abilities and the Swiss, brave and skilled as they were, could never be fully trusted not to sell themselves to the highest bidder. Therefore, I dispatched a secret envoy, Cinthio da Tivoli, to treat with Francis through the good offices of his uncle, the Duke of Savoy.

Once again, my judgment proved sound. Prospero Colonna, condottiere for Milan, was taken by surprise by the French maneuver through Embrun and was captured without a fight. His troops went home. Emperor Maximilian sent not a single soldier or crown to support the League of which he was a member. Upon hearing of the French successes in western Lombardy, Cardona retreated to Piacenza, where he put himself and his troops under the command of Lorenzo (knowing full well that Lorenzo would not directly engage the French).

The Swiss, having seen their supposed allies desert them, treated themselves with the Duke of Savoy and agreed to surrender Lombardy (including Parma and Piacenza) to France for one million crowns.

Just as the treaty with the Swiss was about to be signed, Cardinal Schinner, an implacable foe of France, arrived over the Alps with a fresh contingent of Swiss mercenaries. Rejecting the proposed treaty, he patriotically urged his countryman to demonstrate the force of their character and arms. On the afternoon of September 13, 1515, the Cardinal led 20,000 Swiss in a direct assault upon the French army, which was camped at Marignano.

On September 16, I received a courier at the Vatican with an urgent communication from Lorenzo, informing me that the Swiss had routed the French at Marignano. I immediately summoned Marino Giorgi, the Venetian Ambassador, to give him the news and admonish Venice for having once again chosen the wrong horse in the race. Bibbiena ordered that Rome be illuminated with fireworks in celebration of the great victory.

The next morning, Giorgi had the impertinence to demand of Serapica that I be immediately awakened for an urgent audience. I was still in the midst of my toilet when the arrogant Ambassador barged into my chamber.

"Holy Father," he said sarcastically, "after the example of Christ, I will return you good for evil. Yesterday, Your Holiness gave me bad and at the same time false news; today, I bring in exchange good news which is also true; the Swiss have been defeated."

I was dumbfounded by this intelligence, which I prayed was false. But couriers soon arrived to confirm the worst. Francis himself had led the counterattack upon the Swiss on the morning of September 14 and when the Venetian army under D'Alviano arrived at the field, it was the Swiss who fled and retreated to Milan. There, the coward Maximilian

Sforza surrendered the city and renounced his claims in exchange for a French title and pension.

The situation now closely mirrored that of 1494, when Charles VIII first conquered Milan and then Naples. Alexander had treated with the young king at the Vatican and set in motion the groundwork for driving the French from Italy the next year. I resolved to be even more skillful in my handling of Francis.

Because of my refusal to permit papal troops to attack with the Swiss, Francis still held me in high regard and begged for a personal meeting at the Vatican to seek my blessing and discuss peace between France and the Holy See.

I determined that I would not permit the King and his army to journey south, where it would be within a few days' march from Naples. I was going to propose Florence as a meeting point, but Bibbiena and Giulio convinced me that the presence of the French in Florence might stir up mischief among the enemies of the Medici. They suggested Bologna instead and I agreed with them.

Therefore, I dispatched Cardinal Sanseverino with an invitation to Francis to attend a papal audience in Bologna in early December. The young monarch immediately accepted. I would be remiss if I failed to also report that my beloved sister, Contessina, died last month.

JOURNAL

November 30, 1515

Marignolli

My memoir has now caught up with my life. It is difficult to believe that nearly three years have passed since I assumed the supreme dignity. I should stop writing now. Some distance is required between an event and its retelling so that a proper perspective can be placed upon it. In the passion of the moment, and without knowledge of other intertwined events which might be simultaneously occurring, an accurate picture cannot often be drawn. For example, had I written contemporaneously about my capture at Ravenna and my inflamed fistula, I would have attributed both to the handiwork of Satan. But with the perspective gained from the passage of time, I can see that they were heavenly blessings in disguise because, without both, I would not now be the Vicar of Christ.

I confess, however, that I have grown quite fond of my evening sessions with parchment and quill. It is both a source of relaxation and challenge, a pleasant diversion from the immediacy of the tasks before me. I also derive great enjoyment from the hours I spend in the Vatican library, surreptitiously researching various events of which I have no direct knowledge and my discrete and subtle inquiries to my colleagues regarding their own recollections. It also, I believe, has given me greater understanding upon which to base my own decisions as pontiff.

So, I have reached a compromise with myself. I shall continue to write, contemporaneously recording the events of my life. Then, a decade from now (God willing), I shall return to my jottings and edit them into a coherent and hopefully accurate account.

I write these words from the villa of my friend, Jacopo Gianfigliazzi, at Marignolle, a small town just outside of Florence. I arrived three days ago on my way to treat with Francis at Bologna. The Signoria has organized a festival of unprecedented scope to celebrate my first return to Florence as pope, so I have, at its request, remained here while the preparations are completed. I understand that 2,000 craftsmen have been employed and that Florence's most gifted artists (Sansovino, Sangallo, Bandinelli, Andrea del Sarto, Grannaci and Pontorno) are vying with each other to create the most glorious artistic tributes to me.

This unplanned delay in my travels does not disturb me. My fistula seems to have its own mind and, recollecting its journey from Bologna to Florence to Rome in March, 1513, has decided to inflict the same excruciating pain upon me for the reverse journey. Serapica attends to me thrice daily with the salve prescribed by my doctor, which is slowly reducing the inflammation. Unfortunately, it has done little regarding the foul odor associated with the pus and filth that oozes from the abscess. My perfume and heavy robes help mitigate the embarrassment. Fortunately, no one dares makes an untoward comment in my presence.

December 3, 1515

Florence

On December 1, I made my triumphant entry into the city of my birth. I was greeted by musicians, Lorenzo and all of Florence's notables at the Roman Gate. The procession through the city was led by 100 youths from noble families dressed in finest silk and carrying long silver wands. The eighteen cardinals who accompanied me rode next upon their mules. The Priori themselves carried my sedan chair and canopy. My chamberlains flung silver coins at the crowd. There were twelve massive triumphal arches, richly ornamented with sculptures and paintings on the parade route, along which the entire population had assembled. I stopped often to closely examine the art and give benedictions to the adoring crowds. The Duomo itself had been refurbished for the occasion. Sansovino and Andrea del Sarto had erected a new faux-marble façade, which was decorated with statutes, bas-reliefs and pictures painted in chiaroscuro.

Cardinal Medici presided over Mass, at the conclusion of which I gave my blessing and granted an indulgence to all in attendance. I then proceeded to Santa Maria Novella, where my predecessors Martin V and Eugenius IV had stayed during their residence in Florence. A consistory was held where we discussed the upcoming meeting with Francis. The question of an appropriate gift was raised and the cardinals agreed with my suggestion that the King be presented with Ascanio Sforza's Cross, which is pure gold and encrusted with jewels. It is worth more than 15,000 ducats.

Yesterday was a sad day. In the morning, I attended Mass at San Lorenzo, after which I prayed before the porphyry sarcophagus of my father and tears flowed from my eyes. I then visited the bedside of my brother. Upon hearing last summer that Giuliano had developed a fever, I immediately dispatched two of Rome's best doctors (both Jews) to Florence to attend to him. The reports I had received were not encouraging (galloping consumption was their diagnosis), but I was shocked to see how close to death my poor brother actually was. The consumption was quickly depleting his body of its vital essences and he coughed incessantly into his crimson-tinged handkerchief during our interview. It was clear that Giuliano would be producing no heir before his departure from this earthly realm. I could not tarry long for there was still a great deal to do before my meeting with Francis, but I pledged that I would return to him after Bologna.

December 8, 1515

Bologna

I entered Bologna today. What a difference between the joyous reception I received in Florence and the sullen one I received here. There were no accolades or decorations as my procession made its way to the Palazzo Pubblico. Much animosity remained from Julius' conquest of the city and the cry "Sega! Sega!"° was heard from partisans of the Bentivoglio. Even some local clergymen insulted the Holy Father by their absence from my procession. Paris de Grassis and some of my cardinals suggested I punish them for their insolence, but I was magnanimous and chose to ignore the insult. There were more important issues on my mind.

December 18, 1515

Bologna

My business in Bologna is now concluded and I cannot wait to return to the hospitality of Florence. Overall, I am pleased with the outcome of my interview with Francis. When I arrived at Bologna, the King had ostentatiously taken residence at Parma (my city). I dispatched Lorenzo and four prelates to escort Francis to Bologna. The royal party was met at the border of the Papal States by Cardinals Medici and Fieschi and then by Paris de Grassis and Cardinal Sanseverino at the bridge over the Reno. Paris reported to me that the King failed to approve his suggestions for appropriate protocol and pomp for the visit and even stated that "he cared not a jot for processions." But I would not permit this boy-king to dictate the decorum for his audience with the Vicar of Christ.

Francis arrived in Bologna on December 11, where he was met by all of my cardinals at the Porta San Felice. Cardinal Riario, the senior cardinal, made a brief speech of welcome in Latin. He then was escorted to the Palazzo Pubblico (his apartments were in a separate wing from mine). Unlike the cold reception afforded me, thousands of cheering Bolognese lined the King's procession route and all of the bells in the city were rung.

I observed the procession from the window of my apartment. Francis rode on a dark bay horse decked in black velvet with tassels of gold. He was wearing a robe of silk and silver brocade and a beret of black velvet

---

° Translator's note: "Saw! Saw!" The saw was the emblem of the Bentivoglio family and appeared upon its coat of arms.

with a small black plume – very fashionable in the French style. Cardinals Sanseverino and Este rode on either side of him.

I nominated Cardinals Medici, Bibbiena, Sauli and Cibo to dine with the King, who was then escorted to the Great Hall, where I waited, weighted down by the heavy gold and bejeweled regalia of my office, under which I perspired profusely despite the winter weather. The Hall was overflowing with dignitaries and clerics; so much so that Paris was worried that the floor might collapse. It took the King almost half an hour to force his way through the admiring throng to my throne. He bowed before me, genuflected three times and kissed my foot and hand. I then raised him up and extended him the honor of kissing my cheek.

Francis is a handsome young man of greater than normal stature and full of force and vigor. His complexion is very fine, his nose longish, his hands do not stand out. In short, his appearance is worthy of a ruler. Had the circumstances been different, he might have rekindled the smoldering embers of my passion.

Francis made a short speech in French (another language in which I am reasonably conversant) thanking me humbly for allowing him the privilege of a personal interview with the supreme pontiff and pledging his obedience, as a dutiful son and servant, to all of my commands. I responded, in Latin, attributing this happy and satisfactory moment entirely to the goodness of God.

I then invited the King to take the seat beside me (just as I had done with Isabella) while his Chancellor, Du Prat, delivered the formal discourse of obedience in Latin. Du Prat began with an effusive eulogy to the wisdom, skill and state of the Medici; especially me, to whom God had entrusted the bark of St. Peter, to steer it through the shoals into the haven of safety. He next extolled the Kings of France, who had from old surpassed all other Christian princes in their devotion to the Holy See. He noted that His Majesty, Francis I, in spite of the distain of certain advisors who were of a different mind from himself, hastened over mountains and valleys, forests and rivers, and had run the gauntlet of the Swiss, in order to do homage to the pope, as an eldest son to his father, and the Vicar of Christ, and to lay all that he had at his feet. At the conclusion of this homage, Francis bowed in token of his assent and I commended him for his fidelity.

After the speeches, an endless procession of French nobles bowed before me to kiss my feet and pledge their personal obedience. I only allowed the Dukes of Orleans and Bourbon the privilege of kissing my cheek. When this interminable ceremony thankfully reached its conclusion, I took Francis by the hand and led him to a private chamber, where I left him momentarily to remove my cumbersome vestments and refresh myself.

For the next three days, Francis and I treated privately. While he was always correct and respectful in our conversations, I found him as hard-headed and skillful a negotiator as Alexander himself. I will not attempt to chronicle the back and forth of the discussions each day, but will jump directly to the conclusions. Francis demanded I recognize the French claim to Milan (and order the Swiss to desist in their wars against France), as well as its vassal towns, Parma and Piacenza. Given that all were occupied by French troops, there was little I could do. When I protested that they were fiefs of the Holy See, Francis correctly pointed out that I had ceded them as a wedding gift to Giuliano and Filiberta. When I noted that he had not conveyed the title Duke of Nemours upon Giuliano, he responded that he would immediately do so (which he did). In return, I gave his tutor, Adrian de Boissy, a red hat.

Francis next demanded the return of Reggio and Modena to the Duke of Ferrara, who had been divested of them by the Duke of Urbino (before his treachery) in the last war. I pointed out to him that these were fiefs of the Emperor and that I had recently paid 40,000 ducats for Modena. He conceded that the Duke of Ferrara would have to reimburse me for my costs before the cities were returned to him.

The King also demanded that I recognize his claim to Naples and give my blessing to an invasion to liberate it from Spain. I told him that this was impossible, since a protocol of the League of Mechlin prohibited me from supporting any attack upon Naples. This protocol would not expire for another sixteen months. I intimated that I had no objection to Spain being dispossessed of Naples (but refrained from endorsing France as its replacement).

I, of course, had items on my list. First and foremost, I desired France to lead a new Crusade against the Mohammedans. As a Christian prince, he could scarcely refuse this command. After lengthy conversation, I authorized him to levy, for one year only, a special tax upon the clergy of France, provided all of the receipts were used exclusively to fund the Crusade.

Next, I demanded that Francis recognize and protect the Medici claims to Florence and refrain from any interference in the affairs of Tuscany. He readily assented. I demanded the same for the Holy See's rights to the Papal States, to which he also agreed.

I then, as a matter of courtesy only, informed Francis of my intention to excommunicate the Duke of Urbino and confirm the duchy upon my nephew Lorenzo. This was no surprise to him, since the treacherous Duke had sent Baldissare Castiglione to Bologna to beg the King to not permit this. When Francis protested, I sternly rebuked him. Urbino is and always was a fief of the Church and the Duke its vassal by sufferance. I reminded the King that Francesco Maria had twice treasonably disobeyed direct commands from the Holy Father and had also murdered a prince of the Church. There was no possibility of further discussion and the King wisely withdrew his objection. No other major matters were addressed during our meetings.

In the midst of these discussions, I presided over High Mass at the Cathedral of San Petronio. Francis begged to carry my train and offered to wait upon the Vicar of Christ in the smallest things. I refused his effort to humble himself beneath the dignity of his royal title, but consented to allow him to carry the font of Holy Water in the procession.

A remarkable thing happened during the Mass. A French nobleman suddenly rose and cried out to make a confession. He publicly confessed (as if we did not already know) that he had taken up arms against the Holy See during Julius' war and had ignored the ban of excommunication. He then begged me for absolution. The King himself then rose and made the same confession, followed by dozens more in the congregation. I raised my arms in benediction and granted absolution. The French, joyous to have this blemish removed from their immortal souls, lined up to kiss my feet in gratitude and submission. When Francis knelt before me, he said:

> Your Holiness must not be surprised that all these men hated Julius II, for he was our greatest enemy; in all our wars, we have never had an enemy as terrible as he, for Julius II was indeed a most capable general and far better suited to be such than to be pope.

Although I fully agreed with his assessment, I could not publicly endorse this disrespectful slur upon the memory of my predecessor. I let his comment pass in silence.

The night before the King's departure for Milan, I invited him to dine with me. Bibbiena, Giulio and Cibo joined us, along with the Dukes of Bourbon and Vendome. During the course of the very pleasant repast, Francis requested that I present him with the Laocoon° as a token of our undying friendship. Hiding my astonishment at this audacious suggestion, I graciously agreed. Later that night, I dispatched a messenger to Baccio Bandinelli°, ordering him to sculpt a replica of the statue and ship it to Paris.

° Translator's note: An ancient marble statue that had recently been discovered underneath the rubble of Rome and purchased by Julius for the papal collection.

° Translator's note: One of Florence's lesser sculptors.

December 31, 1515

Fiesole

Another year is drawing to a close, but there is no celebrating at the Medici villa at Fiesole. After bidding farewell to Francis, I departed Bologna for the more hospitable city of Florence. I know that neither of us was overjoyed at the outcome of our conference, but, considering that the League's army had been routed by the French, I am not displeased by the result. The integrity of the Medici claim to Tuscany (and now Urbino) and the Holy See's claim to the Papal States have been recognized by Francis and the southward momentum of the French army has been checked. I am fully confident that I will one day recover Parma and Piacenza for the Church and at least I will be compensated for the loss of Reggio and Modena.

During the month of my absence from Florence, devastating floods had ravaged the city and the heavy rains had destroyed the crops of the surrounding farms. There was no magnificent procession upon my return, just the hollow stares of starving people. I did what I could to help. I raised the ecclesiastical incomes of Florence's clergy and designated its canons as protonotaries of the Holy See. I also donated a jewel-encrusted papal mitre, worth over 10,000 ducats, to the Duomo. I was also forced to severely chastise Cardinals Petrucci and Sauli for their thoughtless luxury and extravagance during this season of dearth.

But it was Giuliano who most saddened me. He was now in the last stages of his illness, appearing utterly shrunken and spent like an expiring candle. I ordered him moved from the Medici palace to our villa at Fiesole, where the air is fresher and the atmosphere peaceful. It is a good place for contemplating one's soul. I resolved to remain with my brother until his passing.

This was a resolution I soon regretted making. Giuliano had only one thing on his dying mind, which he repeated endlessly. He begged me, time and time again, not to deprive Francesco Maria della Rovere of Urbino. He said that upon stopping in Urbino on his journey north to lead the papal army against Francis, he had pledged, in the name of the Medici, that the Duke would remain unmolested in his territory. He cried that he could not go to his grave with a stain upon his honor.

How dare my brother presume to bind the Holy See to his unauthorized promise? He has no standing. He had every advantage in his life and yet elected to fritter it away as a courtier. Nothing he has ever done has advanced the cause of the Medici. The best that can be said for Giuliano is that, unlike my other brother, the idiot Piero, he never did anything to harm us.

Of course I said none of this to Giuliano. Despite all, he is my brother and I love him deeply. Each time he importuned me to change my mind,

I said quietly to him: "Think first upon getting well, my Giuliano, for this is no meet time to vex thyself with politics."

Everyone seems to forget that Francesco Maria twice disobeyed my direct commands. If I show indulgence, others will ape his example and trick and abuse me, presuming upon my lenience, and I would be no better than an owl. I will not let this happen. The scoundrel will be punished.

February 19, 1516

Fiesole

Word arrived today that His Most Catholic Majesty, King Ferdinand, has finally died. This will change everything, as Francis will no doubt now move to wrest Naples from Spain. Giuliano continues to cling to life, although his case is hopeless. As much as I love my brother, I must return to Rome. The affairs of the Church must take precedence over the affairs of man.

I have been remiss in my writing, but, truth be told, little of interest has occurred. I cannot fill these pages with who wore what and what we had for dinner. I never thought I would say it, but I miss the intrigue of the Vatican.

March 1, 1516

The Vatican

I arrived at the Apostolic Palace three days ago and was pleasantly surprised to find a giant preserved rhinoceros awaiting me. My good friend, King Manuel (together with Henry, the only true Christian princes), had tried to send the strange beast to me alive in 1515 but, alas, the galley he was on capsized in a storm off La Spezia. The carcass was recovered and returned to Portugal, where it was embalmed and sent back to Rome, this time without incident.

It is too bad, since the live rhinoceros would have made an interesting companion for Hanno. I am not sure what I will do with him. King Ferrante of Naples used to embalm his enemies and keep them in a chamber next to his bedroom. It is probably beneath the dignity of the Vicar of Christ to keep a stuffed beast in his apartment. I will consult with Paris de Grassis.

Today, I set in motion the legal process to depose Francesco Maria of Urbino. A brief was dispatched commanding him, on pain of deposition and excommunication, to present himself at the Vatican, within eighteen days, to answer the charges against him (which I have previously documented). We will soon see if he has the testicles to appear before me.

March 25, 1516

The Vatican

I am being driven to distraction by scheming women. To no surprise, the Duke of Urbino failed to honor my summons and dispatched, instead, a bevy of surrogates, including his aunt, Elizabetta Gonzaga, Duchess of Urbino, and Isabella d'Este, his mother-in-law (who had worn out her welcome last year). Every day, one of them would arrive at consistory or my apartment to beg and plead for my indulgence. Each day, they attempted to shame me based upon the courtesy afforded my family during our years of exile. Each day, I put them off with kind words. Within hours of their visits, that ambitious shrew, Alfonsina Orsini, would arrive to cajole me to remain true to my intention to invest her son Lorenzo with the duchy.

The map of Europe is about to be redrawn and I cannot free myself of these meddlesome women (not to mention Castiglione, Luigi Gonzaga, Alberto Carpi and half a dozen other advocates). Even Bibbiena has turned on me and is urging leniency. Given his intimate relationship with Isabella, this is not a total surprise, although I believe that he dislikes Lorenzo as well (I do not care much for the boy myself, but one cannot choose one's family).

Poor Giuliano finally expired on March 17 and has been interred at San Lorenzo. I am told that the outpouring of grief by the citizens of Florence was heartfelt. I pray that his soul finds peace. My resident scold, Paris de Grassis, admonished me to withhold any display of grief over the death of my brother "since the Supreme Pontiff is not a man, but a demi-god, and ought therefore always to exhibit a serene and smiling countenance on all occasions to the people." I do not feel like a demi-god today.

March 31, 1516

La Magliana

I am in a complete rage. For reasons I cannot fathom, Giuliano's death has unleashed Ravenna upon my mind once again. Seeking diversion, I went to my lodge at La Magliana for a hunt. As usual, my obsession worked its magic and Ravenna receded. Serapica led me to a large stag that had been wounded in the melee. Taking my sword, I dispatched him with one thrust.

It is well known that, upon a successful hunt, it is my custom to grant petitions. As we were celebrating last evening at the banquet, Duchess

Elizabetta entered the hall unbidden, fell to her knees and once again begged me for indulgence towards Francesco Maria. Never, in all my years of hunting, has a woman of noble blood ever made an appearance. I had been ambushed like the stag. I glared at her in anger and she promptly fainted, hitting her head on the stone floor. Needless to say, all of the hunting party crowded around her, clucking with sympathy.

All eyes were upon me, expecting me to appease the suffering woman. What could I do? My only aim in this sordid affair is the satisfaction of the honor of the Holy See. On the spot, I stated that if Francesco Maria came to Rome, confessed and submitted to my authority, that I would give him a penance which might at first seem hard, but afterwards I would invest his son with the title.

Upon these words, the Duchess made a miraculous recovery and left the hall with a triumphant smile upon her face. No sooner was she gone then Lorenzo was upon me, beseeching me to revoke my promise. I dismissed him with sharp words. I will need time to consider this matter further as more pressing problems currently trouble me.

Francis, in violation of the spirit of my agreements with him, has sent an armed force to assist his ally Venice recover Brescia and Verona from Emperor Maximilian. Maximilian, who received a 125,000 crown loan from Ferdinand just days before he died, has crossed the Alps with a combined German and Swiss army to defend his cities and advance upon Milan. Francis has had the gall to demand a contribution of papal money and arms to defend Milan, while the Emperor has done likewise with respect to Verona.

At this juncture, I know not who is likely to prevail in this contest. I have dispatched Bibbiena as legate to the Emperor and authorized my condottiere, Marc-Antonio Colonna, to take a small army north to assist the Emperor in his defense of Verona. In strict accord with my treaty with Francis, I dispatched 500 Florentine troops to Milan and one month's pay for 3,000 Swiss mercenaries. My obligations to both monarchs have been satisfied.

As I pen these words, a messenger has arrived with news that Leonardo has fled Italy for France. Apparently when Giuliano, his patron and protector, died, the artist became convinced that I intended to do him harm. The old man flatters himself. He has not entered my thoughts since he fled for the marshes. His days as a worthy artist are long past and his reputation outshines his achievements. His presence will not be missed in Italy; let Francis subsidize his sunset years.°

° Translator's note: The *Mona Lisa* was among the works Leonardo took with him to France.

On the subject of temperamental artists, my old friend Michelangelo has been busily at work on the statues for Julius' monumental tomb. Now that Julius' nephew, Francesco Maria, is my enemy, I cannot permit Michelangelo to continue work on this project aggrandizing the della Rovere family for eternity.

Last week, I summoned Michelangelo to an audience with me and Giulio. I ordered him to cease work immediately on the della Rovere contract and to commence work on a new commission of even greater worthiness – a new façade for the Medici church of San Lorenzo in Florence. Any sensible artist would have welcomed this project, but Michelangelo was never sensible. First he refused and then he bargained. He demanded two years' grace to finish the tomb. I refused; the façade must be started immediately. He argued that the della Rovere family would sue him on his contract. I told him that I would personally take care of the della Rovere's. He complained he had spent ten years of his life on the tomb. I told him that he could complete the tomb after the new façade was completed. He continued to resist. Finally, Giulio asked if he no longer desired to work for the Medici. Michelangelo was now boxed. Of course, he answered that he would undertake the commission. I authorized 1,000 ducats for stone and ordered the recalcitrant artist to immediately depart for Carrara to personally select only the most perfect of marbles. I held out my ring for him to kiss as the audience was now over. He departed with tears running down his face. Julius had bent the terribilita artist to his will. I will do no less.

April 25, 1516

The Vatican

No sooner had I returned from my hunt than Castiglione, Francesco Maria's courtier and intimate friend, appeared at my chamber to request that I formalize, in a papal Bull, the unfortunate offer I extended to Elizabetta at La Magliana. He also asked that I provide a written guaranty of the safety of Francesco Maria. I was shocked almost speechless by the audacity of these demands. Here is a man who twice disobeyed direct commands of the Holy Father, who murdered a prince of the Church, who has been excommunicated, his soul dammed for eternity, and who has been divested of all lands and titles. Who is he to demand legal assurances through his agent? How dare he doubt the word of the Vicar of Christ?

Barely disguising my disgust, I said to Castiglione:

> The submission must be unconditional. The Supreme Pontiff does not bargain. Francesco Maria will never trust me unless he realized that I had the power and not the will to harm him; and I could never trust him until I had some proof of his confidence. I pledge my personal word to him and to the Marquis and to as

many cardinals as they pleased, but not in writing; for if I wished to deceive I would do so by Bulls and Briefs, but my personal word could be trusted.

Castiglione rode to Urbino and delivered my message to his master, who dismissed the words of the pope and instead raised an army to resist the Holy See. This final act of disobedience put an end to my long-suffering indulgence of this traitor. I commanded Lorenzo, Captain-General of the Church, to assemble an army and take Urbino and its territories by force of arms. I designated Renzo da Ceri, an accomplished condottiere, to direct the attack upon Urbino with a 14,000 man army. Vitello Vitelli, with 2,000 men, was retained to attack the territories around Lamole and Gianpaolo Baglioni, with a similar force, to attack Gubbio. Stern briefs were dispatched to all of the monarchs of Europe warning them not to interfere in the internal affairs of the Church. We will shortly see what kind of military commander Lorenzo will make.

Since my last entry, Maximilian, with his combined German-Swiss army, successfully defeated the French-Venetian army at Verona and marched upon Milan. He was approaching the city when 10,000 Swiss mercenaries arrived in the service of France. There were now equal numbers of Swiss on each side of the looming battle. The old Emperor, remembering Swiss treachery against Ludovico Sforza (and running out of money), prudently called off the attack and retreated back to Vienna. The status quo had been restored to Lombardy, but both monarchs now unfairly view me with suspicion.

On a lighter subject, Bibbiena took me to his apartment in the Apostolic Palace, where he has commissioned Raphael to decorate his bathing room. The cardinal has selected Venus and Cupid for the subject of the frescoes and Raphael has taken the ancient myth to heart and sketched figures which are quite lascivious. Bibbiena finds it enormously amusing, but I warned him to be careful about whom he admits to his private chamber since the pious would be scandalized by the pagan subject and erotic rendering.

May 2, 1516

The Vatican

It is only by the grace of God that I am able to pen these words. Once the Emperor crossed the Alps in his retreat from Milan, France and Venice renewed their attacks upon Brescia and Verona. Brescia has fallen, but Verona, ably assisted by my condottiere, Marc-Antonio Colonna (whose service I released to Maximilian), heroically resists.

Late last month, my mind unsettled by these unending troubles, I left Rome for a few weeks of fishing and fowling at the mouth of the Tiber near Ostia. I was happily engaged with my rod and tackle when the captain of my Swiss Guards galloped to the edge of the riverbank with ominous news. A raiding party of Moors from Tunis had invaded Ostia and was rampaging through the town. A corsair had detached from the main flotilla and landed just up the river, its infidel marauders intent upon capturing me.

It is beyond belief that God would permit the Supreme Pontiff of His one true Church to be enslaved by the Mohammedans, but I was not content to leave the matter solely in His hands. While a company of Guards remained behind to engage the raiders, I mounted my horse and galloped back to Rome with my personal escort.

I arrived safely, although in severe pain from the rough ride. It galls me to no end that infidels can freely prey upon Christians, while the principal Christian monarchs fight continuously against each other. If France, Spain and Germany spent half of the money they are wasting fighting in Italy for a new Crusade, the Mohammedan scourge could be wiped clean from the earth. I dispatched urgent briefs to all of the monarchs making this point yet again.

June 9, 1516

The Vatican

I pray fervently to God that I am never subjected again to the horrors of the past month. It is scarcely believable that it has been just over three years since I remarked to Giuliano: "God has given us the papacy; let us enjoy it." Looking back, the days of joy I have experienced can be counted upon my fingers, while the days of aggravation and melancholy seem without number.

Within days of my escape from the Mohammedans, I was stricken by a severe case of malarial fever. The lower Tiber is well known for its ill humors, but I would sooner die than surrender my passion for the hunt. My temperature rose alarmingly and paroxysms of excruciating pain wracked my body at regular intervals. I passed in and out of consciousness and my body was plagued with extreme weakness of the muscles. My doctors initially pronounced my prognosis grim and senior cardinals began preliminary planning for a conclave.

At the height of my disability, Fra Bonaventura came to Rome, accompanied by 20,000 of his fanatical followers. In the sixteen years since the execution of Savonarola, a heretical cult of admirers has spread through Italy like a noxious weed. These disciples of the false prophet continue his vituperative attacks upon the Church and similarly captivate the ignorant with predictions of doom.

Fra Bonaventura, an apostate Amadeiti monk, was originally from Subiaco, but wandered throughout northern Italy, acclaiming himself as the Angelic Pope prophesized by Telesphorus, Joachim of Fiore and

Savonarola. In a letter to the Doge of Venice (which the Venetians immediately delivered to the Vatican), Bonaventura described the Roman Church as the "scarlet woman of the Apocalypse" and himself as "chosen by God to be the Pastor of the Church in Zion, crowned by the hands of angels, and commissioned to be the Savior of the World." As such, he excommunicated me and my cardinals and demanded that faithful Christians obey only him.

It is a sad commentary on our modern times that a madman preaching nonsense can attract thousands of followers, but this proves to be the case. His zealots follow him everywhere, kissing his feet and proclaiming him the new Messiah.

I was at my lowest ebb when Bonaventura and his mob of simpletons arrived in Rome and the monk began preaching to crowds of curious Romans. In one address, he predicted that I, five of my cardinals, Hanno and his keeper would all die by September 5 of this year. This blasphemy resulted in his immediate arrest by my magistrates. His thousands of followers milled outside the Castel, eagerly awaiting his martyrdom.

Then, just as the crisis of my illness passed, proving the falsity of his prophesy, Hanno suddenly became ill himself. He lay in his stall, barely able to move, his breathing labored and his body twitching with spasms. He ceased defecating. I was distraught with worry; my own illness quickly forgotten. I rose from my sickbed and had a cot placed by Hanno's stall. I remained continuously by the side of my beloved pet.

I summoned all of Rome's leading physicians to minister to the elephant. They protested they had no knowledge of elephant diseases; one even suggested it was beneath his dignity to tend to an animal. I told the arrogant doctor that a session on the rack would likely change his opinion and that his very life depended upon Hanno's recovery. He protested no more.

As is typical of treatment for humans, Hanno's urine was inspected and his blood was let. But the doctors could arrive at no definitive diagnosis, so the universal treatment of a purgative was prescribed. Unfortunately, the doctors, having no experience with pachyderms, could not reach consensus as to the composition and quantity of the purgative. Finally, it was agreed to administer several gallons of purgative laced with powdered gold.

I do not know why anyone (including me) relies upon physicians. More often than not, the remedy is worse than the disease. Soon after the extremely difficult task of administering the purgative to the protesting pachyderm was concluded, Hanno let out one last moan of pain and died. I was beside myself with grief and anger. I told my chamberlains that I would gladly have sacrificed my own life for Hanno's recovery and ordered him buried in the courtyard of the Belvedere. I briefly considered executing the doctors, but decided to be merciful. This myth of Christ has served us well, but I sometimes find it difficult to accept a God and His Son who would punish so noble a beast as Hanno for no reason at all.

Hanno's mahout was found dead the next day of indeterminate causes (and Cardinals Sanseverino and Vigerio della Rovere are both very ill), so Bonaventura's mob has grown quite agitated with the expectation of his imminent martyrdom and resurrection. Having learned the lessons of history, I did not accommodate them by a trial and execution. Instead, I ordered Bonaventura removed to the deepest dungeon at the Castel, where he is to remain until the rats gnaw his flesh to the bone. I am quite certain that, with the passage of time, his disciples will grow bored and return to their homes.

I have ordered Raphael to immediately cease work on all of his commissions and personally fresco a full-sized portrait of Hanno on the wall at the entrance to the Vatican by the clock tower. This way, pilgrims for a millennium to come will be able to marvel at my wonderful friend and pay homage to him. As is his custom, Raphael immediately agreed. I myself have written Hanno's epitaph, which shall be inscribed upon a marble tablet and mounted next to Raphael's portrait. It follows:

Under this great hill I lie buried

Mighty elephant which the King Manuel

Having conquered the Orient

Sent as captive to Pope Leo X.

At which the Roman people marveled, -

A beast not seen for a long time,

And in my brutish breast they perceived

human feelings.

Fate envied me my residence in the blessed

Latium

And had not the patience to let me serve my

master a full three years.

But I wish, oh gods, that the time which Nature would have assigned to me and Destiny stole away,

You will add to the life of the great Leo.

I must sleep now. My strength still has not returned and my mind will not tolerate further recollection of these dreadful events.

June 12, 1516

The Vatican

For once, there is good news to report. Word has arrived from Urbino that Lorenzo and my army have taken the duchy without a single drop of blood being spilled. As my troops approached, Francesco Maria fled to his in-laws in Mantua and the citizens of Urbino welcomed Lorenzo as their liberator. Pesaro, Sinigaglia, San Leo, Majuolo and the rest of the towns in the duchy surrendered in short order.

Bibbiena has ordered the usual celebrations and illuminations to mark this great victory, but I confess I am still too overcome with melancholy over recent events to participate with any enthusiasm.

August 18, 1516

The Vatican

Francis and Charles are as treacherous and duplicitous as their predecessors. Francis has assembled an armada at Marseilles, under the command of the Spaniard, Pedro Navarro, to attack the Barbary corsairs that are plaguing our coast (and almost captured my person). But, at the same time as I was commending this noble act of Christian unity, the French and Spanish ambassadors concluded a treaty at Noyon (to which the Holy See was not a participant), whereby France and Spain have pledged a permanent cessation of hostilities against each other and a pact of mutual defense. Under the draft, Francis renounces the Anjou claim to Naples in favor of his one year old daughter, Louise, who is to be betrothed to Charles; the marriage to take place when the girl reaches twelve. Until then, Charles pledges to pay Francis 100,000 crowns per year, and then 50,000 crowns per year until a male heir is produced.

By this treaty, France and Spain have agreed upon the partition of Italy. It cannot be permitted to stand. Therefore, I must now once again treat with Maximilian and Henry to undermine Noyon before it is ratified by the principals.

Today, I invested Lorenzo as the Duke of Urbino and the Lord of Pesaro. All of my cardinals, save Cardinal Grimani of Urbino (who has fled Rome), have consented to the transfer of sovereignty from the Holy

See to Lorenzo. The foundation for a Medici state in Italy has been laid. Now I must find a suitable bride for my nephew and pray to the gods that he is manly enough to produce an heir.

December 30, 1516

The Vatican

I have been remiss in my entries, but the last few months have been devoted to non-stop politicking and the situation changes almost daily. There is no joy in my work or in my life; but I must continue to fulfill my destiny. Picking up where I last left off, I opened communications with Henry and Maximilian and a counter-treaty was concluded at London on October 16. This treaty was hostile to the interests of France and Charles was persuaded to join as a party, thereby deserting Noyon.

Francis, displaying his mettle as a diplomat, concluded a treaty with the Swiss at Fribourg, on November 29. The Swiss were now allied with France, rather than the Emperor. Maximilian then countered by adding his signature to Noyon on December 3, as well as making peace with Venice (by returning Verona).

As a result of these machinations and betrayals, all of the monarchs of Europe are supposedly now permanently at peace with one another. That may be what the treaties require, but I can prophesize with certainty that the armies shall soon be marching against one another. In the meantime, I have celebrated the end of dissension between the Christian princes by sending out briefs proposing a united Crusade against the Turks. I have little faith that my call will be heeded.

On the subject of prophesy, I must sadly report that Cardinal della Rovere died on July 18 and Cardinal Sanseverino died on August 7. With Hanno and his mahout, four of the seven deaths predicted by Fra Bonaventura have come to pass. My own prophesy has also proven true – Bonaventura's disciples have long ago deserted Rome. I have no idea whether the monk is still alive in the bowels of the Castel and have no intention of making inquiry.

January 18, 1517

The Vatican

One of the consequences of this rash of peace treaties is that dozens of condottieri and tens of thousands of their soldiers are now out of work. Naturally, this has resulted in a substantial drop in the price for their services, a situation which Francesco Maria has exploited. Borrowing money from the duplicitous Gonzagas, he has been able to retain a sizeable army of hungry and desperate Germans, Spaniards, French and Venetians to recapture Urbino. I received word just two days ago of their march through the Romagna and that the other traitor, Duke Alfonso of Ferrara, has granted safe conduct through his duchy.

I immediately summoned the ambassadors of Venice, France, Spain and the Emperor to protest most harshly this conspiracy against the Church. I dispatched briefs to their masters as well. All disclaimed support of Francesco Maria's actions and pledged their continued obedience to the Holy See. Each promised men-at-arms to assist Lorenzo in repelling the impending attack. I accepted their aid (the Vatican treasury is temporarily in desperate straits and the bankers' rates are forty percent), but do not believe their protestations of innocence for one second. All have sent representatives to a new Congress to be held at Cambrai. Ostensibly, the purpose is to cement the new peace, but the reality is that the monarchs are once again intending to carve up Italy among them.

Lorenzo left Rome today to take command of the troops which have been pledged to my cause. I have retained the condottieri Renzo Orsini, Giulio Vitelli and Guido Rangone to serve under him.

This new year has started badly. My own troops are discontented because I am arrears in their pay. The towns in the Romagna are growing restive and even Florence is in a state of discontent, all owing to the incompetence of the men I appointed to rule them and the need for new taxes to finance St. Peter's, the war in Urbino and the necessary expenses of the Holy See. I cannot be expected to attend to every detail of governance myself. I miss Hanno.

February 8, 1517

The Vatican

Word arrived that Francesco Maria has succeeded in retaking Urbino. My feckless nephew and his scheming condottieri seem intent upon avoiding combat at all costs. I have become the laughingstock of Europe. The fact that this petty duke has humbled the Holy See will only embolden revolution in the Papal States and aggression by the Turks. Julius was right in taking personal command of the papal army. It is the only way to get things done. Unfortunately, my disabilities prevent me from taking to the field. I am too overcome with melancholy to write further.

February 15, 1517

The Vatican

Francesco Maria's personal secretary, Oratio Florida, was delivered to Rome two days ago under heavy guard. Florida and Suares di Lione, a Spanish officer, had requested safe conduct from Lorenzo to deliver a message from Francesco Maria, now in residence at Urbino. Lorenzo granted the safe conduct from his temporary headquarters in Pesaro. He was expecting a proposal for a negotiated surrender, but instead Florida and di Lione delivered a challenge that the two rival dukes resolve their dispute by single combat.

Enraged by the proposal, Lorenzo ordered the two envoys arrested. He was soon forced to release di Lione by the Spaniards in his service, but sent Florida to me for further interrogation. I had him committed to the Castel, where my torturers did their job well. I now know as fact that Francis actively encourages the insurrection and that Charles does nothing to discourage it.

I am desperate for money to combat this international conspiracy. I sent a letter today to my friend Henry for aid. I trust he will not disappoint me.

March 12, 1517

The Vatican

Yesterday, Francis, Charles and Maximilian concluded their negotiations at Cambrai. This treaty poses the greatest threat to Italy and the Holy See in my lifetime. I must redouble my efforts to undermine it. Henry has sent me 50,000 ducats and promises 100,000 more if I ratify the English League. If I do so, I will incite Francis to even more aggressive moves against me. I am in a quandary, but I must have the cash. If my father had not destroyed the Medici bank through negligence and squandered our fortune on frivolity, I would not be in these desperate straits. But the gods have dealt me this hand and I must play my cards as best I can.

Last week, the Vice Chancellor, Sixtus della Rovere, died. I have decided to appoint Giulio as the new Vice Chancellor. I know this will not be well received by the College where Cardinal Medici is rather unpopular, but he is one of the few cardinals I know for certain are loyal to me. They dare not oppose my selection.

March 16, 1517

The Vatican

Today, the work of the Lateran Council came to an end. I issued a Bull pronouncing excommunication upon all persons who should presume to comment upon, or interpret its transactions without a special license of the Holy See. I ordered Cardinal Carvajal, the instigator of the heretic council at Pisa, to preside over its closing service. My humiliation of the old prelate is now complete. My army is finally engaging Francesco Maria's forces. I pray for victory.

March 27, 1517

The Vatican

Lorenzo was seriously injured yesterday at the siege of the fortress at Mondolfo. I am informed that he was directing the placement of canon when he was struck in the back of the head by a ball from the garrison. His prognosis is unknown to me. If he survives, I must hasten my efforts to find him a suitable bride. I cannot allow the Medici line to extinguish for lack of a legitimate male heir. I pray for his speedy recovery.

I dispatched Cardinal Medici to assume control of the papal forces. This may be another blessing in disguise as Giulio has far more military experience and common sense than young Lorenzo. Francesco Maria must not be allowed to usurp Urbino. Tomorrow, I will write briefs to all of the rulers of Europe demanding that they order their subjects to immediately desert his army.

Cardinal Pucci told me the other day that the war will cost at least 800,000 ducats this year and that the Vatican's total income will be only 420,000 ducats. I must be creative, but I am not deterred and will not alter my course. The Lord has always provided for me, notwithstanding any temporary shortage of funds. He will not desert me now.

March 28, 1517

The Vatican

My troubles in Urbino have brought the jackals out of their dens, first among them that arrogant and dissolute cardinal, Alfonso Petrucci. As I have earlier written, Petrucci was the leader of the cabal of young cardinals that chose me as their champion at the last conclave. In his teenaged years, Petrucci was my close friend, even to the point of shared intimacy. But since my election, he has been outrageous in his exorbitant demands for benefices and emoluments and his elaborate and lascivious lifestyle has required me to chastise him on numerous occasions.

Last year, I engineered the removal of his equally arrogant and disobedient brother, Borghese, as tyrant of Siena, who I replaced with his cousin, Raffaello Petrucci, my most loyal Captain of the garrison at Sant'Angelo. Since then, Alfonso has openly expressed his hatred of me and his desire to see me replaced as pontiff. He now complains of the expense of the war in Urbino and my supposed suppression of the rights of the College. He is lucky that I am the pontiff, since either Alexander or Julius would have snuffed out his life by this time.

Petrucci has just left Rome, without my sanction. He will no doubt try and stir up insurrection in Siena. I have ordered my spies to keep close watch upon him.

May 12, 1517

The Vatican

Will I ever again have good news to report? I have been busy corresponding with all of the rulers of Europe, but have made no progress. My spies inform me that a secret annex to the Treaty of Cambrai carving up Italy is about to be signed. Francis gets Lombardy and the north; Maximilian gets Venice, Padua and Tuscany (including Florence and Siena) and Charles gets the south. I would do better to ally with the Turks than these "Christian" kings.

The situation is no better on the war front. Giulio has proven even more indecisive than Lorenzo. My condottieri are playing their traditional game. Their demands for ducats are never ending as they carefully maneuver to avoid decisive combat. Francesco Maria has been emboldened to make forays from Urbino against Perugia and Anghiari, which makes me appear an impotent fool. Lorenzo has fully recovered from his wound, but finds every excuse to avoid returning to the front, despite my direct order to do so. I believe the boy is a coward at heart.

Even Michelangelo treats me like a donkey. Yesterday, I granted an audience to Domenico Buoninsegni, his financial agent in Rome. Domenico informed me that Michelangelo has already wasted half of his advance quarrying marbles that failed to meet his standard. He then tells me the artist requires a contract for six years and 35,000 ducats to complete the San Lorenzo façade and that if it is not acceptable, he will return the 1,000 ducat advance and complete Julius' tomb. As is my custom, I smiled at Domenico and genially told him I would carefully consider Michelangelo's proposal. But I swear to the gods that the sculptor will never again hold a chisel in his hand during my lifetime.

April 21, 1517

The Vatican

Treachery! Treason! Sacrilege! I was right to have ordered a tight watch on Petrucci. My spies intercepted a letter to his secretary, Marc Antonio Nino, in which Alfonso alludes to a conspiracy against my life. I have ordered Nino's immediate arrest and my torturers are primed to exercise their formidable art forthwith. Like my father before me, my geniality and good nature have emboldened my enemies. But unlike Lorenzo, I shall soon demonstrate that I have iron in my spine.

April 22, 1517

The Vatican

My torturers have done their job well. The diabolical nature of the plot takes away my breath and it is only by the grace of God that it did not succeed. Nino confessed that Petrucci has been insane with resentment against me for the reasons I stated earlier. At first, he resolved to assassinate me in consistory, but then changed his plan to poison.

In the last civil conversation I had with Petrucci earlier this year, he suggested I consult with the renowned Florentine surgeon, Battista da Vercelli, regarding my fistula. At the time, my own surgeon, Giacomo di Bartolomeo, had left Rome to visit his birthplace of Brescia. I thanked Alfonso for his concern, but was non-committal in my response. It therefore surprised but did not alarm me when Battista arrived at my apartment to examine my posterior. Since there was no way that I was going to allow a strange doctor to prod and poke my most intimate parts, I sent him away with a purse of ducats for his trouble.

Now I learn that Battista had been bribed by Petrucci to apply poisoned bandages to my wound, insuring a slow but dreadful death. I also know that Cardinal Sauli and Petrucci's henchman, Pocointesta, are parties to the conspiracy. I suspect other cardinals are involved, but my inquisitor and fiscal-procreator, Mario de Perusco, swears to me that the full extent of Nino's knowledge has been obtained. I ordered all involved in the interrogation sworn to secrecy upon pain of excommunication and death.

There is no one I can fully trust save Giulio. I have tripled my guard in the Apostolic Palace and will not venture forth until I know all. Visions of Ravenna are torturing me, but I am trapped like an animal in a snare. There will be no hunting for me until my hunt for co-conspirators has been successfully completed.

May 19, 1517

The Vatican

I could not rest, or even think clearly, until Petrucci was in my hands and the full extent of the conspiracy known. The war, the duplicitous Treaty of Cambrai and all other pressing matters faded into oblivion as I devised my plan. Alfonso and his brother Borghese were safely resident in Naples, but Lattanzio Petrucci was in Urbino negotiating an alliance between the Petrucci's and Francesco Maria.

My envoy was dispatched to Naples with a friendly letter from me inviting Petrucci back to Rome to discuss the possible restoration of Borghese to the government of Siena. Petrucci, knowing of his guilt, was naturally suspicious and demanded a pledge of safe-conduct, with surety from the Spanish Ambassador. I called in the Ambassador and stated that although I knew that Petrucci was treasonably corresponding with Francesco Maria, an excommunicate under interdict, I would do him no harm. The Ambassador was satisfied and Petrucci accepted his surety and returned to the Vatican.

Petrucci, accompanied by his intimate friend Sauli, arrived just a few hours ago with a sizeable train of servants. As soon as the two cardinals were admitted to my antechamber, my guards seized them and dragged them screaming them to the Marocco.° Petrucci cursed me loudly as he was taken from my presence and Sauli furiously tore his rochet to pieces. I ordered them held in complete isolation and secrecy until my interrogators had completed their work.

May 22, 1517

The Vatican

Naturally, news of the arrest of the two cardinals spread through Rome like wildfire. The Spanish Ambassador visited yesterday and protested heatedly that I had breached my pledge of safe-conduct and stained his honor and, by implication, that of Charles. He noisily demanded the immediate release of Petrucci. I quieted the insolent diplomat with a few harsh words and then presented my explanation.

First, I reminded the fuming Ambassador that I had quite specifically pledged to him that I was granting Petrucci safe-conduct in connection with his treasonous communications with Francesco Maria, a pledge which has not been broken. Of course, the Ambassador knew nothing of

---

° Translator's note: The deepest, darkest and vilest of Castel Sant'Angelo's many dungeons.

the plot against my life and was first shocked, and then chastened, when I revealed to him its diabolical nature.

I then recited the irrefutable legal principle that no instrument of safe-conduct, however full and explicit, can be allowed to avail a person who has conspired against the life of a king, emperor or supreme pontiff unless such crime was therein explicitly mentioned. Finally, I noted that the same rule applies to murder by poison, a species of guilt abhorred by all laws, human and divine. The Ambassador could not fault my argument and immediately withdrew his protest and sheepishly departed.

Word arrived today that the surgeon Battista has been seized in Florence and is on his way to Rome in chains and that Pocointesta has been apprehended in Rome. My torturers will have to work overtime.

I had scheduled a consistory today to reveal the plot, but, upon reflection, decided that it was too dangerous to place myself among the cardinals until the full scope of the conspiracy is known. So far, I have learned that Cardinal Riario, who was present at the Duomo on the day my father and uncle were brutally attacked by the Pazzi, was a participant in the plot against me. Petrucci confessed on the rack that he and Sauli had decided to anoint Riario as my successor and disclosed their intention to the cardinal, who neither protested nor exposed the horrific plan. Petrucci says no other cardinals were involved, but I do not believe him.

Riario was ordered to my chamber, where I gently interrogated him for an hour, with Cardinals Accolti and Farnese as witnesses. He disclaims any knowledge of the plot and suggests that men under torture will say anything to end the ordeal. Riario is the most senior cardinal in the College and the richest as well. He has friends everywhere and I must be careful in my handling of him.

I ordered Riario confined within a guarded apartment at the Apostolic Palace, where he is to remain in solitude while he contemplates his sin and the danger to his soul. He is not to be molested in any way and given food and drink consistent with his eminent rank.

Paris was instructed to dismiss the cardinals from consistory and to lock the chamber and post guards at its entrance. I nominated Cardinals Accolti, Farnese and Remolino to make a full investigation and report on the conspiracy. The hour is now late, but I am unlikely to sleep. Nightmares and visions have constantly plagued my mind since this diabolical conspiracy was uncovered. At times, it seems I am going mad.

June 4, 1517

The Vatican

My leniency towards Riario has been for naught. He did not change his story, proving, once again, that stern measures are always required to get to the truth. This morning, I ordered him taken to the dungeon. When my guards arrived, the old man became paralyzed with fear and had to be moved to the Castel on a litter. No sooner had he viewed (and smelled) the vile, rat-infested pit, than a full confession sprang from his lips. I now know the identity of the two other princes of the Church participating in this conspiracy.

Upon first learning of the plot, I summoned Giulio from the papal army to assist me in dealing with the treachery. He arrived yesterday and first briefed me on the war. The situation remains bleak, with my condottieri doing everything in their power to prolong the conflict. The various Spanish, French, Gascon, German and Swiss mercenaries in my employ are fighting more among themselves than against the enemy.

Naturally, my first impulse in dealing with the traitors in the College is to draw and quarter each one of them. But Giulio, being once removed from the plot, has urged a more lenient, but lucrative, approach. By granting pardon to all but Petrucci and Sauli, accompanied by stiff fines, I can both demonstrate my well-known magnanimity while at the same time filling the empty Vatican coffers. Appreciating the merit of his suggestion, I have now settled upon my course.

June 8, 1517

The Vatican

I am exhausted and tormented beyond belief, but I have resolved to record today's events since I know that sleep will not come readily. After Mass, I held a private consistory with the cardinals in residence. For an hour, I channeled the ghost of Julius, raging, bellowing and cursing my unfaithful subordinates. The effect was pronounced. While we were all relatively immune to Julius' outbursts, being frequent and quickly forgotten, none of my colleagues had ever seen me other than genial of disposition in my two decades in the College. I could see fear and guilt in their faces as I delivered my oration.

Leaving unrepeated my intemperate words, I began by bitterly complaining that my life should have been so cruelly and insidiously attempted by those who, having been raised to such high dignity, and who, being the principal members of the Apostolic See, were bound beyond all others to defend me. And yet, those who I could have least suspected, those into whose hands I have entrusted my life, are guilty of this heinous crime. I then reminded them of the kindness and liberality which I had uniformly shown to every individual of the Sacred College, even to a degree which has been imputed to me as a weakness; and yet this was my undeserved reward.

I then outlined the details of the plot which had been confessed by Petrucci, Sauli and Riario and stated that I knew the identities of the other members of the conspiracy. I called upon the guilty to make their peace by a prompt confession; otherwise, they would immediately join Petrucci and Sauli in the Marocco. Silence prevailed in the chamber.

Softening my tone, I stated that however pained I might be by the ingratitude of those whom I had loaded with honors and benefactions, I was willing to forgive them, after the example of Him whose place I fill on earth, provided they would confess their misdeed and ask for pardon. Silence still prevailed. Cardinal Farnese then suggested that each individual cardinal approach me, swear an oath, and whisper in my ear his guilt or innocence. This suggestion was ratified by the College and, one by one, they approached my throne, took their oath and whispered in my ear.

When Cardinal Soderini, whose family instigated the rebellion against the Medici in Florence, whispered in my ear his innocence, his obstinacy enraged me. I pushed him away from my throne and bellowed at him that I knew he was guilty; that I would have pardoned him if an honest confession had been made, but now justice must take its course.

Upon hearing those words, Soderini fell to the floor, groveled towards me and attempted to kiss my feet. Copious tears flowed from his eyes. In halting, pitiful tones, he confessed his part in the plot. He attributed his betrayal to my failure to honor the pledge made at the conclave to marry Lorenzo to a Soderini girl. He then begged for my pardon and implored my mercy.

I ignored the prostrate cardinal and addressed the College: "There is yet another traitor in our midst. He must confess now." When no one spoke, Farnese and Accolti turned to Cardinal Adrian di Corneto and advised him to humble himself and make confession. Like Soderini, he fell prostrate and tearfully confessed his guilt. He claimed a soothsayer had told him that the next pontiff would be a man of common birth named Adrian and therefore believed the conspiracy was sanctioned by divine will.°

As promised, I granted the two traitors my pardon and set their fine at 25,000 ducats, an amount unanimously ratified by the College.

° Translator's note: The soothsayer was correct. Leo's successor was Cardinal Adrian Dedel of Utretcht, no relation to Adrian di Corneto.

June 15, 1517

The Vatican

At consistory today, I announced my intention to expand the membership of the College substantially. As I expected, there was much grumbling and allusions to the pledge made at the conclave not to name additional cardinals (a pledge I had already broken by naming eight, although the College had ratified my selections). I told the cardinals that my pledge is null and void, given that the present College is replete with assassins, traitors and conspirators by silence. I ordered Pocointesta hung tomorrow at the Castel. His complicity in the plot was minimal, so his sentence is merciful. A much worse fate awaits the principal villains.

Soderini and Adrian di Corneto came to the consistory accompanied by bags holding 25,000 ducats. I told them they misunderstood the fine; it was clearly for 25,000 ducats each, not jointly. They insolently sought clarification from the College, but no one dared contradict me. Their faces remained crestfallen throughout the consistory.

Today, I dispatched briefs to the sovereigns of Europe seeking their recommendations of men worthy of elevation to the purple. They must understand that having a friend in the pope is superior to the friendship of a deposed duke.

June 20, 1517

The Vatican

Only twelve cardinals attended consistory today. I was informed that both Soderini and Adrian di Corneto fled Rome sometime last night. Collecting the remaining 25,000 ducats will now be more difficult, but not impossible. I set the notaries to work on the writs to seize their properties.

At consistory, I degraded the principal conspirators, Petrucci, Sauli and Riario, from their ecclesiastical titles, preferments, benefices and properties. There was major grumbling regarding Riario and minor complaints regarding Sauli. Nobody objected to Petrucci being deprived, as his character is inimical to all. Riario's properties alone will go a long way towards closing the gap on the war's financing.

Lorenzo arrived in Rome two days ago. He has fully recovered from his wound, but I was shocked to see the pox of the French boils upon his face and hands. He also coughs incessantly, perhaps a sign of consumption as well. I must redouble my efforts to find him a match before his maladies become too far advanced. I need a male Medici heir; otherwise, all will have been for naught.

June 22, 1517

The Vatican

I am exhausted in mind and body. Today's consistory lasted a full thirteen grueling hours. I first read to the College the minutes of the trial of Petrucci, Sauli and Riario, which has now been concluded. Then, I read to them the full confessions of the three miscreant cardinals. The evidence and the confessions establish beyond any doubt whatsoever that they are guilty of attempted murder by poison, conspiracy and treason. The question was put to the College and all save Grimani of Venice (who fancies himself above the Vicar of Christ and actually raised his voice in anger against me) voted to confirm the verdict.

My secretary, Pietro Bembo, then presented the recommendation for punishment determined by my fiscal-advocate, Justino de Carosis, and my fiscal-procurator, Mario de Perusco: that in addition to forfeiture of their titles, benefices and properties, the three cardinals be turned over to the secular authorities for corporeal punishment. This last recommendation prompted much agitation within the College. Since the universal civil sentence for treason is hanging, drawing and quartering, there was loud remonstrance that a prince of the Church must never be subjected to such indignity.

I angrily reminded the cardinals that I, their Holy Father and Supreme Pontiff, concurred in the judgment and therefore it was correct and just. I pledged to send any cardinal who failed to ratify the recommendation to the Castel to contemplate his error at length. It was only after the recommendation was approved that, in softer tones, I confirmed my inclination to bestow Apostolic grace upon Riario and Sauli.

June 27, 1517

The Vatican

Antonio Nino and Battista da Vercelli received their just punishment today. After one last session on the rack, they were dragged through Rome on hurdles, drawn and quartered with red-hot pincers and then strangled on gibbets suspended from the parapet of the bridge by Sant'Angelo. Had my father shown such fortitude in dealing with his enemies, the Medici fortune would likely be intact today.

I have been inundated with suggestions of men deserving of the purple, as well as pleas for mercy for Riario and Sauli. The negotiations with Riario's family have gone well. A 150,000 ducat fine has been agreed upon, with 50,000 ducats paid now through a loan from Agostino

Chigi and the balance paid over two years and secured by a 150,000 ducat penal surety bond issued by Chigi. In addition, sureties are to be issued by each of the remaining thirteen cardinals, as well as the Ambassadors of Germany, England, France, Spain, Portugal and Venice. It is truly impressive how well-connected Riario has turned out to be. Assuming he pays the first installment, I have agreed to restore him to all of his forfeited offices and dignities.

The same cannot be said for Sauli. Although my brother-in-law, Franceschetto Cibo, his son, Cardinal Cibo and even King Francis have all pleaded for leniency, only 25,000 ducats has been offered as penalty. For that paltry amount, he gets neither his titles nor his freedom, but his life will be spared.

July 1, 1517

The Vatican

Today, the cardinals obediently, but unhappily, ratified the thirty-one red hats I have created (since sufficient titles do not exist, I have appointed a commission to select additional ones). No longer will I have to contend with dissension within the Sacred College, as each of the men I have raised is entirely beholden to me. No longer will a small cabal of ambitious men undermine my rule.

I have neither the patience nor the energy to set forth the credentials of each, but will mention a select few. Among the "political" appointments are Louis de Bourbon, King Francis' cousin, King Manual's seven year old son Alfonso (he must wait until he is fourteen before taking the insignia of office), Adrian of Utretcht and Gulielmo Vick, both championed by King Charles, Pompeo Colonna, Franciotto Orsino, Scaramuccio Trivulzio and Agostino Trivulzio. My family appointments include three of my nephews, Niccolo Ridolfi, Giovanni Salviati and Luigi Rossi. I also gave a red hat to Bianca Rangone's son, Ercole, to show my gratitude for her great kindness to me when I was a prisoner after Ravenna.

All of these men are perfectly well suited by piety, learning and temperament, for the Sacred College. However, the great majority of my appointments are ecclesiastics of the highest degree of worthiness. These include the Vicar-Generals of the Augustinians, Dominicans and Franciscans, Lorenzo Campeggio of Bologna, Giovanni Piccolomini of Siena and Alessandro Cesarini of Pistoia.

July 4, 1517

The Vatican

Alfonso Petrucci was dispatched to Hell this morning. I have taken to heart the concern expressed by many in the College that executing a cardinal in the same manner as a common criminal would set an unfortunate precedent. My chief executioner also sought an audience with me and expressed concern for his soul should he take the life of a prince of the Church. I assured the poor man that one never endangered one's soul by obeying the Holy Father, but, out of compassion, relieved him of his obligation. I assigned the task to Orlando, a Moor in my service who took great delight in his new commission. As befitted his eminent rank, Petrucci was slowly strangled with a purple sash.

I was told by the scandalized priest who presided at the execution that Petrucci cursed me repeatedly and refused to make his confession or receive the sacrament. He said that if he was doomed to lose his life, he cared nothing what became of his soul. It is shocking that such a man could have ever worn a red hat.

August 15, 1517

The Vatican

I earlier wrote that events which might originally appear to be the work of Satan sometimes turn out to be divine blessings. Petrucci's conspiracy appears to be one of those events. The power of the old Sacred College has been broken and the new College is completely subservient to my will. The fines imposed upon the conspirators and the fees received from the new cardinals have brought over 500,000 ducats to my treasury, more than enough to see the war in Urbino through to a successful conclusion. An additional 100,000 ducats has arrived from Henry, being the promised reward for my signature upon the Treaty of London. There is even good news from Germany. Johann Tetzel, a Dominican inquisitor who is my Commissioner of Indulgences for Germany, has exceeded all expectations in his dispensation of indulgences for construction of St. Peter's. The monk is apparently a masterful salesman. It is unfortunate that I must split half of the revenue with Jacob Fugger.

Francis and Charles are both grateful that I honored their nominations for red hats and wise enough to know that, with my pecuniary problems now behind me, there is no profit in continuing to prop up the pretensions of Francesco Maria. Both have pledged to withdraw their subjects from his army and to mediate an honorable surrender of Urbino to Lorenzo. Best of all, Francis has offered his cousin, Madeleine de la Tour d'Auvergne, as a bride for Lorenzo. The marriage is to take place in France as soon as the gifts and wardrobe can be assembled. I pray the boy's maladies are checked until he successfully concludes his connubial duty.

September 30, 1517

The Vatican

I am pleased to record that the war to recover Urbino has now been successfully concluded. True to their word, Francis and Charles have persuaded Francesco Maria to permanently renounce his claim to the duchy and retire in exile to Mantua. Lorenzo is now the undisputed ruler of Urbino, recognized by all. In return, I have graciously granted amnesty and lifted all ecclesiastical sanctions against Francesco Maria and his followers and have paid the arrearage owed to his soldiers (more than 100,000 ducats, but it is money well spent).

With this distraction now resolved, I can return my full attention to the greatest danger facing Christendom – the despicable Turks. In 1512, that bloodthirsty Mohammedan, Selim, seized the Ottoman throne by murdering his father, Bajazet, as well as his brothers and nephews. Once firmly ensconced, the Sultan unleashed vicious successful campaigns against his Mohammedan brethren, including the Sophi of Persia and the Sultan of Egypt.

But his ultimate goal has always been to destroy Christianity. He has made incursions in Hungary, Poland and Italy (I have previously written of his attempt to capture me). Yet, despite this obvious danger to the bodies and souls of all who belong to the Church, no major European ruler save Manuel of Portugal has opposed with arms the Turkish advance. Indeed Venice, whose principal religion is the worship of gold, has entered into a secret treaty of non-belligerence with this son of Satan.

It is folly to sit still and suppose that this ferocious enemy can be conquered by prayers alone. I resolve, in the coming months, to organize the largest and most powerful Crusade ever launched against the infidels. I will not rest until Constantinople, Damascus, Alexandria, Cairo and Jerusalem are back in Christian hands and all Mohammedans have been converted, enslaved or sent to Hell.

October 15, 1517

The Vatican

I called in the Venetian Ambassador this afternoon and demanded that Venice pledge to join the Crusade and provide the naval vessels required to transport the Christian army across the Adriatic. His mealy-mouthed response: "While awaiting special orders from Venice, I must confine myself to generalities." I am not content to wait. I am appointing my able friend, Altobello Averoldo, Bishop of Pola, as Ambassador and papal legate to the Republic to personally deliver my message directly to the Senate.

November 4, 1517

The Vatican

Today, I named a congregation, consisting of Cardinals Carvajal, Remolino, Fieschi, Grassis, Pucci, Medici, Farnese and Cornaro, to address the specifics of the upcoming Crusade. The time has come to move from the realm of proposal to the realm of action. I have invited envoys of all the European rulers to attend the sessions of the congregation, which shall begin in two days. I shall personally preside over its sessions. The Vicar-Generals of the Augustinians, Dominicans and Franciscans have been ordered to command their brethren to forthwith preach the Crusade throughout Europe. There will be no turning back from this godly mission.

November 12, 1517

The Vatican

The work of the congregation has been successfully concluded in an amazingly short period of time (which serves as testament to the justice of the cause). I posed six questions to the cardinals and summarize their responses as follows:

1. Should the war be undertaken? Yes, absolutely.

2. Should it be a war of offense or defense? Offense, as it would show more courage and secure the advantage of an earlier discovery of the enemy's weak point.

3. What obstacles are in the way and how should they be removed? The chief obstacle must come from discord among the princes of Christendom. This must be overcome by a universal peace or a truce for so long as the Holy War shall last. The Pope or the Sacred College must be charged to arbitrate any interim

disputes. The princes must form a league under the Pope, the Brotherhood of the Holy Crusade, and pledge by oath to put down by force of arms those who break the peace. Arbitrators should be appointed now to award possession of the captured lands.

4. Should the war be conducted by all the princes, or only by some; and, if so, by whom? The Emperor and King of France, as the most powerful of the princes of Christendom, must be at the head of the combined powers, but all others should be bound to cooperate in the Crusade according to their strength.

5. By what means shall it be carried on? By the grace of God which shall be prayed for unceasingly. The strength of the army shall be 60,000 foot soldiers (Swiss, Germans, Spaniards and Bohemians), 12,000 light cavalry (Spaniards, Italians, Dalmatians and Greeks) and 4,000 heavy cavalry (French and Italians). Ships shall be supplied by Venice, Genoa, Naples, Provence, Spain, Portugal and England. The budget for the Crusade shall be 800,000 ducats. The princes themselves shall contribute a goodly portion of their income, because it is with them that the enemy mostly concerns himself, taking but little account of the common folk. The monasteries shall give a tenth, two-thirds, or even three-quarters of their income, limiting their private expenditures to the necessaries of life, so that they may dedicate all the remainder to the holy work, for which they are mainly responsible as the possessors of the heritage of Christ. Nobles shall give a tenth and burghers a twentieth of their income. Finally, people who live by the work of their hands shall each give a suitable contribution.

6. How should it be started? By a massive attack upon Constantinople. Troops should be assembled at Ancona and Brindisi and transported across the Adriatic Sea. The remainder of the navy should be based in Sicily, because from thence Greece and Egypt are easily reached.

Memoranda setting forth the recommendations of the congregation are being conveyed to the princes of Europe for their review and ratification. We shall shortly know who the pious rulers are.

December 22, 1517

The Vatican

I have grown increasingly annoyed with Michelangelo, who has been in Carrara for months and has not yet produced a single sketch for the San Lorenzo façade (or quarried a single acceptable marble). All he does is make demands for more ducats and more time through his agent. I summoned him back to Rome for an audience, which took place this afternoon.

After greeting him warmly and bestowing my blessing, I made inquiry on the state of his commission. He showed Giulio and me some preliminary sketches which, frankly, could have been conceived by any draftsman of modest talent. Giulio then informed the sculptor that we have decided not to use marble from Carrara, whose people are rebellious and disobedient (and delinquent in their taxes to the Holy See). Instead, he must use good Tuscan marble from Pietrasanta, which is reputedly the finest in the world.

Michelangelo protested heatedly that it was impossible to transport large stones from the high slopes of Monte Altissimo to the sea for shipment to Rome. The ancient Romans themselves had tried and failed. I responded that no task was impossible for the genius who had conquered the Sistine ceiling. It was only a matter of devoting himself fully to the task.

As might be expected, Michelangelo departed the audience in the height of ill-temper. But I have no doubt that he will succeed in opening up the Pietrasanta quarry; he is too obstinate to admit to the possibility of failure. When he succeeds, it will inure to the benefit of both San Lorenzo and Florence (which holds the rights to the marble within the mountain). It will also keep the chisel from his hand for at least a few more years.

After the artist left, Giulio briefed me on a situation in Saxony (a traditional hotbed of heresy). An Augustinian monk on the faculty of the University of Wittenberg has circulated a pamphlet containing theses attacking the legitimacy of the indulgences which are being so successfully dispensed by the Dominican Tetzel. Giulio tells me the monk suffers from extreme constipation and conceived his excremental arguments while sitting upon the latrine. He is apparently also a drunkard. I laughed and told Giulio that I am sure he will feel differently when he sobers up. Theological squabbles between monks of different Orders are commonplace in that cold, forbidding country.

December 31, 1517

The Vatican

Another year passes, but this is no time for joyful celebration. As yet, not a single prince has responded to the memorandum of my congregation. They all should be excommunicated. The Turks menace Christendom and all they do is plot and scheme against each other. Why does God permit this?

January 20, 1518

The Vatican

The responses from the princes are arriving. I am deeply disappointed, but not shocked. We live in an age ruled by greed and the unholy pursuit of power and riches. Piety and sacrifice are scorned as relics of the past. Francis, while agreeing in principle to the Crusade, wants exclusive control of the funds, with the Crusade tithe raised three years in advance and given to him. He wants exclusive command of the main army (all French) at Ancona and Brindisi, with the Emperor proceeding overland through the Balkans and Charles, Henry and Manuel remaining with the fleet.

Maximilian's proposal is quite different. He recommends a three year war. In the first year, Francis and Henry remain at home, raising the war tax, while the Emperor leads a combined German and Spanish army against North Africa, culminating in the capture of Cairo and Alexandria. In the second year, Francis captures Macedonia and in the third year, Maximilian leads the combined armies against Constantinople. He proposes raising the army by requiring each parish in Christendom to provide one soldier for each fifty residents and financing the Crusade with a tax upon every hearth.

Charles rejects entirely the recommendation of an offensive war and proposes, instead, strengthening the vulnerable defenses in southern Italy (his lands). Henry's response is most peculiar. He warns against any military action, stating he knows that Francis will march his army through Italy, not for the purpose of transporting across the Adriatic towards the Turks, but rather to conquer Italy and depose the Holy Father. I cannot state with certainty that he is wrong.

It is clear that I cannot rely upon these jealous and self-interested princes. Using my spiritual power as the Supreme Pontiff, I must create a great groundswell of support for the Crusade that the princes will be powerless to resist.

February 3, 1518

The Vatican

The Dominicans press me to take action against the Augustinian monk, Martin Luther, who continues to attack Tetzel and the indulgences for St. Peter's. I have now had the opportunity to personally review his ninety-five theses and, while many are harmless, a number are insolent and not in accord with canon law. Luther appears to be a man of talent, albeit misguided.

From my own personal observations of that miserable region, I draw the conclusion that I must proceed cautiously to keep the zealotry of the Saxon clergy and citizenry in check. They have a fundamental bias towards heresy and disobedience to the authority of Rome.

Today, I called in the Vicar-General of the Augustinians, Gabriele della Volta, and directed him to remonstrate with Luther, either by letter or through learned and upright envoys, and urge him to refrain from disseminating his new doctrines. I believe this is the best strategy for extinguishing this new flame so lately kindled.

March 15, 1518

The Vatican

My campaign to convince the princes to participate in the Crusade is proceeding well. On March 3, I named my most persuasive cardinal-diplomats to serve as special legates for the Crusade. Bibbiena will travel to France, Canisio to Spain, Farnese to Germany and Campeggio to England. They will treat directly with the Kings and Emperor and underscore their spiritual obligation to implement the plan developed by the congregation.

On March 6, I issued a Bull explaining in great detail the menace posed by the Mohammedans and requiring all Christian princes to agree to a five year truce, under the severest penalties of the Church. All disputes during the period of the truce will be equitably resolved by the Holy See.

Last Friday, March 12, the first of three great intercessory processions I ordered to beseech God for the Crusade commenced in Rome. All shops were shut and the streets hung with drapery and tapestry. Alters were constructed at the major intersections. The parade began at St. Agostino and ended at Santa Maria in Aracoeli. It was led by the Confraternities of Rome, followed by the religious orders and secular clergy, carrying relics and finally the papal household.

On Saturday, the procession proceeded from San Lorenzo to Santa Maria del Popolo. In this procession, Rome's most sacred relics were paraded through the streets – the heads of St. Andrew and St. Matthew, the Chair of St. Peter, the Holy Lance, the Sudarium of St. Veronica and the fragment of the True Cross from Santa Croce in Jerusalem. These powerful relics will assuredly work their magic with God. The Mohammedans have nothing to compare with them.

Sunday's procession went from St. Peter's (where Cardinal Farnese read the Bull proclaiming the five year truce from the pulpit) to Santa Maria sopra Minerva. All of the ambassadors, bishops and cardinals resident in Rome walked in the procession, as did I. I walked barefoot the entire way to demonstrate my humility before God. The throngs along the route cheered me continuously and I was overcome with emotion by the love for me and passion for the Crusade so evident among the common people of Rome. I stopped often to give my benediction and distribute coins to the faithful.

Upon my return to the Vatican, I ordered the cardinals and generals of the principal orders to organize similar processions in every major city in Europe. Once the princes see their subjects rising up in support of the Crusade, they will be hard-pressed to refuse to do their duty.

April 12, 1518

The Vatican

At consistory today, I gave my blessing to Bibbiena, Farnese and Campeggio, who will depart shortly on their critical missions in support of the Crusade. Cardinal Lang has been pestering me daily to appoint him as co-legate to the Emperor, but I have demurred. I believe Lang fancies himself already as the Supreme Pontiff. He certainly makes no secret of his ambitions. Word has arrived from Venice that the Senate has refused permission for intercessory processions to be held in the city. These duplicitous merchants are intent upon preserving their mercantile relationship with the Sultan, even at the expense of the Church and their mortal souls.

Lorenzo will also depart this week for his marriage ceremony in France. The wardrobe and gifts have been assembled and are of unprecedented magnificence. I am giving Francis a train of thirty-six horses, together with exquisite harness and a slave attendant for each horse. For the bride, a gorgeous matrimonial bed constructed of tortoiseshell inlaid with mother-of-pearl and encrusted with precious stones.

Cardinal Pucci complained that the cost of the wedding has exceeded 300,000 ducats, the Vatican treasury is drained and we are once again beholden to the bankers (each of whom is worse than any Jew). I told him not to worry; God has always provided for me in the past and will do so again, since the cause is just.

Lorenzo's French boils have progressed to an advanced state and his face has been ravaged. Unlike Cesare Borgia, he refuses to wear a mask in public and people of delicate disposition recoil in horror upon observing his visage. I cannot permit any feelings of Madeleine to interfere with completion of the match and production of an heir. If the gifts induce Francis to see the ceremony through, every ducat will have been well spent. One cannot put a price upon peace between France and the Holy See.

April 29, 1518

La Magliana

Thank God my safety is now sufficiently secure that I can venture forth for a hunt. Although the temperature is hot and the fever season approaching, I could no longer constrain my one remaining passion. Today was an excellent day. We began this morning chasing roe-deer and boar, but the pain in my posterior from sitting in the saddle soon displaced the pleasure of the chase. I then switched to my sedan chair and spent the rest of the morning hawking. After a splendid lunch, I let the dogs loose on a cornered deer and watched with delight as they set upon it.

Good news has also arrived from France. The wedding proceeded as planned on April 25 and was a complete success. I am told that the Seigneur de Fleurange declared the jousts and banquets in Lorenzo's honor at the royal castle of Amboise to have been the most sumptuous ever held in France or even in all Christendom. Hopefully, the French boils have not yet corroded Lorenzo's manly parts and a male heir will soon be produced.

June 15, 1518

The Vatican

That impudent Augustinian, Luther, continues to be an irritant. The Dominicans have eagerly forwarded to me the transcript of a sermon Luther breached in Wittenberg questioning my unquestionable right to excommunicate heretics and other enemies of the Church. Luther also sent me a letter defending his execrable theses and professing obedience to my decisions providing they have "their origin in Jesus, without whom you cannot propose or state anything." How dare he suggest that my decisions are anything else but the commands of Jesus? I am His Vicar and Representative on earth. My decisions cannot be questioned or interpreted by a constipated monk.

I do not want to elevate Luther above his station by paying undue attention to his ramblings. But the Dominicans say that his theses are being well-received in Germany (no great surprise) and are being published throughout Europe. This cannot continue. Today, I assigned Girolamo Ghinucci, Auditor-General of Legal Causes to the Apostolic Camera and Prierias, Master of the Sacred Palaces, to undertake a preliminary inquiry as to whether Luther is propagating false doctrines.

I also appointed Leonardo Crivelli as Inquisitor-General of Lombardy. In my brief, I order Crivelli to pay special attention to those who seek to know more than it is well to know, and who think ill of the Holy See; these he must repress with the free use of torture, incarceration, and other penalties, and to pay over their confiscated property to the papal camera, no matter of what condition or dignity they might be. I have been far too lenient with the enemies of the Church. The Church has flourished and prospered for 1,500 years for one reason alone – its doctrines are true and ordained by God. I am the Holy Father of the one true Church, sanctified by the Holy Spirit, and have the duty and obligation to be zealous in its defense. I just wish the so-called Christian princes took their obligations as seriously as I do.

Maximilian has refused to allow Cajetan[°] into Germany unless I appoint Lang as co-legate. No doubt Lang put him up to this. But, given that I have no control over Maximilian, I have given in to the demand and appointed Lang co-legate. With luck, he will be struck by lightening on his journey north. Henry has surprised me by refusing to admit Campeggio to England unless I strip him of all legatine powers and invest them in his chief minister, Cardinal Wolsey, whose naked ambition exceeds that of Lang. Clearly, when I cleaned house last year, I did not sweep the broom with adequate vigor. I am tired of the petty plots and endless scheming that is rampant within the Sacred College.

July 22, 1518

The Vatican

Treachery. I received a letter today from Campeggio. That snake Wolsey has negotiated a separate peace between England and France, to which Charles and Maximilian are being invited to join. There is apparently no provision for the Crusade or for arbitration of disputes by the Holy See. My effort to save Christendom has been undermined by this disloyal cardinal. And Henry and Francis have also betrayed me by keeping their negotiations secret.

[°]Translator's note: Cardinal Farnese had become ill and was replaced as legate by Cardinal Cajetan.

Giulio showed me a letter Michelangelo wrote to him last week. It seems the artist, without consulting me, has purchased land from the Cathedral Chapter in Florence to store the marbles for San Lorenzo that he is quarrying at Pietrasanta (just as I predicted, the obstinate genius has succeeded in opening the quarry and a road to the sea). Michelangelo complains that the Archbishop charged him sixty ducats more than the land is worth, which the Archbishop claims is required by my Bull on procedures for the sale of lands by the Church. The sarcastic artist writes to my cousin: "Now if the Pope makes Bulls to license stealing, I beg your most reverend lordship to have still another made for me." I am of half a mind to have his hands broken. But I have settled upon a more amusing punishment. I will order the marbles sculpted by his competitors in accordance with his designs. Given their placement high in the façade, any imperfections will be imperceptible to the observer. But it will irritate Michelangelo for the rest of his days.

On the subject of irritation, I am irate with Prierias. He has published, without my review, a refutation of Luther's theses. He has entirely botched the job. His logic is flawed, his references to canon law inaccurate and his tone bombastic and filled with invective and innuendo. Luther's theses (which Prierias reprints in their entirety) appear the work of a scholar; Prierias' refutation, the ramblings of an ignorant novice. I understand he is quite proud that he produced his refutation in just three days. He would have done better to work on it for three months.

I do not wish to involve myself directly in this matter, but it will resolve itself successfully only if I take personal charge. I told Ghinucci and Prierias to summons Luther to Rome within sixty days, upon pain of the severest penalties. We will see how this monk fares against the Supreme Pontiff.

August 22, 1518

The Vatican

I have received two disturbing letters from Germany. The first from Cajetan, who is attending the Diet of the Empire at Augsburg, reports that the representatives of the German States have rejected my proposals for a Crusade tax and that Luther is being protected by Frederick, the Elector of Saxony.

The second letter is from Maximilian and is even more disturbing. He reports that Luther's doctrines are being embraced throughout his Empire and that even the princes of the States are in rebellion against the Church. He demands that I immediately excommunicate Luther and put an end to his heretical preaching. He writes that the very authority of the Church and the Empire is at stake. He also desires to abdicate his title of King of the Romans in favor of his grandson Charles. This will make Charles' election as the next Holy Roman Emperor (Maximilian's health is apparently failing) a foregone conclusion.

I cannot permit the thrones of Spain and the Empire to become united in one monarch. Rome is just forty miles from the border with the Neapolitan state, which is firmly under Charles' control. This is far too grave a danger to the independence of the Church.

August 23, 1518

The Vatican

Today, I acted decisively to end Luther's heresy. I dispatched a secret warrant to Cajetan, ordering him to immediately arrest Luther and examine him. If Luther voluntarily surrenders, repudiates and begs pardon for his offenses, Cajetan is authorized to receive him into the unity of the holy mother, the Church. If Luther persists in his obstinacy, he is to be transported to Rome in shackles. I have also commanded Cajetan to banish, curse and excommunicate all who adhere to Luther and to order all Christians to shun his presence. Cajetan is also ordered to excommunicate all prelates, religious orders, universities, communities, counts, dukes and potentates, excepting only Maximilian, who fail to seize Luther or who condone his heresy. I have sent a copy of the warrant to the Vicar-General of the Saxon Augustinian Order with instructions to bind Luther hand and foot and forthwith deliver him to Cajetan.

I have also sent a secret letter to Frederick. In it, I intimate that if he withdraws his protection of Luther, he will be my choice as Maximilian's successor. This would be a perfect outcome.

September 10, 1518

The Vatican

My instincts have proven true yet again. I received a letter today from Cajetan. Maximilian has been pressing the Electors to pledge their votes for Charles as his successor and all but Frederick have agreed. Frederick has met with Cajetan and agreed to turn Luther over to the Church for trial. However, he insists that the trial be held in Augsburg; otherwise, the nationalistic tendencies of the Germans will become inflamed and his own standing with the other Electors will be diminished.

I dispatched a reply to Cajetan authorizing him to preside at the trial as my legate. I also awarded Frederick the Golden Rose, the highest honor I may bestow upon a temporal ruler. Frederick will make an excellent Emperor.

November 8, 1518

The Vatican

The greatest curse in my life is not my suppurating fistula, although it pains me every day. It is not the memories of Ravenna, which cripple my mind and make life unbearable. It is not even the loss of everyone I have loved (and Hanno) and the resulting melancholy that is my unwanted companion. No, the greatest curse in my life is that I have constantly been surrounded by incompetent men upon whom I am forced by necessity to rely.

My instructions to Cajetan were simple and clear: either accept Luther's complete and unequivocal recantation of his heretical doctrines or clap him in chains and transport him to Rome. So what did Cajetan do in Augsburg? He allowed Luther to goad him into a three day long academic debate over obscure theological principles. Even worse, at the end of the debate he conceded that Luther was correct that there were no definitive papal decretals on the precise nature of indulgences. And worst of all, he permitted Luther to leave Augsburg and return home to Wittenberg under the protection of Frederick.

Cajetan has backed me into a corner. To prove Luther a heretic, he suggests I must first issue a Bull setting forth the Church's definitive position on the theological underpinnings of indulgences. In the Bull *Unigenitus Dei Filius*, Clement VI ruled that the pope, as the keeper of the keys, may dispense indulgences for the remission of sins from the treasury of indulgences composed of the merits and sufferings of our Lord Jesus Christ and the Saints. Luther suggests that indulgences grant remission of only temporal penalties (penance remits the guilt) and that the pope, as keeper of the keys, does not directly release the merits from the treasury, but rather petitions God to do so.

This scholarly debate is of no interest to me. Whether I release the merits or petition God to release the merits is irrelevant so long as the ducats from their dispensation continue to flow to Rome, because Raphael is insatiable in his demands for cash for St. Peter's, which is no doubt the most expensive building project in the history of the world (as well it should be as the new home of the Church).

Today, I promulgated the Bull *Cum Postquam*, which adopts Luther's interpretation but which unequivocally establishes the pope's right to dispense indulgences. If he continues to preach against the campaign for St. Peter's, he will, by his own admission, be committing heresy and be subject to excommunication.

So now, I have reversed the situation and boxed Luther and Frederick into a corner. Luther dares not openly contradict the Holy Father and Frederick can no longer protect him if he does. The irony of the situation is that if Ghinucci, Prierias and Cajetan knew their canon law as well as Luther, this entire controversy could have been quietly resolved months ago and Luther would today be lecturing in Wittenberg and groaning on the latrine, unknown to the world at large.

November 15, 1518

The Vatican

Maximilian, Francis and Charles, who betrayed me by signing Cardinal Wolsey's Treaty of London last month, have been unceasing in their recent demands upon me. Maximilian is now holding his support for the Crusade hostage to my crowning him Emperor. Since 1508, he has technically been only the Emperor-Elect because he has never found the time to travel to Rome for the coronation ceremony; now he is too ill to travel south and wants me to journey north. He wants this to cement Charles' claim to the crown after his death. Charles wants a dispensation from the ancient Bull that prohibits the crowns of Rome and Naples from residing in one sovereign (over my dead body will he get this).

But it is Francis who vexes me most. Since the marriage between Lorenzo and Madeleine, he has treated me as the lesser relation. Every day, I have granted the king some fresh favor. No sooner is it bestowed than he presses some new and weighty demand upon me, as if he had received nothing before. He has awarded benefices in Milan without my knowledge or blessing; he has conspired with the traitor Duke of Ferrara; he has clandestinely encouraged discord within the Papal States. Now, he not only wants me to block the crowning of Maximilian and the election of Charles, but he wants the crown of the Empire for himself.

I am not in humor of granting the requests of any of these princes. At least not until there is something of substantial value for the Church. In any case, I have firmly settled upon Frederick of Saxony as my choice for Emperor (although I keep this intelligence to myself).

Today, I appointed one of my chamberlains, Karl von Miltitz, who is a Saxon himself, as papal nuncio to Frederick. He will travel to Germany to deliver the Golden Rose, as well as two dispensations annulling the effects of illegitimate birth for Frederick's bastard sons; patronage notes for ecclesiastical offices for Frederick to dispense; and blank Bulls of Excommunication for Frederick's political enemies. In return, Frederick must silence Luther and pledge his obedience to the Holy See after his election.

November 29, 1518

The Vatican

Francis has apparently become discomfited by the silence from the Vatican and now fears that I will endorse the claims of Charles to Naples and the Empire. A letter arrived today from Bibbiena which reports an entirely new and more favorable attitude of the king towards the Holy See. He has pledged to subordinate his own candidacy for Emperor in favor of any choice I might make, so long as it is not Charles. He has renewed his pledge to commit a sizeable French army to the Crusade (and to personally lead it), provided I release to him personally the second Crusade tenth to finance it. I have written Bibbiena that I am amenable to releasing the taxes, provided he pays 100,000 ducats to Lorenzo to help with his living expenses. We shall see what happens.

December 15, 1518

The Vatican

Last month, I referred Maximilian's request to be crowned Emperor outside of Rome and Charles' request for a dispensation to wear the crowns of both Naples and Rome to the Papal Master of Ceremonies and the Papal Protonotary for their review and recommendations. Today, they presented their reports to the full Congregation of the Sacred College. They have recommended, on the basis of clear precedent, that both requests be denied as incompatible with canon law. The Sacred College debated the recommendations for six hours. While the cardinals had every wish to be conciliatory and honor the requests of the monarchs, the difficult and important legal issues presented necessitated additional careful study. Thus, the matter was deferred to a later meeting.

I shall write Maximilian and Charles tomorrow pledging to do everything within my power to facilitate a prompt and favorable vote by the College, which, of course, is a mandatory legal prerequisite. Certainly, I personally have no objection to traveling to Verona or Mantua to conduct the coronation, but am deeply concerned that such a journey might unduly tire the Emperor. I shall send copies of my letters to Francis and Bibbiena, which may help speed conclusion of a treaty of friendship between France and the Holy See.

January 15, 1519

The Vatican

It is a pleasant change to report that a new year is starting off well. I received a report from Miltitz, who has met with Luther. Luther has finally admitted his errors and the grave damage to Christianity which might flow from them. He has pledged to maintain silence regarding his doctrines, provided I silence his opponents. Tetzel, Prierias and Cajetan have caused me sufficient embarrassment already by their incompetence, so muzzling them is no burden. Luther will write to me a letter of contrition and publish a document calling upon his followers not to view his writings as attacking the Roman Church and urging them to remain subject to the Church. I could not ask for a better outcome.

The treaty between the Holy See and Francis has been completed and is awaiting Francis' signature. In it, I have authorized Francis to control the second tenth and Francis is required to repay 100,000 ducats within four years. Francis and Holy See pledge the mutual defense of their possessions and the sharing of all state secrets. Francis specifically acknowledges the spiritual jurisdiction of the Holy See in Milan. The treaty contains no specific obligation on my part regarding the upcoming election for Emperor. There is a secret annex between the Medici and Francis which fixes Lorenzo's titles, territories and compensation (including the 100,000 ducats) and pledges Francis to defend the Medici interests in Italy.

My letter to Charles has also had its intended effect. Charles has proposed a secret treaty of alliance between Spain and the Holy See. In it, he agrees to protect the States of the Church (and the possessions of the Medici) in exchange for the Holy See acknowledging and protecting the possessions of the King (including Naples). He also proposes to support the Crusade and I have authorized him to tax a tenth upon the Spanish clergy. Once again, there is no obligation on my part to support his bid for the crown of the Empire.

As I see no inconsistency between my treaties with Francis and Charles (my only desires are for universal peace within Christendom and a successful Crusade against the Mohammedans), I intend to sign both treaties. Now, I can only pray that neither of these Christian princes deals treacherously with the Vicar of Christ, a possibility which I unfortunately cannot rule out.

January 23, 1519

The Vatican

News arrived today that Maximilian died on January 12. He was a difficult man, but I shall never forget his kindness during my sojourn in Germany. The effectiveness of my recent diplomacy will shortly be put to the test. I will send secret instructions to Cajetan to support the candidacy of Frederick, or if he shall falter, Elector Joachim of Brandenburg or the King of Poland. Under no circumstances shall the efforts of Charles or Francis to secure the crown be supported. It would be helpful to have Giulio at my side as I navigate these treacherous shoals, but he has hastened to Florence where Lorenzo has taken critically ill. Madeleine is with child; may God grace us with a boy.

January 29, 1519

The Vatican

Developments have taken a serious turn for the worse. Charles is emptying the treasury of Spain in his effort to win the crown. The Bishop of Plock° advises me that five Electors have confirmed their pledges to Charles. Frederick has neither the financial resources nor the popularity to stop Charles. At this late date, Francis is the only viable alternative. I called in the French Ambassador today and told him that the Holy See will actively support Francis' bid for the crown. I hope it is not too late.

March 14, 1519

The Vatican

Francis is spending ducats freely, but the election is not swinging in his direction. The Germans seem adamant in their preference for a countryman to be the next Emperor. I authorized Francis to offer the Electors of Treve and Cologne red hats for their votes. Today, I personally offered Albert of Brandenburg, Archbishop and Cardinal of Mayence, the position of permanent legate to Germany should anyone other than Charles be elected. I am hopeful, but not optimistic, that the tide may change.

One positive development from Germany is that the promised letter from Luther has arrived. In it, he writes: "Before God and all his creatures, I bear testimony that I neither did desire, nor do desire to touch or by intrigue to undermine the authority of the Roman Church and

---

° Translator's note: Maximilian's special envoy to the Vatican.

that of your Holiness." I trust the promised publication to his followers will follow soon and this matter laid to rest.

April 14, 1519

The Vatican

Madeleine has given birth to a girl. God willing, Lorenzo will survive long enough to plant another seed. I am tired and will perhaps write further tomorrow.

April 29, 1519

The Vatican

God has forsaken the Medici. Madeleine is dead of plague and Lorenzo is soon to follow. The only males beside me in whom the undiluted blood of Cosimo and my father still flows are my brother Giuliano's bastard son Ippolito and Lorenzo's bastard son Alessandro (whose mother is a Moorish slave and is thus unfit to continue the line).

I have done my best to follow in the footsteps of our Lord, Jesus Christ, and to bring honor upon his Church, but have fallen short. I believe that God Himself, the Blessed Virgin and the Holy Apostles have always known my good intentions. I confess that sometimes, like other men, I have yielded to the frailties of the flesh, but confirm and thank God for His mercies. God has given and now taken away from the Medici. Although I am deeply distressed to see our line extinguished, I must thank God that He has delivered me from the service of the secular world, so that I might now think only of the profit and exaltation of the Holy See. Henceforth, I belong no more to the House of Medici, but to the House of God.

I dispatched Giulio back to Florence to attend to Lorenzo's deathbed and the rule of the city. I am sure he will do his usual excellent job.

May 6, 1519

The Vatican

Lorenzo has gone to his Maker today. Given the cruelty of the French boils, his passing is a testament to God's mercy. Two days ago, I received a letter from the Archbishop of Florence seeking the financial assistance of the Vatican in repaving the floor of the Duomo. I shall instruct Giulio to deliver Michelangelo's marbles to be broken up into tiles. I have lost interest in the new façade for San Lorenzo. I only wish I could be in the room when Giulio informs the ill-tempered artist of my decision.

June 5, 1519

The Vatican

For four months, I have done everything within my power, and more, to promote Francis for the crown. How does this ungrateful prince reward me? By writing a letter, received today, admonishing me against incorporating Urbino in the States of the Church and asserting that it belongs to Lorenzo's infant Catherine, "whom he regards as his own daughter." Urbino has always been a fief of the Church and must revert to its native condition. I will not have the French king asserting ownership of such a strategic duchy on this nonsensical basis. He should take care for his mortal soul.

Francis has abused my friendship and betrayed our agreements, but will do so no more. His efforts to obtain the imperial crown have fallen short. I shall now turn my full attention to improving the Holy See's relations with Charles, whose election is now inevitable. It makes no sense for me to knock my head against a stone wall.

June 11, 1519

The Vatican

Today was a welcome change from the political intrigue that has occupied my days since the Electors assembled in Frankfort. Raphael and his assistants have completed the fifty-two fresco panels depicting stories from the Old and New Testaments on the arches of the Vatican loggia. I inspected them this morning before authorizing final payment.

Knowing of my great delight in nature, Raphael portrays many animals including lions and horses and unicorns and peacocks. He even includes a wonderful portrait of Hanno rubbing himself against a tree. Raphael's Eve is a vision – were I so inclined, I am sure she would induce heat within my loins.

Raphael has once again demonstrated his superior virtuosity. I prophesy that a millennium from now, long after Leonardo and Michelangelo have been forgotten, Raphael's genius will still be universally celebrated. I cannot wait for his tapestries, which are now being woven in Brussels, to be hung in the Sistine Chapel. No longer will people have to strain their necks to observe the most beautiful art in Christendom.

June 17, 1519

The Vatican

I met today with the Spanish Ambassador and informed him that I was sending instructions to all papal legates and nuncios to support Charles' candidacy for the imperial crown. I also suggested that the Sacred College would vote to approve a dispensation for Charles to wear both the Roman and Neapolitan crowns in exchange for giving the Holy See a veto over any Spanish expansion within Lombardy or Tuscany. Caroz was very favorably inclined towards my proposal and will forward it to Charles immediately.

July 5, 1519

The Vatican

Word of Charles' election to the imperial dignity reached Rome today and bedlam is reigning in the streets. As I write, I can hear singing and music and cries of "Spain, Spain" from large armed bands of celebrating Spaniards, who are being encouraged with wine and coin by the Spanish prelates in the city. The Germans, angry that the Spanish are usurping the Hapsburg as one of their own (and consistent with their war-like character), have taken to attacking the celebrants with clubs and swords. The French are walking about like dead men, muttering that somehow I am responsible for this international catastrophe. This does not bode well for continuation of the peace that currently prevails within Italy. It will take all of my diplomatic skills to prevent the two headstrong young monarchs (Charles is only nineteen) from going at each other.

July 10, 1519

The Vatican

I contend that the two most powerful weapons in Satan's arsenal are academic theologians and the printing press. If one looks to the origins of virtually every heresy promulgated since the Resurrection, one finds an arrogant professor, with too much time on his hands, who professes to have discovered some new interpretation of Scripture that the Holy See has somehow overlooked. Heresies can now spread with lightening speed thanks to Gutenberg's press. Notwithstanding my Bull (and Alexander's as well), prohibiting the printing of any book, tract or pamphlet without prior approval of the Holy See, Luther's heretical works are everywhere. As Christ himself discovered, many men will trade their souls tomorrow for a handful of silver today.

Miltitz and I skillfully negotiated an end to Luther's agitation, but now another self-regarding professor, Johann Eck of Ingolstadt, may single-handedly have ruined our delicate arrangement. Without consultation with the Vatican, Eck issued a series of theses in opposition to Luther's and challenged the monk to a debate at the University of Leipzig. This action has of course violated my agreement to keep Luther's opponents silenced.

Reports of the debate have been pouring into the Curia and the news is not good. Eck demolished Luther's arguments with unassailable logic and references from Scripture and canon law. Luther, his own ego inflamed, now adopts the heresy of Hus and the Bohemians outright, declaring that it is not necessary to salvation to be obedient to the Roman Church and that the pope has no more spiritual authority than any other man.

While Eck carried the day theologically, I fear that Luther, now subject to excommunication and execution by the indisputable words of his own mouth, will fancy himself the new Savonarola and embark upon an even greater campaign of slander against the Church. This is not a good time for a theological war, given that a real war may break out at any moment.

July 19, 1519

The Vatican

I received a letter from Charles, which I read to the College at consistory today. The letter is quite modest in tone and Charles professes his good-will and submission to the Holy See. I shall craft an equally flattering reply. We shall see what happens.

August 15, 1519

The Vatican

I returned Urbino and Pesaro to the States of the Church today. However, at Giulio's suggestion, I gave the fortress of San Leo and the district of Montefeltro to Florence as reward for its financial contributions in the war against Francesco Maria. As I predicted, Giulio is doing an excellent job administrating Florence as the papal legate to Tuscany. All is quiet within the city and the Medici are universally revered. Francis will no doubt be outraged by my action, but he is scarcely in any position to oppose me. Charles would like nothing better than an opportunity to prove himself a defender of the Church.

October 26, 1519

The Vatican

Giulio has returned to Rome, leaving quiescent Florence temporarily in the capable hands of Cardinal Passerini. He has brought with him Catherine, the five month old "Duchessina" of Urbino. The infant brings all the catastrophes of Hell with her presence, but she is nonetheless an adorable little baby. Not since Julius brought young Federico Gonzaga to the Vatican as his hostage and catamite has a child graced its corridors with laughter. I must ponder what use to make of her.

I was wrong about Francis. I thought my annexation of Urbino would provoke outrage, but instead it has provoked fear, a most unexpected but welcome outcome. He now is terrified by the possibility of an alliance between Charles and the Holy See and, through his Ambassador, Saint-Marceau, has negotiated a new treaty of strictest secrecy. In it, I pledge to defend France with all of my weapons, both temporal and spiritual, and to refuse to Charles the investiture of the crown of Naples in conjunction with that of the Empire. On his part, Francis agrees to defend the States of the Church (including Urbino) with all of his might and to withdraw his protection from the Duke of Ferrara, whose treachery against the Church has not been forgotten or forgiven. Francis signed the secret pact on the 22nd. He has now begun work on a secret triple alliance against Charles among France, the Holy See and Venice. I warned Saint-Marceau that Venice also must renounce its support for Duke Alfonso.

December 26, 1519

The Vatican

Seven of the ten tapestries I commissioned have arrived from Brussels and are hung in the Sistine Chapel on its lower walls. In honor of St. Stephen's Day, I ordered the Chapel opened so that the public may marvel at them. A special gallery has been constructed near the left entrance so that women may view them.

The tapestries are woven from the finest silk and gold threads and mirror precisely Raphael's cartoons (at a cost of 150,000 ducats). The work is so exquisite that it is almost impossible to believe that the scenes are woven and not painted.

Raphael, at my suggestion, has depicted stories from the lives of the Apostles. In the wide border beneath each scene is a corresponding scene from my own life. Raphael portrays my exile from Florence and the looting of the Medici palace; my capture at the Battle of Ravenna; my escape from the French and journey in disguise across wild Apennine passes; my triumphal entry into Florence after the sack of Prato; and my reception at the conclave that elevated me to the supreme dignity.

From cardinals and ambassadors to lowly bakers and fishmongers, everyone is struck dumb by the magnificence of these hangings. Paris de Grassis remarked to me that by universal consent, there is nothing more beautiful in the world. It will no doubt gall Michelangelo that his ceiling painting has been eclipsed by these miraculous works of art. I can hardly wait for the remaining three hangings from the first set and the ten from the second set (depicting the life and death of Christ and corresponding scenes from my papacy) to arrive from Brussels.

January 9, 1520

The Vatican

At consistory today, the subject of Luther arose. It is the consensus of the College that Luther has kindled a fire which may be very difficult to quench. One of the officials of the Curia made an impassioned speech that the mortal enemies of the Holy See will seduce all of Germany with Luther's errors and that efficacious steps must be taken against this hydra. He declared that I must authorize the Auditor of the Camera to take all legal steps to ensure the coercion of Luther and his followers and to compel them to give an account of their religious opinions; failing which they should be declared to be heretics. He concluded by saying that religion itself will be undone unless the evil is grasped in its beginning and the incurable wound cauterized.

I confess that I am still of mixed opinions regarding this matter. While Luther's theses are undoubtedly heretical, he was under control until that pompous ass Eck undid all of my good work at Leipzig. If I excommunicate him, he will be viewed as a martyr by many. It will be like Savonarola all over again. I still prefer to take a political approach to this problem. Now that Charles is Emperor-Elect, he may be willing to silence Luther to cement his friendship with the Holy See. Only one-quarter German blood courses through his veins.

February 1, 1520

The Vatican

The pressure from the Curia on this Luther matter continues to grow. Today, I appointed a commission of Franciscan Observantines under the direction of Cardinals Carvajal and Accolti to make recommendations regarding Luther. I charged them to also investigate Elector Frederick of Saxony, Luther's principal sponsor and protector. It must be made clear that princes too have some risk in this matter. Otherwise, Luther will remain emboldened, believing that the secular arm will afford him protection from the religious.

February 11, 1520

The Vatican

Never in the history of the Curia has a commission ever acted with such dispatch. The unanimous recommendation is that Luther be declared a heretic and excommunicated. This is not the timing I desire, so I appointed a new commission today to make a more deliberate study of the issues involved. I have appointed ten eminent university theologians to the panel, which should ensure no end of jealous fighting among the wordsmiths. In the meantime, Cardinal Riario has personally appealed to Elector Frederick to bring Luther to heel and the Vicar-General of the Augustinians has ordered Luther's superior, Staupitz, to muzzle the monk.

March 5, 1520

The Vatican

With Francis and Charles both vying for my friendship, the time has come to put the Papal States back in good order. The petty tyrants of the Marches have taken advantage of the unsettled political situation in Europe to defy the authority of the Holy See and reassert their ancient prerogatives. In doing so, they have trampled upon the people with rapacious cruelty. As shepherd, I cannot sit back while my flock is abused.

I have engaged my distant cousin (also the son-in-law of my sister Lucrezia), Giovanni de Medici to lead the papal troops. Giovanni distinguished himself militarily during the Urbino war. I intend to deal with the most vicious of the despots, Gianpaolo Baglioni of Perugia (of the notorious and degenerate Baglioni family) myself. Last month, I invited Gianpaolo to an audience, but the suspicious tyrant sent his son, Malatesta, in his place to determine the safety of the summons. I assured the youth that my intentions were pacific and gave him a safe-conduct for his father, which Camillo Orsini, Gianpaolo's new son-in-law, vouched for.

March 17, 1520

The Vatican

The news from my namesake is excellent. Ludovico Uffreducci of Fermo has been put to death, as have the Lords of Recanati and Fabriano. Ettore Severiano of Benevento and the other petty tyrants have fled for their lives. Good government can at last be restored to the Marches.

Gianpaolo Baglioni arrived in Rome yesterday with a large retinue. Today, I summoned him to an audience at the Castel Sant'Angelo, where the Captain immediately arrested him upon arrival. During the trial of Cardinal Petrucci, a secret letter had been produced conclusively linking Baglioni to the conspiracy against my life. Thus, the safe-conduct was null and void according to the legal precedents I have previously described. I am sure that after my prosecutors complete their examination, Baglioni's confession will reveal many other crimes and atrocities.

Another visitor arrived in Rome today, this one unbidden. Johann Eck arrived from Germany, no doubt to urge my commission to recommend the severest sanctions against Luther. Given Eck's brilliant defense of Church doctrine at Leipzig, it will be difficult not to receive him with warm praise, but in truth he has done the Church more harm than good.

March 26, 1520

The Vatican

Two days ago, I summoned Raphael to the Vatican to discuss what appear to be serious structural faults in the upper loggia of the Apostolic Palace (so much so that I have taken temporary refuge in the apartments of Cardinal Cibo). He was in good spirits and excellent health. Today, I received news that he has fallen ill. My doctors report that he has over-exerted himself with his mistress, Luti, and is suffering the ill effects.

April 2, 1520

The Vatican

Yesterday I presented a play to which Rome's leading citizens were invited. Upon Giulio's recommendation, the play was *La Mandragola*, written by Cesare Borgia's Florentine apologist Machiavelli. I had no idea Machiavelli has such a talent for comedy.

The play takes place over a twenty-four hour period. Callimaco, a Florentine who is living in Paris, overhears a fellow Italian tell of the incredible beauty of Lucrezia, the wife of Nicia, a rich merchant. Compelled to see this beauty himself, Callimaco returns to Florence, where he sees Lucrezia and resolves to possess her.

Callimaco retains the services of Ligurio, a crafty marriage broker, who devises a wonderful scheme. Ligurio visits Nicia and convinces him that a certain doctor has a potion made of mandrake root that will cure Lucrezia's barrenness (Nicia desperately wants an heir). Callimaco, pretending to be that doctor, convinces Nicia that the potion will be effective, but that the first man who copulates with Lucrezia will die of a poisonous aftereffect. He suggests that Nicia get an innocent dupe to sleep with his wife and absorb the poison.

Nicia agrees, but Lucrezia is reluctant to go along with the scheme. Callimaco and Ligurio, using Nicia's money, bribe Friar Timoteo, who, with the assistance of Lucrezia's mother (who desires a grandchild), convinces Lucrezia that taking the potion is fulfilling God's will. That night, Nicia "captures" an innocent man on the street (Callimaco in disguise), who then has his way with Lucrezia.

The next morning, Callimaco reveals the fraud to Lucrezia. Lucrezia is pleased that Callimaco will not die and is highly satisfied with his performance as a lover. She agrees to continue the affair.

Thus, the play has a happy ending because everyone gets what they desire. Callimaco get Lucrezia. Lucrezia gets a capable lover and, eventually, a child. Her mother gets a grandchild. Nicia, who remains ignorant of the hoax and continued affair, gets an heir. And Ligurio and Friar Timoteo get sizeable fees.

The play was a welcome diversion from the weightier issues that confront me. I laughed so hard that tears rolled down my cheeks; something that hasn't happened since Baraballo was crowned Arch-Poet and paraded on Hanno. After the performance, I told Giulio to reward Machiavelli with a commission and gave him authority to pay the author up to 300 ducats.

April 3, 1520

The Vatican

Raphael has taken a turn for the worse. He is being bled and given purgatives, but is sinking. God cannot be so cruel as to take him from me at the peak of his powers. I pray that if God needs another artist in Heaven, he takes Michelangelo instead.

April 7, 1520

The Vatican

Raphael has gone to the angels. I am distraught beyond comprehension. Never has there been an artist of such genial temperament and exquisite skills. Bembo has penned an epitaph: "Here lies that famous Raphael by whom Nature feared to be conquered while he lived, and when he was dying, feared herself to die." I confess I sometimes find it difficult to understand the way in which our Lord does His business. I cannot help but wonder when my own summons will come.

April 25, 1520

The Vatican

The demons of Hell are running loose in my mind. Raphael's death has deprived me of all spirit. Only a hunt may revive my attention to the affairs of my holy office. I will depart for La Magliana tomorrow. Although fever season is approaching, I fear it not. My life is in the benevolent hands of the Lord.

May 2, 1520

La Magliana

It is well known within the Curia that I loath to be disturbed with business during a hunt. Yet today, Eck (who may be excused for his ignorance given that he is not resident in Rome), arrived and presented me with a working draft of the Bull against Luther. Cardinal Accolti has been its principal author. I just finished a cursory reading and judge it acceptable. Despite the vitriolic attacks upon Luther by Eck and his allies within the Curia, the Bull does not excommunicate the monk, but expresses the Church's willingness to receive Luther back to its bosom as a prodigal son if he renounces the errors set forth in his writings within sixty days. It lists forty-one specific errors of doctrine and bans all faithful to read, praise, publish or defend any of his heretical ideas.

Eck expressed dissatisfaction with the benevolent tone of the Bull, but I reminded him that Luther's followers would like nothing better than to see him martyred. I will not be complicit in elevating this monk beyond his station. But I am confident that Charles will work with me to suppress Luther and his fellow zealots as it is in both his temporal and spiritual interest to do so.

May 15, 1520

La Magliana

Another fine day of hunting has revived my spirits. I may not ever return to the Vatican. Tonight, Giulio, sensing the elevation of my mood, presented me with a personal plea, which in accordance with my custom will be difficult to refuse.

Last year, he commissioned construction of a small chapel at the rear of San Lorenzo to honor our fathers, Lorenzo and Giuliano. Now, he seeks my permission to engage Michelangelo to decorate the chapel. He argues that no living artist can better glorify their memories. With my beloved Raphael now gone, it is a statement that I cannot dispute.

As much as it galls me to reward the insolent artist with a new commission, I owe it to my father and uncle to provide them the best. And, of course, benevolence and forgiveness are noble qualities, particularly in a pontiff. I granted Giulio's request, but told him that I also want memorials in the chapel to my brother Giuliano and nephew Lorenzo (his father Piero can continue to rot at Monte Casino).

La Magliana

June 3, 1520

The trial of Gianpaolo Baglioni has been concluded and he has been turned over to the secular authorities for execution of sentence. Tomorrow, the people of Perugia will rejoice that the tyrant has been dispatched to Hell. The College has met four times during my absence to debate and revise the Bull on Luther. It arrived yesterday and, after the day's hunt, I personally wrote a more dramatic opening paragraph:

> Arise, O Lord, and judge your own cause. Remember your reproaches to those who are filled with foolishness all through the day. Listen to our prayers, for foxes have arisen seeking to destroy the vineyard whose winepress you alone have trod. When you were about to ascend to your Father, you committed the care, rule, and administration of the vineyard, an image of the triumphant church, to Peter, as the head and your vicar and his successors. The wild boar from the forest seeks to destroy it and every wild beast feeds upon it.

I shall title the Bull *Exsurge Domine*.°

July 8, 1520

The Vatican

As a courtesy, I sent a copy of the Bull to Elector Frederick (the official Bull is being carried to Germany by Girolamo Aleandro, whom I have appointed Nuncio-Extraordinary and Ambassador to Charles V and the other Sovereigns of Germany). In my covering letter, I reiterate that the scabby sheep must not infect the flock. I close the letter with a personal plea: "We exhort you to induce him to return to sanity and receive our clemency. If he persists in his madness, take him captive." I

° Translator's note: "Arise, O Lord."

have now done all I can to resolve this matter amicably. It is now up to Frederick and Luther to grasp the hand which I have extended to them.

October 15, 1520

The Vatican

Luther has, by his own hand, sealed his fate. I have received from him a letter, written before *Exsurge Domine*, which makes reconciliation impossible. While the letter praises me in the most gratifying terms, Luther's attacks upon the Church cannot be tolerated. He writes (among many other libels):

> It is indeed as clear as daylight to all mankind that the Roman church, formerly the most holy of all churches, is become the most licentious den of thieves, the most shameless of all brothels, the kingdom of sin, of death, and of hell; the wickedness of which not Antichrist himself could conceive.

Frederick, his protector, has answered my July letter, refusing to arrest Luther and instead insisting that Luther be given an opportunity to defend his teachings before an impartial panel of University theologians in Germany. Ulrich von Hutten, that most vociferous humanist and enemy of the Church, has now endorsed Luther's heresy as his own. Only Charles holds the key to quarantining this pestilential outbreak before it infects all of Europe. Aleandro will deliver this message personally to Charles when he attends the coronation on October 23. He will also carry my secret plan for an alliance to drive the French from Lombardy.

October 18, 1520

The Vatican

I met today at the request of Francis' Ambassador, Saint-Marceau, who presented me with a most alarming proposal. Francis has apparently decided to launch an invasion against Naples, not for himself but for some undisclosed "third party." He offers me part of Naples and part of Ferrara for my endorsement and cooperation. This bodes evil.

From the moment he ascended the throne, Francis has dealt treacherously with me. He has broken his promises; ignored the prerogatives of the Holy See in Milan; interfered with the elevation of the Bishop of Lieges to the purple; conspired with the Duke of Ferrara and other enemies of the Holy See; and opposed the return of Urbino to the bosom of the Church. He has even demanded that young Catherine be sent to France under his guardianship.° These French are as unbearable as allies as they are formidable as enemies. I will not allow this scheming wolf into the Italian pasture.

Today, of course, I was my usual genial self with the Ambassador and advised him that I need to reflect upon Francis' interesting proposal. We will see how far Francis can be pushed to secure my friendship. It is now clear as day that war is coming. The problem is that Charles poses at least as grave a threat to the Holy See as Francis. I shall engage a large contingent of Swiss mercenaries to supplement my Swiss Guards. I must be prepared for all contingencies.

October 25, 1520

The Vatican

I signed the charter for the College of Cavalieri di S. Pietro today. Cardinal Pucci has found 401 men who will pay 1,000 ducats each to become its founding members. This will help relieve the burden of the Urbino war loans and pay for the Swiss.

November 2, 1520

Palo

Today, All Souls' Day, marks the start of the greatest hunt in history. The country surrounding La Magliana has insufficient game to satisfy the 1,000 men I have invited to participate, so I have taken Felice Orsini's (Julius' natural daughter) magnificent castle at Palo, which is situated on the sea but surrounded by vast oak forests which teem with wolves, boar, stags, roe-deer, hares, goats and hedgehogs. The skies are full of birds and the sea of fish. It is like paradise on earth. Only the glum expression of Baldassare Castiglione mars the jovial mood. His wife has just died. Castiglione is here on behalf of his master, Julius' catamite Federico Gonzaga, the new Marquis of Mantua, who desires appointment as Captain-General of the Church. But Federico is weak; more a woman than a man (although no one could accuse his mother, Isabella d'Este, of weakness). Also, he is a strong partisan of Charles and I still do not know how my hand will ultimately play out in this game between Francis and the Emperor-Elect.

° Translator's note: Catherine de Medici grew up to become one of the most powerful women in French history. At the age of fourteen, she married Francis' son Henry (later to become king) and gave birth to three future kings of France and one queen of Spain.

November 3, 1520

Palo

Today, the first full day of hunting, was marvelous. The weather was perfect. An immense quantity of game was driven through the narrow opening in the sailcloth fence. A giant wolf raced directly at my horse, but my guards drove him away. I was not frightened in the least. The poet Postumo had a far graver encounter. A savage boar knocked him to the ground and nearly gored him. Fortunately, many hunters were close by and lanced the boar. On a lighter note, one of my knights, Licaba, apparently blinded by the excitement of the melee, mistook one of his favorite hounds for a wolf and speared him. At the banquet, I presented the errant knight with the carcass of his dog, to the great amusement of all the company.

November 5, 1520

Palo

Today's hunt was marred by an unfortunate incident of violence. Two of my guests, Falloppio and Lica, quarreled over possession of a slain boar and came to blows. Poor Lica had his eye put out and his howls of pain ruined the mood. As the Bible commands, I ordered Falloppio's eye gouged out in compensation.

November 10, 1520

Palo

Word arrived from Rome that Bibbiena died yesterday. It is no great surprise since he has not been well. Now I have but two links remaining to my childhood – Giulio and Michelangelo. It was a mistake to have sent Bibbiena to France. He always had a weakness for luxury and was highly susceptible to flattery. Francis had no trouble in beguiling Bibbiena into becoming his lackey and tool. Since his return to Rome, Bibbiena has been useless as an advisor and dangerous as a French spy. I believe he also entertained pretensions to the triple tiara. I shall not permit his death to darken my mood, which has finally been elevated from the depths of melancholy.

Today was an exceptional day. We went down to the sea near Santa Marinella and took to barges beneath a steep cliff. My gamesmen drove a great number of stags, boars and goats over the cliff edge and my guests slew them as they fell to the rocky shore. The sea ran red with their blood.

November 14, 1520

Palo

A letter from Charles arrived today, written on the day of his coronation and pledging perpetual fealty to the Holy See. I replied after the day's festivities. My reply begins: "As there are two planets in heaven, the sun and the moon, so are there two great dignitaries on earth, the Pope and the Emperor, to whom all other princes are subject and owe obedience."

Aleandro's latest report arrived with the same messenger. He has nothing but positive things to say about Charles and his desire to serve the Holy See by enforcing the writ against Luther. Immediately after his coronation, Charles issued an imperial edict requiring the burning of Luther's books. But Aleandro also reports that he was unable to officially serve the Bull *Exsurge Domine* until just a few days ago. Disobedient German clerics refused to accept it and mobs of armed students and fanatical supporters of Luther prevented him from publicly posting it. It seems all of Germany has gone mad. I must now wait until the end of the year before I can officially excommunicate the heretic.

November 16, 1520

Palo

Two incidents involving my Orsini relations occurred today. Valerio Orsini, the sixteen year old son of my hosts, chased gallantly after a stag but the beast evaded him. The petulant youth burst into tears at his failure. Fra Mariano, my buffoon, attempted to cheer the boy with jests, but Valerio was inconsolable. His parents were greatly embarrassed by this unmanly display.

At dusk, a vulture was spied aloft hovering against the gold and crimson of the western sky. Cardinal Orsini's falconer released the Cardinal's favorite peregrine, which darted upward in pursuit of its larger but less attractive opponent. While we gazed rapturously at this aerial combat, an immense eagle suddenly sailed into the ken, which in turn assailed the Cardinal's falcon. The falconer immediately sounded the return whistle, but the plucky falcon engaged the king of birds, which slew it. The lifeless mass of blood-stained feathers dropped with a thud at the feet of the weeping trainer.

Cardinal Orsini, rising to the occasion, decreed that the falcon be buried with full honors of war upon the battlement of some lofty tower. Her chains and jesses shall lie beside her tomb and an achievement bearing the proud arms of Orsini shall mark the spot, above which skulls of doves and herons shall yearly be suspended for a votive remembrance of the bird's past victories.

November 30, 1520

Corneto

The game surrounding Palo has become exhausted, so the party has moved to Cardinal Corneto's vast estate. Giulio has returned from Rome with another 1,000 guests, but the surrounding woods can easily accommodate 2,000 hunters. A tragic but amusing incident involving the Cardinal's favorite kennel-man, Lancetto, occurred today. Lancetto, who is overly fond of wine, was chasing down a boar when he threw his spear and accidentally slew one of his best hounds. Horrified by his clumsiness and maddened by wine, Lancetto, with a might effort, leaped upon the back of the flying boar and attempted to strangle it with his bare hands. But the boar threw Lancetto off and gored his prostrate body from head to foot. Lancetto's corpse was brought back to the Cardinal, who anointed the face with his finest wine and proposed this epitaph for his faithful servant: "Here lies Lancetto, whose death-wound was the work of a wild boar, or rather of the wine-cup."

December 20, 1520

The Vatican

I wish I had never returned from the hunt. Politics and heretics have undone all of its good. Francis and I continue to negotiate our secret treaty through our ambassadors. He now offers me all of Ferrara and a strip of the Neapolitan coast to the Garigliano River. Naples itself will be given to his infant son Henry, who will marry Catherine when the two come of age. He also offers to contribute one-half of the pay of the 6,000 Swiss mercenaries I have retained and who will arrive next spring. In return, I must allow the French army unrestricted passage through the Papal States and Tuscany.

This proposal might be enticing if I believed that Francis had any intention of honoring it. In any event, the Venetians must agree to join in the treaty, since the Republic is allied with the Duke of Ferrara. The negotiations will continue. Meanwhile, I have given Charles' Ambassador, Manuel, written assurance that I will not enter into any agreements adverse to the interests of the Emperor for three months.

At this point, I need Charles more than Francis. Aleandro writes that Luther publicly burned the Bull *Exsurge Domine* and added other books of canon law to the fire. Luther has published a pamphlet declaring me the Antichrist. Aleandro also reports that nine-tenths of Germans shout for Luther and the balance hold the Roman Court in deadly hatred. Worse, Charles has agreed with Elector Frederick that Luther should be given an opportunity to defend his doctrines within Germany.

Charles must be made to understand that Luther's dangerous doctrines threaten all order and authority, temporal as well as spiritual. I informed Ambassador Manuel today that if Charles insists on Luther being given an opportunity to defend his doctrines, I will give the monk a safe-conduct to Rome, where a body of learned men would be selected to speak and dispute with him.

I have given instructions to Aleandro to remind Charles that Luther's sixty day period of grace under *Exsurge Domine* has now expired and it is a mortal sin for any Christian to have contact with him. I also instructed him to request an imperial edict extending the ban on the works of Luther to include those of von Hutten and Luther's other supporters. I sent a large quantity of ducats with my instructions to assist Aleandro in his dealings with the German rulers.

January 3, 1521

The Vatican

Today, I signed the Bull *Decet Romanum Pontificem*, which unconditionally excommunicates Luther and his followers. I sent a special brief to the Inquisitor-General of Germany ordering him to proceed with energy and all of the tools at his disposal against all obstinate Lutherans, including those of electoral dignity. I also sent a brief to Charles, requesting that he secure the execution of the Bull.

January 30, 1521

La Magliana

Good news from Germany. Aleandro reports that Charles will enforce the Bulls against Luther at the Diet of Worms. Luther will not be permitted to attend unless, prior thereto, he makes a full recantation of his heretical doctrines. I sent a letter of thanks to Charles, expressing my joy that he was rivaling Constantine, Charlemagne and Otto in his zeal for the honor of the Church.

I signed the secret treaty with Francis today, doing so with a clear conscience. I will not be the first to break its terms since I know that Francis has no intention of abiding by it. He has not an honest bone in his body. A cold wind is blowing from the sea, but I would rather freeze to death at La Magliana than return to the Vatican.

February 15, 1521

The Vatican

The impudent Venetians continue their arrogant defiance of the Church. The Council of Ten has rejected the terms of the secret treaty with France, electing instead to support the traitorous Duke of Ferrara. My lot now lies entirely with Charles. Worse, it has suspended the execution of witches condemned by the Inquisition. Thousands of convicted witches crowd the jails in Brescia and other towns under Venetian control (25,000 witches attended the Black Sabbath on the plain outside Brescia, but only seventy have been burned to date). The Council has voted to have each conviction reviewed by secular jurists. Today, I signed the Bull *Honestis*, which orders the excommunication of any officials and the suspension of religious services in any community that refuses to execute, without examination or revision, the sentences of my inquisitors. I shall bring Venice to heel by one means or another. If the Church cannot freely exercise its spiritual authority in the battle against Satan, the salvation of mankind will be lost. I will not permit this.

March 28, 1520

The Vatican

I listed Luther today in the Maundy Thursday Bull.° I am very disappointed with Charles. The Diet has been in session for two months, but the Luther issue is not yet concluded. Charles has bowed to demands by the Electors that Luther be summoned to Worms to explain himself. If the Emperor is able to effect so little against one man who is in his power, what can the Church and Christendom expect of him in a fight against Turks and infidels?

I called in Manuel today and admonished him that his sovereign had been badly advised in summoning Luther to appear at Worms. I told him it was impossible that Luther be received even in Hell, and that he would do well to warn his imperial master, in every letter he wrote, not to take this matter lightly.

° Translator's note: An annual Bull which announces the excommunication of heretics as well as listing the external enemies of the Church.

April 25, 1521

The Vatican

Praise be to God. Truth and reason have prevailed at Worms. Luther, bewitched by Satan, refused to recant. Charles rose to the occasion. The dispatch arrived today. His exact words:

> A single monk, led astray by his own folly, rises against the faith of Christendom. I will sacrifice my kingdoms, my power, my friends, my treasures, my body, my blood, my spirit, and my life in putting a stop to this iniquity. I am about to send back the Augustinian, Martin Luther, forbidding him meanwhile to cause the least tumult among the people; I will then proceed against him and his adherents, as against manifest heretics, by excommunication, by interdict, by all means fitted to ruin them. I call upon the members of the States to conduct themselves like faithful Christians.

I could not have asked for a more forceful statement. While Charles must, to honor his safe-conduct, allow Luther to leave Worms unmolested, I trust that he shall soon bring the full power of the Empire down upon Luther and his followers.

I am not so well pleased with the treaty which Manuel presented to me today. Charles has altered the draft language in a thousand places. He has stricken the language regarding the return to the Holy See of Parma, Piacenza and Ferrara, which is absolutely unacceptable. I am not yet convinced of his courage or even his good faith. Giulio suggests that Charles spent so much in his campaign for the crown that the Imperial treasury is nearly empty and he is intentionally delaying the negotiations while he recovers financially. Manuel assures me that the differences are minor and easily resolved and that Charles remains ready and able to prosecute the war.

May 8, 1521

The Vatican

I have modified the draft treaty with Charles, adding back the clauses regarding Parma, Piacenza and Ferrara and adding a provision requiring Charles to defend the Medici in Tuscany. We shall see how Charles reacts.

The French Ambassador has confided to me that the Swiss have become signatories to the secret treaty between France and the Holy See that I signed in January. If true, this changes the balance of power.

However, my Swiss have arrived and know nothing of an alliance with France. Henry has sent me a letter urging neutrality in the upcoming war between Francis and Charles. He states that England will remain unaligned and that the two monarchs will exhaust their armies and fortunes in the conflict.

It offends God that these Christian princes are preparing to fight yet again when the Turkish menace is greater than ever.

May 16, 1521

The Vatican

Charles signed the Edict of Worms last week. The last legal prerequisite to the suppression of Luther is now in place. His writings will be burned throughout the Empire and the Inquisition and Imperial authorities will root out and destroy the heretic and his adherents.

My spies confirm what I have always known – that Francis will not honor his commitments in the secret treaty. Marshal de Lautrec° was overheard saying that "he would leave nothing to the Pope except his ears." And my spy in Duke Alfonso's court reports that French envoys meet with the Duke almost daily.

I met today with Francis' diplomatist, the Count of Carpi. Of course, I disclosed nothing of my new intelligence to him. I did hand him a case, under lock and diplomatic seal, which I asked him to deliver to my nuncio in Paris. I told him it contained detailed instructions for the nuncio regarding the upcoming offensive against Charles. I did not tell him the case was full of blank papers.

May 29, 1521

The Vatican

I have cast my lot. Today, I signed the treaty with Charles and delivered it to Manuel with instructions that it is to remain secret until I authorize its release. The treaty has been greatly improved in recent weeks. My grand-nephew Alessandro (his mother may be a slave, but his paternal blood is pure Medici) is granted the duchy of Civita di Penna° and Giulio a 10,000 crown a year pension, payable from the Archbishopric of Toledo.

° Translator's note: Commander of the French forces in Milan.

° Translator's note: A town near Naples.

June 7, 1521

The Vatican

At consistory today, the Edict of Worms was read to the College. Aleandro was charged to deliver my warmest thanks to the Emperor and all who had contributed to the carrying out of that important measure. We then proceeded to the Piazza Navona, where Luther's picture and writings were burned.

June 10, 1521

The Vatican

The war has begun. Francis has lent his arms to the insurrections against Charles in Navarre and Luxemburg. In Italy, 2,000 Spanish soldiers under the command of Girolamo Adorno were dispatched in Spanish and papal galleys against Genoa. Unfortunately, the doge Fregoso had somehow received foreknowledge of the plan and fortified the harbor so that the galleys could not make landfall and were forced to retire. I have sent 10,000 ducats to Francesco Guicciardini, my governor of Modena, to pay to Girolamo Morone, chancellor to the exiled Duke Maximilian Sforza, who has raised an army at Reggio in support of the allied cause.

June 24, 1521

The Vatican

French forces arrived before Reggio two days ago and were repulsed by the troops of Guicciardini and Morone. Francis has now had the audacity to attack the Papal States and the time has come to reveal my treaty with Charles.

June 27, 1521

The Vatican

At consistory today, I disclosed Francis' diabolical attack on Reggio and my treaty of alliance with Charles, the defender of the Church at Worms. Some cardinals objected, but they are in the pay of France. I received from Manuel a beautiful white palfrey as a token of Charles' esteem.

I met today with Prospero Colonna, whom Charles and I agree will take supreme command of the allied forces. Federico Gonzaga, who has continued to press for appointment and has renounced his ties with France, will be confirmed as Captain-General of the Church. Guicciardini will be Commissary-General of the army; the Marquis of Pescara will command the imperial cavalry and Giovanni de Medici the papal cavalry. All together, the allied forces will exceed 20,000 men-at-arms.

As usual, I am short of funds, so I will pledge the Vatican's silver plate once again. I may also sell a few red hats. But I will not allow an insufficiency of ducats to interfere with success.

July 20, 1521

The Vatican

Cardinal Schinner reports that the Swiss Cantons have honored their treaty with Francis and 4,000 men are marching south to Milan. There are now Swiss on both sides of the conflict. I know they will not fight each other, but do not yet know whom they will betray, Francis or me. I sent a brief to the Cardinal urging him to take every action necessary to assure the loyalty of the Swiss to the Holy See. I told him to engage as many additional Swiss troops as possible regardless of the cost. The majority of Swiss must be on the allied side. I have just dispatched Cardinal Pucci to Zurich as special nuncio. He carries with him many strongboxes of gold. These money-loving Swiss will understand the import of this action.

Venice has rallied to Francis' defense, sending to Milan 8,000 foot and 900 horse soldiers under the joint command of Teodoro Trivulzio and Andrea Gritti. Duke Alfonso supports him as well.

Francis himself is foaming with rage against me. He has issued a sacrilegious mandate forbidding the transfer to Rome of any income from French bishoprics or abbeys. Charles urges me to excommunicate Francis for this unlawful act, but I hesitate to take this final step. I do not entirely trust Charles. Luther still remains alive, pouring out his venom. I confess that this war is causing me unbearable anxiety. I am unable to sleep at night or concentrate during the day.

August 1, 1521

The Vatican

My concern regarding Charles, which I have freely expressed to Manuel, has prompted Charles to write to me. In his letter, he pledges to make no agreement with Francis without my prior consent. I am not convinced; words on paper have little meaning in this treacherous age.

The King of Hungry writes that the Turks are pressing against his borders and mistreating his subjects. Although it deeply depresses me, I must reply that I can do nothing regarding the Turks until the French have been driven from Italy. I have written both the Kings of Portugal and England for assistance, but have small belief that either will heed my call. Portugal is naturally antithetical to Spain and Henry is content to perch like a vulture on the branch and then scavenge the carcasses.

Prospero Colonna reports that the allied forces are assembling at Bologna and that he will soon have sufficient strength to launch an attack on Parma. I pray that he shall have complete success in returning to the Holy See that which belongs to it by the grace of God.

August 28, 1521

The Vatican

I am stricken with fever. My head and bones ache constantly. My mind is barely able to function. The doctors are concerned and recommend bleeding and purgatives. I have refused, bearing in mind the example of Julius, who recovered from fever without such interventions. I have seen too many men die from the cure rather than the disease.

The news from the war remains unsettling. My troops lay siege to Parma, but cannot (or will not) take it. The intentions of the Swiss continue to be opaque. They take gold from everyone, but no one yet knows who they will betray. Charles sends me no money for the troops in the field. I now belief that Giulio was right. Charles has spent so much money on his own affairs that he has none for ours.

That traitor Alfonso has taken the field with his army and captured Finale and San Felice. He threatens Modena. My spies tell me that he encourages Francesco Maria to launch a new attack upon Urbino. Will Federico, my Captain-General, remain loyal to me and put down his cousin? No man can be trusted. Just writing about the war has increased my agitation. I must rest.

September 4, 1521

The Vatican

My fever has broken and my strength is rapidly returning. I was entirely correct to ignore the recommendations of the physicians. But that is the only good news to report.

A large contingent of Swiss arrived to reinforce the French garrison at Parma and the Duke of Ferrara presses with his artillery. Colonna has withdrawn his forces from Parma and assumes a defensive posture near Reggio. He reports that his troops are threatening mutiny due to lack of pay. Nothing arrives from Charles.

With my temporal weapons failing, I must exercise my spiritual ones. Today, I signed a Bull proclaiming excommunication and interdict against Francis and his generals if they do not lay down their arms and return Parma and Piacenza to the Holy See within fifteen days. Francis merits the tortures of perdition. He has used the funds reserved for the prosecution of the Crusade to attack his fellow Christians; he has violated ecclesiastical liberties; he has seized the revenues of the Church; he has attacked Reggio; he has arrested Florentine merchants in Lyons; he has kept unjust possession of Parma and Piacenza. I fear that Francis cares not a jot about his soul. But I am convinced that his generals do. I shall never forget how they begged for my absolution while I was in Milan as a prisoner.

September 16, 1521

The Vatican

I am rapidly losing all confidence in Charles. The boy has no courage. The Church's campaign to quench the flames of Luther's pernicious doctrines is proceeding well everywhere except Germany. His works and followers have been suppressed in The Netherlands, in Poland, in Spain, in Portugal and in England. The faculties of the Universities at Oxford, Paris, Louvain and Cologne have condemned his teachings. Henry has written a book in Latin condemning Luther, *A Vindication of the Seven Sacraments*, which is dedicated to me. Even my arch-enemy Francis has ordered Luther's works burned.

But Charles temporizes, notwithstanding his bold words. Luther continues to pour out filth from Saxony, protected by Frederick. I sent instructions to Leandro to meet with Charles as soon as possible. He is to tell the Emperor that if the injunction of the Edict of Worms is disregarded now, while the ink with which it was written is scarcely dry, what would the Elector of Saxony dare not do when Charles departs from Germany? If matters are not taken in hand now, at the beginning of the evil, the last state of things will be worse than the first.

Leandro is also to remind Charles that he is seriously delinquent in his obligations for the war. There are only 6,000 German soldiers in the field and they are without pay. The allied army cannot be permitted to crumble. I shall dispatch Giulio to the troops as legate to rally them to God's cause.

September 30, 1521

The Vatican

Giulio resists my order to travel to the front. I believe he privately thinks our cause his lost. For the first time ever, I had to put my instructions to him in writing, not as his cousin and best friend, but as the Holy Father and Vicar of Christ. He must do his Christian duty. I cannot lose this war.

October 5, 1521

The Vatican

At consistory today, I awarded King Henry VIII and his posterity the title "Defender of the Faith" for his great service on behalf of the Roman Church. I also announced an indulgence for every man who reads *A Vindication of the Seven Sacraments*. I shall press Henry once again to join the alliance against France. I shall promise him Paris.

October 10, 1521

The Vatican

Cardinal Pucci arrived back from Zurich today, without his strongboxes but with wonderful news. He has procured the services of an additional 12,000 Swiss, who depart now for the war with Cardinal Schinner at their head. This will assure the defeat of the French.

He tells me the gold he left with the Swiss (and another 100,000 ducats which he personally advanced) is just a retainer and thousands of ducats are due to them in the field. He says that the Vatican has exhausted all sources of credit and provided this list of current obligations:

Bini Bank	200,000 ducats
Strozzi Bank	150,000 ducats
Gaddi Bank	32,000 ducats
Ricasoli Bank	10,000 ducats
Cardinal Pucci	150,000 ducats
Cardinal Armellini	100,000 ducats

Cardinal Salviati	80,000 ducats
Datary Turini	16,000 ducats
Serapica	18,000 ducats
Camillo Gaetani	10,000 ducats

I understand Pucci's concern, but reminded him that Chigi's sons have not yet been tapped this time around. I also explained that once my troops occupy Milan, the fabulous riches of that city will promptly repay these debts. I reiterated to him my fervent belief, proven true countless times, that God takes care of my debts – my job is to spend as necessary to protect His Church and glorify His name. I also said it was of great comfort to me that so many noble and pious men were no doubt praying daily for my continued good health and success in the war. Pucci did not seem overly amused by my little jest.

October 15, 1521

The Vatican

Each day, messengers arrive from the war front. One messenger reports that success is imminent; the other moans that defeat is inevitable. Castiglione has taken an apartment at the Belvedere and I consult him regularly as he is an expert on military matters. He assures me that such differences are normal in the confusion of maneuvers. This does nothing to settle the fierce anxiety that paralyzes me. Charles is still silent; I am convinced he is negotiating behind my back with Francis. I fear casting my lot with him was a monumental error. Worse, Giulio is silent. Without reports from my cousin, I am totally in the dark as to the truth of the situation. I pray that God will give me the strength to bear this burden. The future of His Church hangs in the balance.

October 17, 1521

The Vatican

Joyous news. A report has finally arrived from Giulio and he is optimistic of a successful outcome. He leads the troops personally and reports that the Swiss will shortly join the papal army at Gambara. I pray he is correct. Francesco Maria continues his attempts to raise an army to retake Urbino. When the primary battle has been won, I shall turn my full attention against him and his traitorous cousin, the Duke of Ferrara. Both men will pay with their lives.

October 26, 1521

The Vatican

My organs are in revolt against me. My heart, my liver, my eyes, my brain and my stomach are all failing. My fistula leaks. My left leg twitches uncontrollably. I am too weak to rise from my bed. I fear I am on the verge of death, but Bonet attributes the malady to nothing more than anxiety over the state of the war. He prescribes the only cure possible. I must hasten to La Magliana and divert my mind with a hunt.

October 31, 1521

La Magliana

The restorative powers of the countryside are evident already. My strength is returning. Castiglione arrived from Rome today with remarkable news. Normally, I cannot abide the interference of business while I hunt, but today's news made my heart sing with joy.

Francis had dispatched a baggage train with 300,000 ducats for Marshal de Lautrec at Milan. However, the King's mother, the Duchess of Angouleme, has appropriated the ducats for her own use. Thus, Lautrec cannot pay his Swiss, who most assuredly will now desert.

November 15, 1521

The Vatican

I returned to the Vatican to attend consistory, principally because Castiglione warned me that rumors are rampant in Rome that I was critically ill. Today, the cardinals saw me in full vigor. At consistory, I confirmed the appointment of Duke Giovanni Maria da Verano as Admiral of the Papal Fleet. He paid 10,000 ducats for the title, money which is vital at this critical juncture. Tomorrow, I shall attend a memorial service for Cardinal Riario, who has finally died and then return to La Magliana.

November 23, 1521

La Magliana

Zeus and Artemis° were not kind to me today. A cold damp wind has blown in from the sea and the morning's chase had little to show for the effort. I spent the afternoon tending to my hawks, rabbits and ferrets. I continue to

Halleluiah and praise be to God. A messenger just arrived with an urgent report from Giulio. Lautrec has evacuated Milan with the French garrison. Victory is at hand. The news is spreading rapidly throughout the estate. A gang of my guards is preparing a bonfire in the courtyard. Guns and fireworks are being discharged into the air. Men are singing and cheering and clamoring for me. I shall go to the balcony and give them my benediction.

November 24, 1521

La Magliana

I was up all last night watching the celebrations from my window and have paid the price with a chill. My head and bones ache, but it has not dampened my spirits, which soar. Castiglione arrived today with more wonderful news. Not only has Milan fallen, but Parma, Piacenza, Pavia, Novara, Tortona, Alessandria, Cremona and Asti have all thrown open their gates and declared their eternal allegiance to the Holy See. Giovanni de Medici is now chasing Alfonso eastward and will not stop until Ferrara itself is restored.

I called for Paris de Grassis and told him to arrange for a consistory of thanksgiving on Wednesday and great celebrations throughout Rome. He answered that it was not customary for the Holy See to celebrate the result of any battle waged between two Christian monarchs, unless the Church had some special interest at stake, but in such a case the Pontiff himself, as head of the Church, would naturally be the best judge. I laughed heartily at his drollery and answered that the Church has every reason to rejoice. Paris then declared that it was my manifest duty to return to the Vatican and give public thanks to the Almighty for the benefits lately obtained. I shall return tomorrow.

° Translator's note: Ancient Greek gods of weather and the hunt.

November 25, 1521

The Vatican

Today has been a most exhausting day. I returned from my lodge in the afternoon and great crowds lined the roads, cheering me as loudly as they did upon my assumption of the throne. I spent so much time greeting them and offering benedictions that I wager I walked several miles in total. But the weather is glorious and the sun is shining; evidence that even the Lord rejoices at this great victory.

At the Vatican, the College greeted me with great reverence as cannon boomed in salute from the battery at the Castel. I accepted the congratulations of the Imperial Ambassador and remarked to him that I rejoice more over the capture of Milan than I did over my own election to the supreme dignity.

Giulio's private secretary approached me after consistory with most interesting news. He reported that Duke Maximilian Sforza proposed to Giulio an exchange of Milan for Giulio's red hat and benefices (which total over 50,000 ducats per year). With Giulio ruling Milan and Alessandro ruling Tuscany, the power and fortune of the Medici will be unrivaled. It will also permit Giulio to marry and produce a legitimate male heir. I am concerned that Charles will find the arrangement objectionable, but Francis, while defeated, still remains a powerful force. And I am sure my friend Henry would have no objection. I will ponder this proposal further.

November 26, 1521

The Vatican

At a private audience with Cardinal Trivulzio and his nephew this morning, I suddenly was taken with a shivering fit and had to break off the interview and return to my bedchamber. My physicians have completed their examination and pronounce my ailment nothing more than a continuation of the cold I caught at La Magliana. Given that they are usually wrong, I suppose I should now worry. In any event, I will rest for awhile. I have scheduled cards with Cardinals Pucci, Salviati, Ridolfi and Cibo tonight and my mind must be sharp for the game.

TRANSLATOR'S AFTERWORD

Leo was right to distrust the diagnosis of his physicians. He retired early from his card game, complaining of headache and chills. Later that evening, while listening to musicians from his bed, he lost consciousness. Over the course of the next four days, he drifted in and out of a coma. On the morning of Sunday, December 2, 1521, Leo died in his bed at the Apostolic Palace. Historians differ as to whether he received the final sacraments.

As usual in such cases, Leo's unexpected death prompted suspicions of poison. An autopsy was performed, but the surgeons were divided as to his cause of death. Most modern authorities believe he died from the same virulent strain of malaria that killed Alexander VI, but given Leo's obesity and multitude of medical problems, even a cold might have precipitated his final decline. Leo was buried, without pomp or an elaborate ceremony, in the crypt of St. Peter's where he joined many of his predecessors.

The simplicity of his funeral was prompted by the financial panic that gripped the Vatican, Rome and, indeed, much of Italy. The Vatican had been stripped bare during Leo's illness and not a ducat remained in the treasury. Half-consumed candles left over from Cardinal Riario's recent funeral were recycled for use in Leo's procession.

Leo was the most profligate spender in papal history, burning through over 5,000,000 ducats in less than nine years. More to the point, he died owing over 850,000 ducats to a large assortment of banks, cardinals, friends and relatives. Virtually all were ruined.

The sizeable Florentine community in Rome promptly packed up and left town. Joining them were thousands of newly unemployed artists, poets, musicians, construction workers, decorators, craftsmen, translators, curators, Curia bureaucrats, cooks, servants, jesters and buffoons. The magistrates closed the gates and issued an edict banning further exodus, but it did not stem the tide. The papal army deserted for want of pay and Francesco Maria della Rovere and the other petty tyrants of the Papal States quickly recaptured their fiefs.

Cardinal Medici hurried from Milan as soon as news arrived of his cousin's death, intent upon claiming the triple tiara for himself. But the Medici's principal enemy, Cardinal Soderini, arrived first and organized a powerful block in opposition to Giulio. When none of the other major candidates, including Cardinals Wolsey and Farnese, could assemble the required votes, the traditional elderly compromise candidate was selected. In this case, it was sixty-three year old Cardinal Adrian Dedel of Utretcht, Emperor Charles' former tutor. The election of a "barbarian" precipitated riots in the streets. Little was known about the Flemish professor, who had never even been to Rome. Adrian was so ignorant of

Rome that, upon learning of his election, he wrote the Vatican and requested that suitable lodgings be found for him to rent.

Adrian VI (keeping his Christian name as pope, he fulfilled the soothsayer's prediction) arrived a full eight months after his election and the cardinals soon realized they had made a grave mistake. Adrian was the antithesis of Leo. Where Leo was a spendthrift, Adrian was a tightwad. He gave Paris de Grassis exactly one ducat each day to run the papal household. He brought an old Flemish crone with him to cook his frugal meals and make his bed. Vast sections of the Apostolic Palace were ordered closed. Adrian issued edicts regulating the dress, hairstyles and ethics of cardinals and members of the Curia. He was an extremely pious man who attempted to seriously address the complaints set forth by Luther and other critics of the Holy See. Of course, his reform efforts were opposed and undermined at every turn.

Adrian died just eighteen months into his papacy (the suggestions of poison had perhaps somewhat more credibility this time). There was great rejoicing in Rome that the failed experiment in barbarian rule had come to an end. Garlands were left at the door of Adrian's physician and there was talk of erecting a statue in the doctor's honor. The Sacred College voted the following epitaph for Adrian's tomb: "Here lies Adrian VI, whose greatest misfortune was that he became Pope."

The conclave to select Adrian's successor was among the longest and most contested in history. For sixty days, the cardinals were locked in the Sistine Chapel while Giulio bribed and maneuvered to put together the necessary votes. It was a testament to Medici diplomacy and influence that Francis, Charles and Henry all finally endorsed his candidacy. Giulio took the name Clement VII upon his election.

During Leo's papacy, many believed that Giulio was the real brains and power behind the throne. Leo was just too amiable, fun-loving and distracted by the hunt, theatre and music to have crafted the agile, if somewhat underhanded, statesmanship that had kept Italy relatively independent and free of bloodshed during his reign.

Clement's handling of the foreign monarchs put that notion to the lie. While the chronology of his papacy is beyond the scope of this *Afterword*, suffice it to say that Clement vacillated and procrastinated and ultimately picked the wrong horse in every diplomatic and military contest. The net result was the infamous Sack of Rome in 1527. The troops of Charles V ravaged the city and Clement was a prisoner in his own Castel Sant'Angelo for six months.

After reconciling with Charles (courtesy of a 400,000 ducat bribe), Clement obtained his freedom, but the temporal power of the Vatican was forever crushed. However, the Medici family was not. Charles lent Clement his imperial army to assist in returning Florence to Medici rule (shortly after Leo's death, the Medici had been expelled for the third time and the Republic restored). In 1531, Clement installed nineteen year old Alessandro de Medici (now believed to be Giulio's bastard, not Lorenzo's) as Duke of Florence (a title purchased from Charles).

Alessandro was assassinated by his distant cousin, Lorenzino de Medici, in 1537, who was in turn murdered by an assassin hired by Cosimo I de Medici, the son of Leo's condottiere, Giovanni de Medici. Cosimo I assumed rule of Florence and purchased the title Grand Duke of Tuscany from Charles.

Unlike his ancestor Cosimo and his direct descendants, Grand Duke Cosimo I made no pretence of recognizing republican institutions and ruled as an absolute feudal lord. Cosimo I appropriated the Palazzo della Signoria from the Florentine government as his private residence and commissioned construction of the Uffizi Palace to house his administrators. When his wife Eleonora complained about the lack of a garden, he moved to the Pitti Palace across the Arno and constructed the famous Boboli Gardens in the backyard.

Cosimo I and his heirs accumulated unimaginable wealth during their two century rule; far more than the senior line of the family. The last Medici, Anna Maria, died in 1743, bringing to an end one of the most remarkable dynasties in history.

It is not easy for a person of casual interest to find detailed information about Leo's life and papacy. This is perhaps not surprising. The Vatican reached the zenith of its wealth, temporal and spiritual power during the rule of Julius II. Leo squandered this inheritance and left the papacy bereft of its former influence (although to be fair, St. Peter's Basilica and many other churches, monuments and public works in Rome owe their existence to Leo's beneficence). The Roman Catholic Church has yet to recover from the downward spiral that Leo helped precipitate. The *Catholic Encyclopedia*'s entry on Leo concludes with uncharacteristic understatement: "The only possible verdict on the pontificate of Leo X is that it was unfortunate for the Church."

The public section of the Vatican's official website has few links on Leo and most relate to his numerous appearances in Raphael's works (there is no mention of Leo driving Leonardo from Italy or stifling Michelangelo during his potentially most productive years).

Within the Vatican itself, the only evidence of Leo's reign can be found in the magnificent frescos in the Raphael Rooms (the Loggia frescoes are not open to the public).

Leo no longer rests with ninety-two other pontiffs at St. Peter's. On June 6, 1542, his bones were removed from the crypt and transferred to Santa Maria sopra Minerva. Leo no doubt feels right at home in a church built directly over the ruins of an ancient Roman temple dedicated to the goddess of art, poetry and music.

In the church, small placards in Italian and English identify the many notables interred within its walls and floor (perhaps assuming that visitors cannot translate the Latin inscriptions chiseled in the marble). But there is no placard or inscription by the marble edifice to the left of the main alter. Only the Medici palle and the poorly executed statue of an obese man with bulging eyes and papal keys identify the monument as Leo's final resting place. Ironically, the statue was carved by Baccio Bandinelli, the second-rate sculptor whom Leo ordered to forge a copy of the Laocoon for Francis.

There is a little more evidence of Leo in Florence. Of course, the Medici palle are nearly ubiquitous throughout the city. When Grand Duke Cosimo I appropriated the Palazzo della Signoria as his personal residence, he commissioned the artist Giorgio Vasari to decorate one of its rooms in honor of his mother's Uncle Leo. Here can be found scenes from many of the episodes that Leo described in his secret memoir.

The history of human civilization is not one of linear forward progress. Rather, there are long periods of stasis punctuated by brief bursts of intense change as man transitions from one socio-economic paradigm to another. During the Renaissance, Europe transformed from a highly decentralized feudal/agricultural society to a mercantile society in which power began to become concentrated in emerging nation-states.

Everyone is familiar with the glories of the Renaissance – the magnificent art and architecture, the rebirth of literature, humanism and science, the invention of the corporation and the emergence of the middle class. But there was also a dark side to this fascinating period of human history. As D.H. Lawrence observed: "The fairest thing in nature, a flower, still has its roots in earth and manure."

The Renaissance was a time of enormous inequality among men. Corruption was endemic in every aspect of life; everything could be bought, sold or fixed. It was a time of extraordinary violence and the rich could literally get away with murder. Warfare was constant, both between and within ruling families. Women were treated as chattel and bartered and sold for political and financial gain. Non-Europeans were exploited and enslaved. Sexual predation of all kinds was widespread and the rulers cynically outlawed the very practices that they regularly engaged in.

The Roman Catholic Church was the Renaissance's dominant institution and thus both the virtues and vices of the time were concentrated and magnified within it. As we gaze upon the treasures within Italy's churches and museums, we give scant thought as to how all this beauty came to be.

Leo was indeed a true son of the Renaissance. His father Lorenzo is perhaps the most famous single personage (aside from the great artists) of this golden age and Leo spent his entire life trying to surpass his father's accomplishments. Leo never gave a moment's thought to fiscal discipline and, while he accomplished much with the millions of ducats he spent, he bankrupted the Church in the process. Leo was so inured to the corruption that permeated his society that he never considered it problematic. He waged indefensible wars to build a family empire because his predecessors had done the same. He lied and cheated and stole because everyone he knew was also lying and cheating and stealing. He used torture freely because the Church believed in its efficacy. And while Leo was obsessed by the perceived threat from Islam, he was blind to the far graver threat to the Church posed by Luther and other reformers disgusted by its institutional rot. The Roman Catholic Church has not and may never regain the moral authority that was once unquestioned.

Are there any contemporary lessons to be learned from this five century old tale? Probably not.

READER AIDS

SELECT BIBLIOGRAPHY

Ady, Julia Cartwright, <u>Isabella d'Este, Marchioness of Mantua, 1474-1539: A Study of the Renaissance. Volume: 2</u>, John Murray, 1903.

Bedini, Silvio, <u>The Pope's Elephant</u>, Penguin Books, 1997.

Bellonci, Maria, <u>Lucrezia Borgia</u>, Phoenix Press, 1939.

Brucker, Gene, A., <u>Renaissance Florence</u>, University of California Press, 1969.

Burchard, Johann, <u>At the Court of the Borgia</u>, The Folio Society, 1963.

Creighton, Mandel, <u>A History of the Papacy During the Period of the Reformation</u>, Longmans, Green and Co., 1887.

Crompton, Louis, <u>Homosexuality and Civilization</u>, Belknap Press, 2003.

De Rosa, Peter, <u>Vicars of Christ</u>, Poolbeg Press, 1988.

Gilbert, Creighton, <u>Complete Poems and Selected Letters of Michelangelo</u>, Princeton University Press, 1980.

Gobineau, Arthur, <u>The Renaissance: Savonarola Cesare Borgia – Julius II – Leo X – Michael Angelo</u>, G.P. Putnam's Sons, 1913.

Hibbert, Christopher, <u>The House of Medici, Its Rise and Fall</u>, Harper Perennial, 1974.

Kitts, Eustace John, <u>In the Days of the Councils</u>, Archibald Constable & Co., Ltd. 1908.

Lea, Henry Charles, <u>A History of the Inquisition of the Middle Ages. Volume: 3</u>, Harper & Brothers, 1888.

Machiavelli, Nicolo, <u>Florentine History</u>, J. M. Dent & Co., 1912.

Mallett, Michael, <u>The Borgias</u>, Academy Chicago Publishers, 1987.

Martines, Lauro, <u>April Blood</u>, Oxford University Press, 2003.

McCabe, Joseph, <u>Crises in the History of the Papacy: A Study of Twenty Famous Popes Whose Careers and Whose Influence Were Important in the Development of the Church and in the History of the World</u>, G. P. Putnam's Sons, 1916.

Mee, Charles, White Robe, Black Robe, G. P. Putnam's Sons, 1972.

Partridge, Burgo, A History of Orgies, Prion Books Ltd., 1958.

Pastor, Ludwig, The History of the Popes from the Close of the Middle Ages, Volume VI, Second Edition, B. Herder, 1902.

Pastor, Ludwig, The History of the Popes from the Close of the Middle Ages, Volume VII, B. Herder, 1908.

Pastor, Ludwig, The History of the Popes from the Close of the Middle Ages, Volume VIII, B. Herder, 1908.

Peters, Edward, Inquisition, University of California Press, 1988.

Pignotti, Lorenzo; The History of Tuscany, Young, Black & Young, 1826.

Plumb, J. H., The Italian Renaissance, Mariner Books, Houghton Mifflin Company, 2001.

Rocke, Michael, Forbidden Friendships, Oxford University Press, 1996.

Roeder, Ralph, The Man of the Renaissance, Time Life Books, 1933.

Roscoe, William, Life and Pontificate of Leo the Tenth, Fifth Edition, Henry G. Bohn, 1846.

Roscoe, William, Life and Pontificate of Leo the Tenth Part II, Fifth Edition, Henry G. Bohn, 1846.

Roth, Cecil, The History of the Jews of Italy, Jewish Publication Society of America, 1946.

Schevill, Ferdinand, The Medici, Harper Torchbooks, 1949.

Stone, Irving, The Agony and the Ecstasy, Doubleday, 1961.

Vasari, Giorgio, The Lives of the Artists, Oxford University Press, 1991.

Vaughan, Herbert M., The Medici Popes: Leo X and Clement VII, Methuen & Co., 1908.

Villari, Pasquale, Life and Times of Girolamo Savonarola, Charles Scribner's Sons, 1888.

249

Zimmermann, T. C. Price, Paolo Giovio: The Historian and the Crisis of Sixteenth-Century Italy, Princeton University Press, 1995.

THE HOUSE OF MEDICI

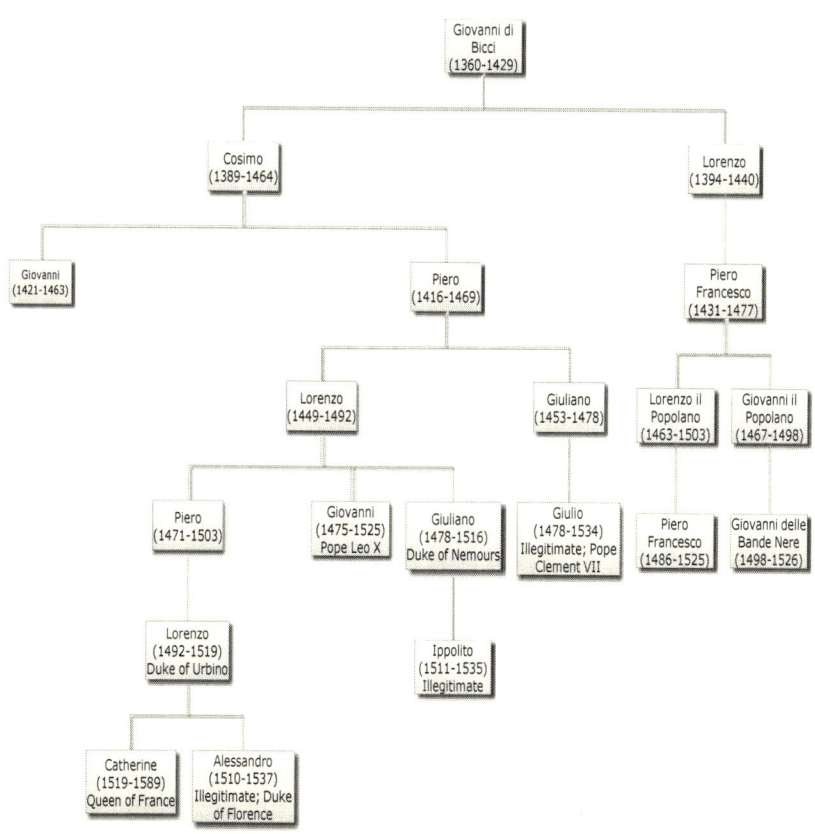

THE HOUSE OF BORGIA

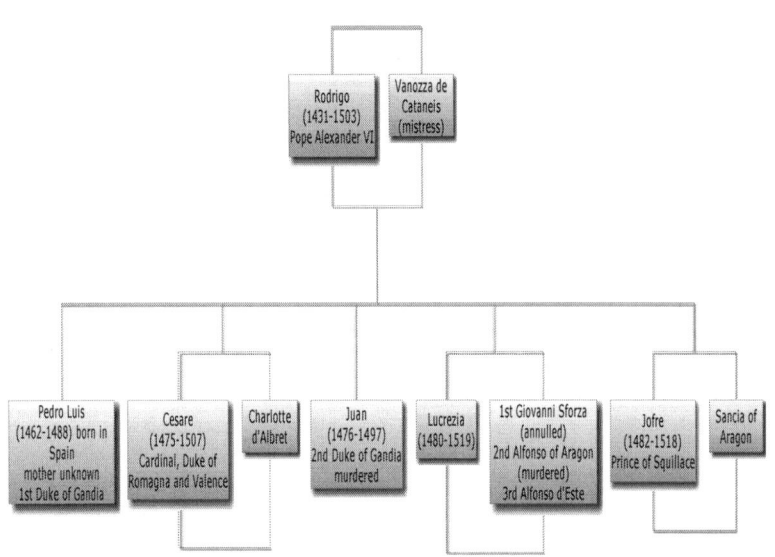

The Della Rovere Family

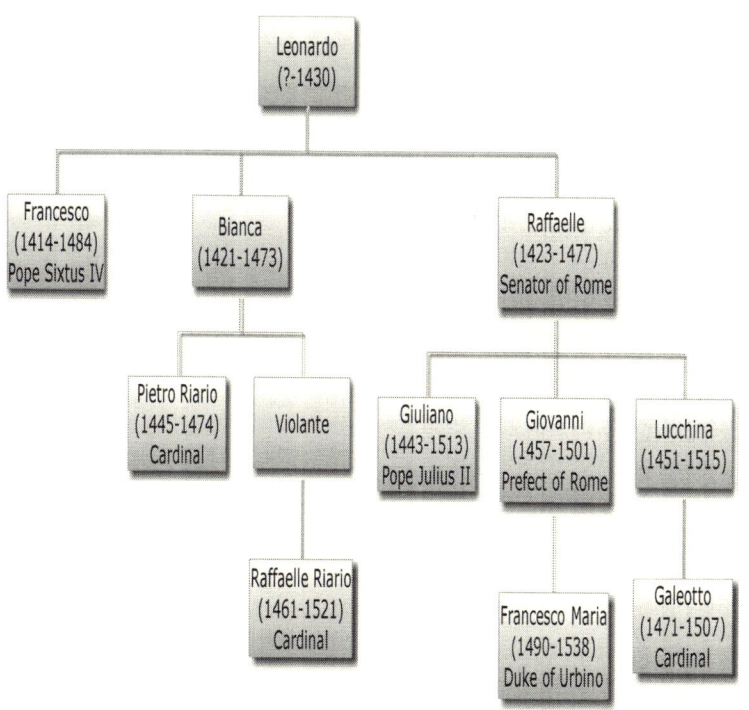

THE HOUSE OF SFORZA

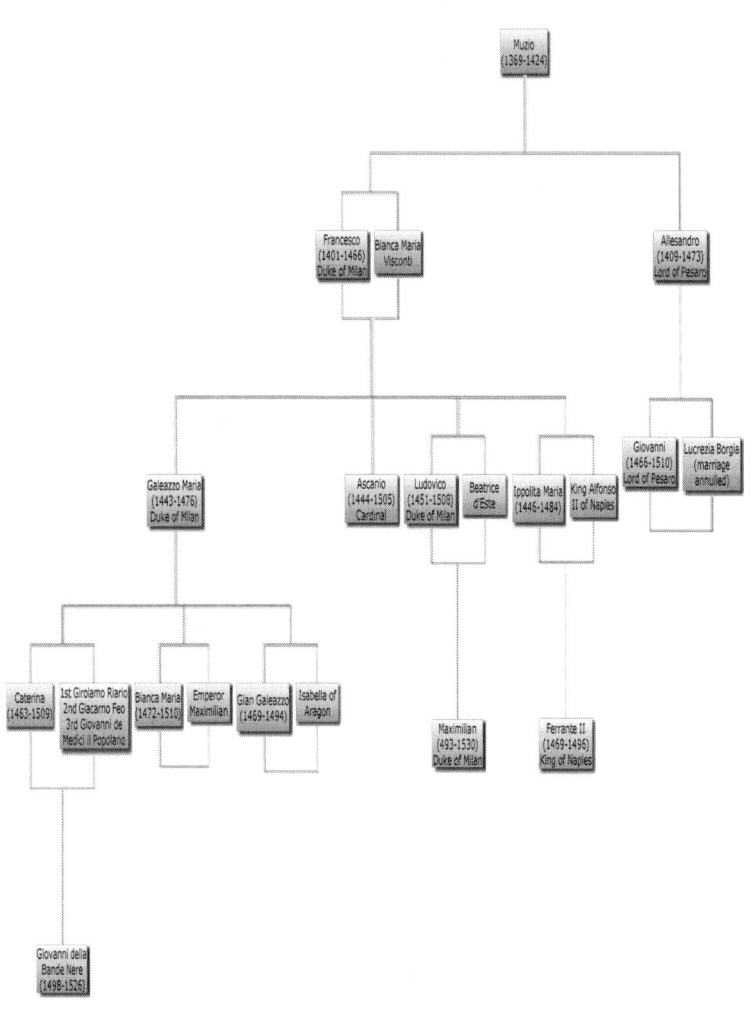

THE HOUSE OF ESTE

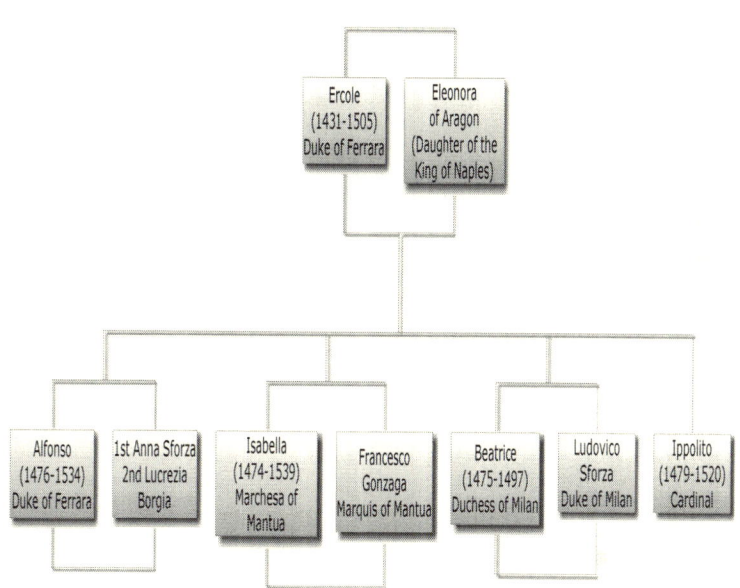

Printed in Great Britain by
Amazon.co.uk, Ltd.,
Marston Gate.